THE BOLD VEGETARIAN

Also by Bharti Kirchner

The Healthy Cuisine of India: Recipes from the Bengal Region
Indian Inspired: A New Cuisine for the International Table

THE BOLD
VEGETARIAN

150 Inspired International Recipes

by Bharti Kirchner

HarperPerennial
A Division of HarperCollinsPublishers

FIRST EDITION

Designed and illustrated by Barbara Balch

Library of Congress Cataloging-in-Publication Data
Kirchner, Bharti.
    The bold vegetarian: 150 inspired international recipes/by Bharti
Kirchner.—1st ed.
        p. cm.
    Includes index.
    ISBN 0-06-095056-0
    1. Vegetarian cookery. 2. Cookery. International. I. Title.
TX 837.K53 1995   94-43950
641.5'6336-dc20

95 96 97 98 99 ◆ /RRD 10 9 8 7 6 5 4 3 2 1

FOR UNCLE SUKUMAR, *KAKABABU*,
WHO ALWAYS BELIEVED IN ME,
AND
FOR TOM

CONTENTS

ACKNOWLEDGMENTS

It would be difficult, if not impossible, to write a cookbook without the help and encouragement of others, and certainly it would be a lot less fun. My husband, Tom Kirchner, has stood beside me through the long hours of work, tasting and critiquing each recipe, some more than once. My family in India has been equally supportive. I can think of no better compliment than having an accomplished cook like my sister, Tapati, prepare my recipes when she entertains.

I would also like to thank Shau Lee Chow, Yvonne Gunawardene, Gary Boynton, Dr. Wyveta Kirk, Dick Gibbons and his critique group, Leon Billig and his critique group, Mimi Gormezano, and the Seattle National Writer's Club.

One of the greatest satisfactions I have experienced as a writer has been the feedback from the readers of my two previous books. Through letters, telephone calls, and spontaneous chats, they have recounted to me specific recipes and anecdotes they have enjoyed. I am grateful for their encouragement.

Finally, I would like to thank my editor, Susan Friedland, who suggested a book I have always wanted to write.

INTRODUCTION

Creating a World Cuisine

It was a soft, warm evening in Singapore when I first grew aware of an emerging world cuisine. I was strolling through Newton Food Circus, a collection of outdoor food stalls in central Singapore. It teemed with life as locals and foreigners alike gathered there to feast. A sari-clad Indian woman and a Malaysian woman in a sarong kabaya chatted as they inspected the delectable array of fresh tropical fruits: sliced mango, papaya, and pineapple, skewered jackfruit, and delicate litchi; all temptingly displayed in a kaleidoscope of colors and aromas. A Chinese man in a suit and a Westerner in jeans both headed toward the same satay grill, drawn by a tantalizing smoky odor of grilled shrimp, chicken, and onions.

At another booth, an Indian cook deftly flipped a flat bread in the air and dropped it back on a large heated griddle, while joking in Hindi with his brother who was kneading the dough.

"What kind of bread are you making?" I asked in English. "*Prata*," he said, which I recognized as *paratha*, a rich pan-fried bread popular throughout Northern India. Even the scent was the same.

The next booth held a sign that read, HOKKIEN MEE. Hokkien is the largest ethnic Chinese group in Singapore, known for hearty peasant soups. I had never tasted Hokkien-style cooking. An elderly Chinese man sat at a table, hunched over his Hokkien *mee*, a clear soup with smooth, glossy noodles, attractively garnished with bright green slivers of scallion. This was his evening meal and he cupped his hands around the bowl as if to protect its warmth.

A Malaysian drink vendor persuaded me to buy a purée of fresh papaya poured over crushed ice. This she did without speaking English, simply by handing me a chilled glassful—cold, delicately sweet, and unforgettable. Stall after stall displayed dishes I'd never tasted before, many I'd never heard of, all existing in harmony. Eventually I decided on a supper of Hokkien *mee, prata,* and a coconut cake, one of Singapore's specialties. I was surprised that these dishes could be brought together so conveniently in a single meal and equally surprised that perhaps there wasn't a typical Singapore meal. Here at the crossroads of Asia, I had just had my first exposure to a world cuisine.

That memorable evening was one of the inspirations for this book. In it I have collected numerous vegetable dishes in which ideas, techniques, and ingredients flow freely from culture to culture. My criteria are variety, nutrition, ease of preparation, and good taste. The recipes call for easily obtainable seasonings, which enhance the flavor of the ingredients. I have also converted some famous meat dishes to vegetarian versions.

The recipes that follow are my invitation to an exciting way of cooking, and the resulting dishes will be full of color, flavor, texture, and aroma. A world cuisine, an adventure in eating, is at your fingertips.

THE BOLD VEGETARIAN

BASICS OF VEGETARIAN COOKING

A friend once confided that she could prepare beef bourguignon with little thought and making chicken cacciatore was almost second nature. "But when it comes to vegetables," she admitted, "I'm stumped."

The attitude is not uncommon. In the West, meat in some form is usually the centerpiece of a meal. Yet the preparation of vegetables is usually simpler than that of meat or fish. What's more, with the wide variety of vegetables available in supermarkets today one need never be at a loss for tasty, meatless meals.

In the following section you will find some essential information on methods, equipment, and techniques used in the preparation of vegetables by cooks throughout the world. Although this is not a comprehensive treatment of the "basics," it should get you through the areas most likely to cause confusion.

Cooking Methods

BLANCHING. Blanching involves plunging vegetables briefly into boiling water to soften them slightly, and, in the case of greens, to intensify their color. They are then dipped into cold water to stop the cooking process.

GRILLING. Grilling imparts a roasted, nutty quality to vegetables. Grilled vegetables can serve as side dishes or be used as ingredients in dishes that require further cooking, such as a quiche or stew. You can use wood chips, such as oak or hickory, or mesquite charcoal to impart a unique smoked flavor if grilling outdoors.

Cut onions in quarters and skewer them. Smaller onions may be grilled whole. Halve tomatoes and squeeze out the seeds before grilling. Marinate vegetables in olive oil or a good vinaigrette for 30 minutes, if desired, and drain. Or coat them lightly with oil to ensure even cooking. (Long-cooking vegetables such as carrots, potatoes, and sweet potatoes may require steaming beforehand. Potatoes need not be peeled, as their skin is rich in nutrients. Quick-cooking vegetables such as onions, bell peppers, and zucchini may benefit from blanching, that is immersing in boiling water for 2 to 3 minutes to soften them slightly.)

Arrange the vegetables on a fine mesh barbecue grid, one that goes on top of a grill and prevents food from falling through the grate. Skewer the small pieces for ease of handling. Turn them frequently and let cook until they can be pierced easily and are browned in places. These tasty bites are best served hot.

Grilling brings out the natural sweetness of some fruits and they can serve as side dishes or light desserts. To grill fruit, slice it and, if you wish, baste it with balsamic vinegar or a fruit vinegar of your choice. Peel pineapple, but grill pears, apples, and peaches with their skin on. Small pieces can be skewered and cooked in the same manner as vegetables.

SIMMERING. Simmering is cooking in liquid just below the boiling point, and is a technique commonly used for grains, beans, and vegetables. The ingredients are generally cooked, covered, over low heat, with the liquid in the pot gently bubbling but not boiling vigorously. Open the cover occasionally and check to see that only a few bubbles break the surface; adjust the heat if necessary. A vigorous boil may ruin the texture of food. On the other hand, if the temperature is too low, the dish will not cook.

STEAMING. Steaming is cooking food in a tightly covered pot over, but not immersed in, a small amount of boiling water. The steam cooks the food. You may use a pot specifically designed for steaming, or you may improvise by placing a perforated metal steaming basket in the bottom of one of your general-purpose pots. Make sure the pot you use has a tight-fitting lid. Add about ½ inch water to the pot, place the steaming basket with the vegetables in the pot, cover, and bring to a boil over high heat.

When steam begins to escape, reduce heat to medium-low and start timimg. Adjust the heat so that the steaming is gentle. Root vegetables such as potatoes, carrots, and turnips may take 15 minutes or more, depending on how thickly they are sliced; hearty greens such as mustard or collard about 5 minutes; broccoli and cauliflower, 6 to 7 minutes.

STIR-FRYING. Stir-frying is quickly cooking food in a small amount of oil over high heat, tossing and turning the food constantly. For more details, see "Stir-Fries and Quick Entrées," page 109.

TOASTING NUTS, SPICES, AND GRAINS. Toasting enhances the flavor of nuts, whole spices, and grains—ingredients often used in vegetarian cooking. This is best done in a cast-iron skillet on top of the stove. Baking them is another option. Spread your selection in a single layer in an ungreased skillet or on a baking sheet. Stirring often, toast over low heat or bake in a 350-degree oven for 5 to 15 minutes, checking frequently to prevent burning. When the color begins to change, remove from heat immediately and transfer to a cool plate. In the case of spices, the change in color will be accompanied by a noticeable aroma. Be careful not to burn the ingredients; they will become bitter and acrid.

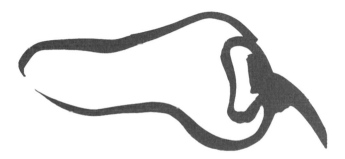

Tips

USE THE FRESHEST POSSIBLE INGREDIENTS. It is the quality of the ingredients that will determine the final result, regardless of the cooking techniques. Freshness is a vital quality in both fruits and vegetables. This is why chefs in the better restaurants shop daily for their produce and, in some cases, even grow their own. For a home cook, frequent shopping may be inconvenient. Keeping this in mind, basic items like roots and tubers need not be purchased more than once a week, if properly stored. Other items, particularly leafy greens or bean sprouts, should be purchased as fresh as possible.

CONTROL THE HEAT AND DON'T OVERCOOK. The most common mistake people make when preparing vegetables is overcooking. Carrots and cauliflower rapidly lose their texture when boiled instead of simmered. When cooked for too long, cabbage, broccoli, and Brussels sprouts not only become mushy, but develop an odor that many people find unpleasant.

SPICES AND FLAVORINGS ARE ESSENTIAL WHEN COOKING VEGETABLES. Salt and pepper alone may not be sufficient seasoning, especially when you are cutting down on oil and butter. If the vegetables are fresh, simple steaming and light spicing will bring out their natural flavors. Bolder spicing will transform vegetables into a richly flavored Indian *korma* or Southeast Asian *sambal*.

STRIVE FOR VARIETY. Combine vegetable dishes with an eye to complementary colors, flavors, and textures. An eggplant dish goes well with red lentils. Grilled sweet potatoes combine well with many tofu dishes. A yellow-orange vegetable like butternut squash is delicious with sautéed leafy greens. When serving cooked vegetables, a crisp green salad is a delightful companion.

PREVENT YOGURT AND COCONUT MILK FROM CURDLING. Exercise caution when using these two ingredients, often called for in vegetarian sauces. They will separate when exposed to high heat for more than a few seconds, ruining the texture and appearance of the dish. Once yogurt or coconut milk is added, the dish must be finished over low heat. Combine either with a small amount of flour before adding it to sauces to prevent separation.

GARNISH DISHES LIBERALLY. Visual appeal increases the enjoyment of food. Not everyone wants to spend time shaping a radish into a rose, but many simple yet elegant garnishes are easily achieved. Chopped cilantro, carrot slices, sweet onion rings, and toasted pecans all increase the attractiveness of vegetable dishes and add new dimensions of flavor and texture.

SERVE VEGETABLES AT THE APPROPRIATE TEMPERATURE. Part of the art of serving food is to ensure it is brought to the table at the correct temperature. A green salad is better served slightly chilled. On the other hand, most chutneys and salsas develop their fullest flavor when served at room temperature.

The time of the year also influences the appropriate serving temperature for a dish. The Zucchini Vichysoisse that is so refreshing served chilled in summer provides warmth and comfort when served steaming hot on a crisp autumn evening. On a balmy day, a plate of sliced, vine-ripened tomatoes, drizzled with olive oil, is a tasty treat; but on a blustery winter day, a side dish of fragrant roasted potatoes is much more satisfying.

USE "SERVING SUGGESTIONS" AS GUIDELINES. The Serving Suggestions following each recipe in this book list complementary dishes, but do not necessarily attempt to provide a meal that is nutritionally balanced. Use your own good sense and creativity when planning a meal.

A
VEGETARIAN
PANTRY

Unusual Vegetables, Spices, and Flavorings

ARUGULA (ROCKET OR ROQUETTE): Italians, and most recently Americans, use the long, arrow-shaped dark green leaves of this plant in salads and pasta dishes. They have a sharp, yet agreeable taste.

ASAFETIDA: Asafetida is the dried sap from the roots and stems of several species of giant fennel. It is sold in rocklike chunks or as a powder in Indian groceries. The raw spice has a strong odor, but once cooked it mellows to produce a tantalizing, musky garliclike flavor.

ASIAN PEAR: This crisp, juicy relative of the European pear is native to China and Japan, and is now widely grown in the United States. It is shaped more like an apple than a pear, yet has a delicate sweet taste that is definitely "pear." It comes in many varieties, with colors ranging from pale yellow to dull russet brown. Although sometimes called an "apple pear," it is not a hybrid.

BLACK BEAN SAUCE: A thick purée of fermented soy beans, it is used widely as a seasoning in Chinese cooking. It is carried in Asian markets and many neighborhood supermarkets.

BLACK SALT: This reddish-gray salt from India has a complex, earthy flavor. Indian groceries sell it in lump form and a more convenient powder. Don't try to use substitutes because of its unique flavor. Omit, if not available.

BOK CHOY: Crisp with a delicate mustardy flavor, this vegetable of the cabbage family is a staple in Chinese cooking. Instead of forming a tight head like cabbage, it more resembles Swiss chard. The large leaves are dark green and shiny, and the thick white ribs are tender and succulent. The entire vegetable is edible. It is available in Asian markets and many American supermarkets.

BLACK MUSTARD (BROWN MUSTARD, RED MUSTARD): Round hard mustard seeds from India have a pungent flavor and vary in color from dark brown to black. They are used both whole and ground, and are considered more flavorful than the yellow mustard common in the West. Whole seeds are sautéed at the beginning of the cooking process until they pop and release their essence to the oil. They may also be ground, moistened with water to form a thick paste, and allowed to stand for 10 minutes to develop their flavor. Then the paste is added to a dish to form a sauce.

CHICK-PEA FLOUR (*BESAN*): This flour is made by grinding chick-peas and sieving the husks, presenting a powdery texture similar to cornstarch with a nutty flavor. It is widely used in Indian cooking to make batters, for thickening, and in breads, and is always available in Indian groceries. Refrigerate this perishable flour in a sealed container. Wheat flour is *not* a substitute.

CHILE, DRIED: These are dehydrated whole ripe chile peppers. The slender dried red variety is available in jars in the spice section of most supermarkets. I sauté these whole chiles at the beginning of the cooking process to flavor the oil. A much wider range of dried chiles is sold in Latin American and Asian markets and well-stocked supermarkets. These are generally softened by toasting and soaking, and their flesh is extracted to be used in many dishes. In this book, I use the following types: The flat, wide *ancho* chile is brownish to dark red in color and has a mild to moderately hot, smoky, faintly sweet flavor. *Chipotle* chiles are smoked and dried jalapeños and are *extremely hot*. They can be purchased dried or, more commonly, canned in a spicy sauce. Ground chipotle powder is now available in natural food stores and some supermarkets. Together with Indian spices, namely, mango powder, black salt, and asafetida, this smoky hot powder forms an intriguing spice mix, sort of an Indo-Mexican chili powder.

Pasilla chiles are brownish black, long, and wrinkled. Their flesh is more intensely hot than that of the ancho and also have a hint of smokiness. Note that anchos are frequently mislabelled as pasillas.

CHILE, FRESH: Fresh chiles range in color from green to bright red. Their flesh is juicy and their flavor is considerably different from their dried counterparts. They are best stored in a plastic bag in the refrigerator. Handle all chiles, especially fresh ones, carefully. Be extremely careful not to let the juices of the chiles come in contact with eyes, lips, or other mucous membranes of the body via the fingertips, as they contain a potent, highly irritating oil that can cause extreme discomfort. Wear rubber gloves if possible, or wash hands thoroughly after handling them.

My recipes call for the following varieties of fresh chiles: The *habanero* is a highly flavored variety reputed to be the hottest of all chiles. The fruit is tapered and lantern-shaped, and varies from pale yellow through yellowish orange to bright red when completely ripe. Seed and dice this chile and use sparingly. Look for fresh or dried habanero in supermarkets and Latin American markets. The most common chile in American supermarkets is the *jalapeño*. It has a shiny, dark green exterior, medium-thick skin and matures to red. Their hotness varies. The *serrano* chile is a thin, flavorful pepper, hotter than most supermarket jalapeños and a good substitute for them if you desire a more fiery taste.

COCONUT MILK: Coconut milk is derived by soaking shredded fresh coconut in hot water, then straining the mixture through layers of cheesecloth to produce a milky white liquid used to flavor soups and sauces. It is also sold canned in Asian markets, and is increasingly available in Western supermarkets. For the recipes in this book, canned coconut milk is adequate. Before measuring, be sure to stir the contents of the milk to mix the thin watery liquid at the top and the thick creamy layer that settles to the bottom during storage.

COUSCOUS: A tiny grainlike wheat pasta of North African origin. It becomes light and fluffy when cooked, and can be substituted for rice or millet. It is typically prepared by steaming or boiling, and is served as an accompaniment to stews.

CURRY LEAVES: Curry leaves are not related to curry powder. These small aromatic leaves are indispensable to the cooking of southern and western regions of India. They are usually sautéed with black mustard seeds at the beginning of the cooking process to flavor the oil. They are more commonly sold dried, but are occasionally found fresh in Indian groceries. The fresh leaves have more flavor. If you are fortunate enough to find them, use them as soon as possible and refrigerate any leftovers in Ziploc plastic bags. They will last up to two weeks. If you have a food dehydrator, you can dry any surplus as you would parsley or coriander. There is no substitute for curry leaves.

CURRY POWDER: Curry powder refers to a standard blend of spices sold in supermarkets. In the West, it is used in preparing Indian dishes as a substitute for the custom blended spices an Indian cook would tailor to each individual dish. There are three standard varieties: mild, medium, and hot, depending on the amount of chile in the mix. All contain turmeric, which gives them a characteristic yellow color. Other spices include cumin, coriander, cloves, cardamom, fennel, ginger, fenugreek, and black pepper. The curry powder used in Southeast Asia may include lemon grass, coriander root, and shrimp powder. Because curry powders and curry pastes are now readily available, I haven't included instructions for preparing them at home.

As mentioned, Indian cooks don't use standardized curry powder. They prefer, instead, to combine different seasonings for each dish to enhance the flavor of the main ingredient. The blend for potatoes, for instance, would be different from that for eggplant. Because the use of curry powder is widespread, I use it occasionally in this book, supplementing it with extra seasonings as required.

FENUGREEK: These brownish yellow, squarish seeds have an agreeably bitter taste, somewhat akin to burnt sugar. Fenugreek is widely used in India in vegetable dishes and is available in Indian groceries, natural food stores, and some supermarkets.

FETA CHEESE: This crumbly goat cheese has a sharp, salty taste. It is available in cheese shops and Middle Eastern groceries. In my salad recipes I use it in small amounts as a garnish.

GAI LAN (CHINESE BROCCOLI, CHINESE KALE): This leafy plant is 10 to 14 inches high, with succulent stems and a small head of flower buds that closely resembles tiny broccoli florets. When fully ripe, the buds open into white or sometimes yellow flowers. The entire plant is edible. When shopping for gai lan, look for unopened flower buds and smooth stalks. Broccoli raab is an excellent substitute for gai lan, and in a pinch, regular broccoli will do. Gai lan is available in Asian markets.

> **TO PREPARE GAI LAN FOR COOKING:** Before cooking you can separate large stalks of gai lan and halve them lengthwise. Or you can follow Chinese cooks, who leave the stalks whole for a more elegant presentation, but snap off the tough bottom ends.

GARAM MASALA: These words literally mean "hot spices," because they raise the body heat. This aromatic mixture from India consists of roasted and ground cinnamon, cardamom, and cloves, and can include black pepper, nutmeg, coriander, and other spices. This spice mix is added at the last moment, putting the finishing touch on many dishes. Don't confuse it with curry powder, whose content and use are entirely different. You can buy garam masala at any Indian grocery.

GHEE (CLARIFIED BUTTER): Ghee is a rich cooking medium from India that imparts a nutty fragrance to dishes. It does not burn at high heat. This clear golden liquid is made by gently cooking unsalted butter until the milk solids separate from the fat and fall to the bottom. Because of its saturated fat content, I usually specify ghee in my recipes only as an optional flavoring. Don't substitute vegetable ghee, often sold in Indian and Middle Eastern groceries, as it contains nearly as much saturated fat and lacks the distinctive flavor.

TO PREPARE GHEE: Heat 1 pound unsalted butter in a heavy pan over very low heat, allowing it to simmer without stirring. A smooth white foam will soon cover the surface as the milk solids separate from the fat. The soft foam will gradually become crusty, turning yellowish initially and then light brown. In 45 minutes to 1 hour, when the butter has stopped foaming and much of the crust has settled to the bottom, remove from heat. Strain the contents of the pan through 4 or more layers of dampened cheesecloth pressed into a large sieve, holding it over a bowl. Make sure none of the sediment gets through the cheesecloth. If it does, refilter it. Store the golden liquid, ghee, in a covered container in the refrigerator. Discard the sediment. Ghee will solidify during storage and must be liquefied before using. It may be softened by placing the covered jar in a pan of warm water for 5 to 10 minutes. Melt it in a small saucepan over low heat before sprinkling it over cooked vegetables or grains.

Yield: 1½ cups

TO PREPARE SPICED GHEE: This flavored ghee is excellent as a table sauce. Even a small sprinkling greatly enhances cooked grains, especially rice, baked potatoes, and steamed or grilled vegetables. Heat 2 to 3 tablespoons of ghee and sprinkle ⅛ teaspoon asafetida powder over it. For variety, also add a dash of black salt and ground cumin.

Because ghee fetches a high price in India, a popular saying is: "If you are adding ghee to a dish in your dreams, why not pour a lot?"

GINGERROOT: This aromatic rhizome has a light brown skin and pale yellow flesh. It imparts a clean, lively taste to dishes, and is an essential ingredient in many of my recipes. I prefer fresh gingerroot and only occasionally use powdered ginger (also called ground ginger), which has a milder flavor. When using gingerroot, make sure it is minced or grated, because it will not blend with the sauce if left in large pieces. A food processor or a mini chopper makes for easy preparation. A hand grater can be used, although it takes longer. Store unpeeled gingerroot in the vegetable bin of your refrigerator.

GROUND RED PEPPER: This fiery red powder, also called cayenne pepper, is best bought from an Asian or Latin American market. Supermarket varieties will do, but they are less flavorful.

HOISIN SAUCE: A thick, sweet, spicy sauce from China, hoisin is made from soy beans, garlic, and various spices. It is used in stir-fries and is available in Asian markets and some supermarkets.

JICAMA: This large tuber has a coarse brown inedible skin that peels away easily. The edible white flesh is crunchy, juicy, and faintly sweet. You can eat it raw, sprinkled with lime juice, ground red pepper, and black salt, or use it like a potato. It retains much of its crispiness even when cooked.

KALONJI SEEDS (NIGELLA): These blue-black seeds from India have an onionlike flavor and closely resemble onion seeds, but they are not related. They add a peppery flavor, crunchy texture, and a dash of color to vegetable preparations. Most Indian groceries carry them.

KASHA (BUCKWHEAT GROATS): In the United States, kasha refers to buckwheat groats, the seeds of the buckwheat plant. These seeds become light and fluffy when cooked and make an excellent pilaf. Kasha is hearty, has a pleasant nutlike aroma, and cooks quickly. It is rich in protein and many vitamins and can be found in health food stores and many supermarkets.

MANGO POWDER (AMCHOOR): Made by pulverizing dried, unripe mangoes, this brown powder adds a delightful tartness to dishes. It can be bought from Indian food shops.

MILLET: This tiny, round whole-grain is pale yellow in color and becomes fluffy like rice when cooked. It grows well in poor soil and in harsh climatic conditions. Since ancient times, it has been used as a staple in Africa, Northern China, and parts of India. It is sold in natural food stores and some supermarkets.

MIRIN: A sweet, syrupy rice wine from Japan, mirin is used only for cooking. It is excellent in marinades and stir-fries.

MISO: A thick, pungent paste of Japanese origin, miso is made from fermented soy beans or grains such as rice or barley. It is used as a base for soups, stews, and marinades, and is reputed to aid digestion. Miso comes in several varieties—white, red, brown, or beige—and each has varying degrees of saltiness. In my recipes, I use the dark red variety, which has a strong flavor and rich, meaty taste. Miso should be used sparingly because of its high salt content.

NAPA CABBAGE (CHINESE CABBAGE): This tasty member of the *Brassica* family, native to China, is barrel-shaped and creamy white to pale green in color. It is more tender than regular cabbage and has a more delicate flavor. Napa cabbage cooks quickly, but is also excellent shredded and served raw in salads.

NORI: Seaweed that has been dried into thin, purplish sheets comes from Japan, and is used most commonly for wrapping sushi and also as a garnish for rice or soups. It is usually gently toasted before using.

> **TO TOAST NORI:** Place several nonoverlapping sheets of seasoned nori in an ungreased skillet over low heat. Within a few seconds, nori will change color and become crisper. Remove immediately to avoid burning.

OILS: I use the following types of oils in these recipes: *Canola oil* is high in both monounsaturated and polyunsaturated fats, and low in saturated fats. It is relatively flavorless and can be used for general-purpose cooking. The high smoke point of this oil makes it suitable for frying. The fine-flavored *hazelnut oil* is excellent in vinaigrettes. *Mustard oil* is a deep golden, pungent aromatic oil from India that enhances bean and vegetable dishes. Indian groceries sell both pure mustard oil, which is stronger, and mustard-flavored blended oil, a milder oil that is a mixture of mustard and soybean oil. Either may be used in recipes calling for mustard oil. I use monounsaturated *olive oil* often, especially when preparing dishes from the Mediterranean countries and the Middle East. Because of its distinctive aroma and flavor, it can clash with Indian spices, but I have found situations where the two can work together. *Dark sesame oil* is amber-colored, with a strong aroma, and is prized as a flavoring in Chinese cooking. In my recipes, I use it in small amounts as a seasoning and in salad dressings. It can be purchased in Asian markets and some supermarkets. In some recipes, I use the pale yellow Indian *light sesame oil* called *gingely*, which has a delicate aroma and flavor. It is sold in Indian groceries. The variety sold in natural food stores can be substituted. *Walnut oil*, with its warm, nutty flavor, is highly prized in France. It is excellent in salad dressings and for briefly sautéeing vegetables.

OLIVES: Olives are sold either green (unripe) or black (ripened on the tree). My recipes use purple-black Kalamata (Calamata) olives, which are firm, juicy, and flavorful and have a rich, briny taste. Even a small amount enhances stews and salads. These olives are sold pickled in brine and oil in gourmet shops and some supermarkets.

PAPAD OR PAPADDUM: This spicy, paper-thin lentil wafer from India can be served as an appetizer or side dish. It is delicious with or without a chutney. Traditionally it is deep-fried, but I prefer baking it oil-free (page 24).

PINE NUTS (PIÑON NUTS, PIGNOLI): These are soft, white, oval nuts that resemble a large grain of rice, with a flavor and texture similar to macadamia nuts. I toast them lightly and use them as a garnish.

PLUM SAUCE: This sweet, hot sauce from China is made with plums, chiles, sugar, and spices, and is used as a dip or in cooking. In my recipes, I use plum sauce for seasoning or glazing. It is available in Asian markets, natural food stores, and some supermarkets.

POLENTA: This is the Italian name for yellow (not white) cornmeal. Yellow corn grits, sold in natural food stores, can be substituted, but medium or finely ground cornmeal cannot.

POMEGRANATE SYRUP (POMEGRANATE MOLASSES): The tart ruby red pomegranate fruit is much appreciated in Asia. Its juice is cooked to form a rich, tangy syrup for flavoring soups and stews. It is sold in Indian and Middle Eastern grocery stores.

QUINOA: A tiny, beige, round grain, similar to millet, it has been used since ancient times in the high Andes region of South America. It has one of the highest protein profiles of any grain. Prior to cooking, it must be rinsed several times to remove a naturally occuring, protective bitter residue called "saponin." Quinoa becomes light and fluffy when cooked, and readily takes on the character of other ingredients in a dish.

RED LENTILS (EGYPTIAN LENTILS): These tiny, lens-shaped lentils with a salmon-pink color are used on a daily basis in many parts of India. When cooked, they turn pale yellow. They cook much faster than the greenish brown lentils found in supermarkets.

> **TO PREPARE RED LENTILS FOR COOKING:** If you have bought red lentils from a bulk store, spread them out in a single layer on a large cutting board, cookie sheet, or even a piece

of newspaper. Pick out any stones or small debris that might be present and discard. Transfer the lentils to a bowl and rinse thoroughly several times in cold water, or until the water runs clear.

RICE VINEGAR: See **Vinegars.**

ROSE WATER: This flavoring, popular in India and the Middle East, is extracted by distilling fresh rose petals at the height of their fragrance. Only a splash is needed to enhance ice creams, rice dishes, and teas.

SAFFRON: The most expensive spice in the world, saffron comes from the inner part of flowers of a small crocus and has a wonderfully intense, fragrant aroma with bitter overtones. Usually a pinch is dissolved in a spoonful of warm water or milk to release its bright yellow color and distinctive flavor. This water is then used in cooking. Saffron threads, rather than saffron powder, give better results.

SAMBAL OELEK (SAMBAL ULEK): This Indonesian ground chile paste, is available in Asian markets. In my recipes, I use it not only for hotness, but for its rich, complex flavor. Red chile paste available in Indian food stores is an adequate substitute, but it can be much hotter.

SESAME SEEDS: Both the black and white sesame seeds make a crunchy garnish when roasted. In Asian markets, roasted sesame seeds are available in jars, but toasting raw sesame seeds just before using achieves the best result. Ground sesame seeds are excellent as a flavoring and sauce thickener. A delightful garnish called *gomasio* is made by roasting the seeds and partially grinding them with coarse salt.

> **TO ROAST AND GRIND SESAME SEEDS:** Place white sesame seeds on an ungreased griddle or skillet over medium-low heat. Toast them until they are lightly browned, stirring often. Remove from the heat and grind to a powder in a spice grinder or mortar and pestle.

SAMBHAR POWDER (SAMBHAR MASALA): This essential seasoning from South India is most often used in preparing sambhar, a thick lentil sauce that is always served at a main meal. Sambhar powder is made by grinding coriander, fenugreek, black mustard seeds, and dried red chiles. Indian groceries carry this ingredient.

SOBA: These are thin, dried, brownish gray buckwheat noodles from Japan. They have a rich, hearty taste and are enjoyed hot or cold with a dipping sauce. They are sold in Asian markets and natural food stores.

SUMAC: This tart red powder has a sharp, sour flavor and is made from the edible berries of a special variety of sumac bush. It resembles chili powder in appearance. Sprinkle it over rice, slivered onions, or cucumber salads.

TAHINI: Also called sesame butter, it is made by puréeing toasted or raw sesame seeds. Stored in a sealed container in the refrigerator, it will keep indefinitely.

TAMARIND: The brown, intensely sour pulp of the tamarind fruit is much appreciated in India, Southeast Asia, and Latin America for its complex tart flavor. Asian markets and Indian groceries sell tamarind as a dried block that needs further processing, and they also sell a ready-made concentrate in a jar. In my recipes, I use the concentrate for convenience. Lemon or lime is not a substitute for tamarind.

TEMPEH: This Indonesian meat substitute made from fermented soy beans is sold in flat, ½ inch-thick slabs. It is produced by a natural aging process and contains active enzymes to make it more digestible. Rich in protein, it is one of the few vegetarian sources of vitamin B_{12}. Tempeh can also be made of beans and grains. Buy it in Asian markets, natural food stores, and some supermarkets.

TOFU: Tofu is made by extracting soy milk from cooked soy beans and adding a curdling agent. The square cakes, which are fragile and have the consistency of custard, are sold as "soft," "firm," and "silken," depending on their texture. Tofu is an excellent protein source for vegetarians.

VINEGARS: I use the following types of vinegars in this book: Delicate *rice vinegar* is distilled from rice and is lighter, sweeter, and far less acidic than common cider vinegar. It is ideal for salad dressings or cooking, and is sold in Asian markets and many supermarkets. Aged Italian *balsamic vinegar* has a deep, complex flavor with a hint of sweetness. It is excellent in vinaigrettes, or simply sprinkle it over fresh fruit or steamed vegetables as a delightful counterpoint to their natural sweetness. Buy one of the finer brands from well-stocked supermarkets or gourmet food shops. Rich, red *raspberry vinegar* is flavored with raspberries and is milder than red wine vinegar. It is excellent in salad dressings and is available in gourmet food shops and some supermarkets.

WILD RICE: Wild rice is long, narrow, and ricelike. It is not a rice but an aquatic grass found in North America. In this book, I use wild rice as an ingredient for burgers, in salads, and in pilafs.

> **Whatever the benefits of fortune are, they yet require a palate fit to relish them.**
> —*Montaigne*

APPETIZERS AND SNACKS

Appetizers and snacks occupy a prominent position in most cuisines. People from all levels of society enjoy an endless variety of tasty finger foods: from *mezza* in the Arab countries and *namkeen* in India to *tapas* in Spain. In Spain, a culinary subculture has evolved based on *tapas*—green olives, pimientos, stuffed eggs, marinated onions, cheese puffs, vegetable pâté, little fish or meat pies. Madrid is known for its *tapas* bars, and people often spend an entire evening traveling among these establishments, sampling tidbits of food.

One early evening in Madrid I shared several *tapas* with friends. We chatted about the weather, the traffic, the neighbors, each new *tapa* leading the conversation in a different direction.

Over a tiny plate of caramelized garlic cloves someone asked, "Did you know that Carmela fell in love with Manolo?" I wanted to hear the rest of the tale and hoped these tidbits would last as long as the story.

Before long we moved on to another place where we nibbled on tender, cured olives and discussed movies. The taste of olives invigorated me, and I looked forward to the food and conversation yet to come. There I learned that with the right company and the right combinations of appetizers, nibbling can become a social art.

Snacking is equally popular in India. One of my earliest childhood memories is the first time I visited a street fair, or *mela*, with my sister. This was in Krishnanagar, a town in Northern Bengal famous for its yearly *mela*. The city was crowded with people from nearby villages. Artisans displayed toys finely sculpted from clay, wood, bamboo, or straw—all hand-painted. Musicians played drums and children danced.

People clustered around food vendors who prepared a wide variety of sweet and savory snacks. One seller grabbed my attention by lifting a luscious, rose-colored ball of sweetened farmer's cheese called *chanabora* from a pot of fragrant, gently simmering sugarcane syrup. This treat was a specialty of the fair. A customer good naturedly complained, "These *chanaboras* are a bit smaller than last year's, don't you think?"

"The price of sugar has gone up, you know," replied the seller, smiling. "Why don't you have another one?"

I bought a simple clay doll from one vendor and argued with my sister over how to split a spicy mixture of roasted nuts and lentils, called *dalmoot*. Then all for myself I bought an intensely sweet pastry made with milk and sugar and shaped like a miniature Buddhist temple. But I couldn't eat it all and had to share it, too, with my sister. To my surprise, doing so filled me with contentment.

Although my clay doll broke even before I reached home, my spirits were high. That night my dreams were of the fair: the toys, the crowd, the jubilation, and the snacks. Some things in life should never change.

Korea is another country where snacking is fun. The day I arrived, the ice-covered streets, smooth as slate, seemed ominous in the predawn haze. I reached my hotel in Seoul, tired from an overnight journey. Chilled by a wind with a Siberian bite, I wanted something warm to eat.

At a busy intersection, a street vendor roasted chestnuts. A cloud of steam rose from his mobile cart and slowly floated skyward through the bitter air. My heart danced. As I stood huddled in the crowd, another vendor, who specialized in grilling sweet potatoes, opened a stall. One by one, vendors began selling a variety of snacks. A common language was unnecessary to make purchases. I pointed; they handed me food in exchange for a few Korean won and a polite nod. My fingers came to life when I grasped the hot packets, and my soul was warmed by friendly eyes.

In the next several days, I discovered more Korean cuisine, with its penchant for garlic, hot chiles, and grilled food. Between meals I kept returning to that first street vendor for freshly roasted chestnuts. Seoul became another food adventure. The snack recipes in this chapter come from diverse cultures. They can be served as hors d'oeuvres, picnic food, side dishes, or combined for a full meal.

SPEEDY SNACK AND APPETIZER IDEAS

With a ready supply of convenient munchies like those listed below, you're ready for a "snack attack" at any time. Many of these ideas also work well as appetizers.

Bite-Size Raw Vegetables and Salsa

Along with carrot and celery sticks, serve jicama, fresh mushrooms, and scallions. Also include lightly steamed stalks of broccoli, cauliflower, or Swiss chard. Serve with Ancho and Red Pepper Salsa (page 216).

Fresh and Dried Fruits with Garnishes

Sprinkle fresh apple or pear slices with crystallized ginger powder (prepared by grinding crystallized ginger in a blender or food processor until reduced to a coarse powder). Enjoy ripe peach or mango slices with Honey Pecans (page 85). Among dried fruits, consider apple and banana chips, dried persimmons, nectarines, and pineapples—all available in well-stocked supermarkets and natural food stores. You can prepare these fruit chips at home if you have a food dehydrator by following the manufacturer's directions.

Chutney-Topped Rice Cakes

To improve the taste of rice cakes, heat them for 5 to 8 minutes in a preheated 350-degree oven. Top with Mint-Cilantro Chutney (page 213) or pile with Marinated Carrot Chutney (page 214).

Roasted Chestnuts

Late autumn or winter, when chestnuts are available, roast them by placing on an ungreased baking sheet in a preheated 350-degree oven for 20 to 30 minutes. Or steam chestnuts by placing in a steamer basket for 20 to 30 minutes, or until tender. Before baking or steaming, cut an X with a sharp knife over the "eye" to keep the steam inside from exploding. Shell and enjoy.

Papads (or Papaddums)

Papads are spicy, paper-thin lentil wafers, sold in Indian groceries. In India they are traditionally deep-fried, but I prefer to bake them oil-free, not only for nutritional reasons, but for their superior crispy texture and nutty flavor. Arrange the papads, nonoverlapping, on a large baking sheet. Bake at 350 degrees F for 5 to 15 minutes, or until crisp and medium brown in color. Handle them gently, as they tend to be brittle. Serve alone or with Chile Chutney (page 212) or Chipotle Barbecue Sauce (page 228).

Spicy Roasted Chick-peas

This is a popular snack from India, one that can also be served with a meal. Combine 1 tablespoon canola oil with a dash each of turmeric and ground red pepper, 1 tablespoon freshly squeezed lime juice, ¼ teaspoon each of asafetida powder and mango powder, ½ teaspoon ground cumin, and black salt or regular salt to taste. Toss 1½ cups cooked chick-peas (or one 14-ounce can, drained) with this mixture. Arrange chick-peas in a single layer on a baking sheet and pour any remaining sauce over them. Bake in a preheated 350-degree oven for 15 to 18 minutes, or until thoroughly heated. Serve hot or at room temperature.   *Yield: 3 to 4 small snack servings.*

FIVE-SPICE NUTS
China

Chinese five-spice is a fragrant powder consisting of star anise, fennel, cassia (similar to cinnamon), cloves, and Szechwan pepper. The spices are roasted before grinding. This aromatic powder is often used in preparing rich stews and in barbecues. Here it is sautéed with sugar and nuts to produce an unusual snack.

2 teaspoons canola oil
¼ teaspoon Chinese five-spice powder (available in
    Asian markets and some supermarkets)
1½ teaspoons sugar
4 ounces red-skinned peanuts, pecans, or whole walnuts
    (1 cup)

Heat oil in a medium skillet until sizzling. Add five-spice powder and sugar and stir until sugar is dissolved. Add nuts. Cook, stirring constantly, until the sugar-spice mixture has formed a glaze around the nuts, 3 to 5 minutes. Transfer to a platter and allow to cool before serving. It is best served the same day. *Yield: 1 cup*

SERVING SUGGESTIONS: Serve alone as a snack or with Indian-Style Roasted Potatoes (page 32). As an appetizer, team with Spicy Roasted Chick-peas (page 24) and Papads (page 24).

GARAM MASALA VARIATION: An alternative to five-spice is Indian garam masala, a ground mixture of cinnamon, cardamom, cloves, and other spices. Substitute it in the above recipe for the five-spice powder.

CARAMELIZED GARLIC
Spain

In Spain this dish is most commonly prepared with onion, but it works equally well with garlic. For those who love garlic, this delightful appetizer sets the mood for a fine meal. It can also be served as a side dish.

3 to 5 whole heads garlic, cloves separated and peeled
    (about 30 cloves)
1½ cups Vegetable Stock (page 45) or canned
    vegetable broth
1 bay leaf
2 teaspoons brown sugar
1 tablespoon ghee or butter
Salt and freshly ground black pepper to taste

1. Preheat oven to 350 degrees F.

2. Bring the garlic cloves, stock, and bay leaf to a boil in a medium saucepan. Simmer, covered, until garlic is tender, 10 to 12 minutes. Drain in a colander, retaining the cooking liquid. Arrange the garlic cloves in a single layer in a lightly oiled 9 × 13-inch cake pan.

3. Cook sugar in a medium-size skillet over medium heat, stirring often. In a few minutes the sugar will melt and start to thicken. Add ghee and 2 tablespoons of the garlic-cooking liquid and bring to a boil. (Use the remaining garlic-cooking liquid to prepare grains or in soups.) Pour mixture over the garlic cloves. Bake 15 to 25 minutes, or until the sauce is thick. Remove from oven and let stand, covered, for a few minutes to thicken the sauce. Season to taste with salt and pepper. Serve warm or at room temperature.

Yield: 4 small servings

SERVING SUGGESTIONS: Serve with hot baguettes or pile on top of baked potatoes. Meat eaters can enjoy these garlic cloves with grilled chicken accompanied by a green salad and grilled vegetables.

SEAFOOD VARIATION: For a taste treat, arrange these garlic cloves over sautéed scallops and serve as an entrée or appetizer. In this case, you can use the leftover garlic-cooking liquid to prepare rice and serve along with the scallops.

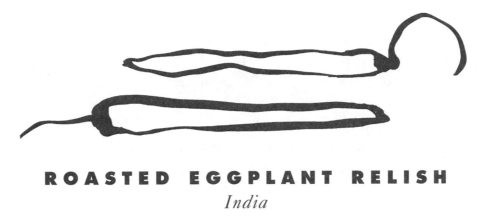

ROASTED EGGPLANT RELISH
India

Here the versatile eggplant absorbs the fragrance of Indian spices to produce a robust appetizer. Since the eggplant is softened by roasting, it soaks up less oil, which lowers both fat content and calories.

1 pound eggplant, unpeeled, cut in half lengthwise
2 tablespoons canola oil
2 whole dried red chiles
1 cup finely chopped onion
¼ teaspoon ground turmeric
2 teaspoons ground cumin
½ teaspoon salt
1 teaspoon sugar
½ teaspoon tamarind concentrate
Chopped scallions for garnish

1. To roast eggplant, place it cut side down on a baking sheet lined with a piece of aluminum foil. Preheat broiler. Broil 12 to 20 minutes, or until eggplant is soft to the touch and the skin is wrinkled. Allow to cool. Using a fork, carefully extract the pulp. Discard skin. Shred the pulp coarsely and place in a large bowl along with any juice that accumulates. Set aside.

2. Heat oil in a medium-size skillet and sauté dried chiles until blackened, turning once. Add chopped onion and cook until richly browned but not burned, 8 to 10 minutes, stirring constantly. Add turmeric, cumin, salt, and sugar and stir to distribute evenly. Add the reserved eggplant pulp and juice. Simmer, covered, 7 to 10 minutes to blend the flavors, adding a little water if the mixture sticks to the bottom. Stir in tamarind. If the mixture is a little watery, remove eggplant with a slotted spoon to a large bowl, leaving any juice in the skillet. Over medium heat, cook until thick. Return eggplant to the skillet and mix well. Remove from heat, discard chiles, and let sit covered for 10 minutes. Garnish with scallions. This is best served warm. It can be prepared ahead and refrigerated, but reheat gently before serving.

Yield: 4 servings

SERVING SUGGESTIONS: Serve as an appetizer with crusty bread and Mint-Cilantro Chutney (page 213). At lunchtime, stuff into pita pockets with sliced tomatoes and sweet onion rings for a tasty sandwich. You can also serve this as an entrée with brown rice and Slow-Roasted Tomatoes (page 36).

CROSTINI WITH CHUTNEY
Italy/India

Crostini is the popular Italian toast, full of crunch, flavored with garlic and olive oil. It is often served alone, but the bite of an accompanying herb chutney gives it an added zest. This eye-catching pair makes a most inviting starter for any meal.

8 to 12 slices (½-inch-thick) Italian bread
2 tablespoons olive oil, or 1 tablespoon butter and
    1 tablespoon olive oil (for a richer flavor)
3 to 5 large garlic cloves, forced through a garlic press
1 teaspoon fresh tarragon, thyme, or other fresh herb of
    choice, or ½ teaspoon dried herb of choice
Sprinkling of Romano, Parmesan, or other grated hard
    cheese of choice
Mint-Cilantro Chutney (page 213)

1. Preheat the oven to 350 degrees F.

2. Arrange the bread slices on a large baking sheet. Bake for 10 to 14 minutes, or until golden, turning once.

3. Meanwhile, combine oil, garlic, and herbs in a small pan and heat gently just until warmed through. Remove bread from the oven, but don't turn the oven off. Brush each piece with this mixture, sprinkle with cheese, then return to the oven for another 6 to 10 minutes. Serve immediately with chutney on the side.

Yield: 8 to 12 slices; 4 appetizer servings

PECAN MUSHROOM PÂTÉ
France

A vegetarian friend once complained that she attended a party where the only pâté served was made with poultry liver. In my experience, this is usually the case, so I set out to develop a vegetarian version. The final result was this pâté with a rich, meaty taste and texture, similar to the French version on which it is based.

1 tablespoon olive oil
1 cup minced onion
3 to 5 large garlic cloves, minced
1 pound fresh mushrooms, stems trimmed, coarsely
    chopped
2 tablespoons canned vegetable broth
¾ cup pecans, lightly toasted and ground to a coarse
    powder in a blender or food processor
1 teaspoon regular or vegetarian oyster sauce, or more
    according to taste
1 scallion, very thinly sliced
Salt and freshly ground black pepper to taste

1. Preheat oven to 350 degrees F. Oil a small 7½ × 3½ × 2-inch loaf pan and set aside.

2. Heat oil in a medium skillet until sizzling. Sauté onion and garlic until onion is lightly browned. Reduce heat slightly. Add mushrooms and broth and cook, covered, 5 to 8 minutes, or just until mushrooms are soft. The skillet will now contain the vegetables and liquid from the mushrooms. Remove the vegetables and drain thoroughly over the skillet. Reduce the liquid remaining in the skillet by simmering uncovered over medium heat for a few minutes, until very thick. Set aside. Allow vegetables to cool to room temperature.

3. You can use either a food processor or blender to purée the vegetables. A food processor will produce the final result more quickly. If using a food processor, place the vegetables and liquid in the container and pulse a few times until a meal-like consistency results. If using a blender, purée the vegetables along with the liquid until smooth, adding a small amount of broth if the mixture becomes too thick to process. Remove to a bowl, add ground pecans, oyster sauce, and scallion and mix well. Season to taste with salt and pepper.

4. Spoon mixture into the prepared pan and bake for 30 minutes, or until a toothpick inserted near the center comes out clean. (If using a blender you will need to bake longer, 1 hour or until the top is set.) The pâté will feel soft to the touch. Allow to cool on a rack for 15 minutes. It may be served at this point, but the consistency will be more like a thick spread. Alternatively, if you wish to serve the pâté in slices, refrigerate (in the pan) until firm, about 2 hours (4 hours or more if using a blender).

Yield: 4 to 6 servings

SERVING SUGGESTIONS: Offer as an appetizer with celery and carrot sticks and Garlic Toast (page 41) or assorted crackers. To serve as an entrée, cut into ½-inch-thick slices and top with Peppery Tomato Sauce (page 230); accompany with Pesto-Laced Broccoli (page 120) and Indian-Style Roasted Potatoes (following recipe). Or spread on toasted bagel halves for a delicious sandwich.

SHIITAKE MUSHROOM VARIATION: Bits of darker mushrooms create a trufflelike effect and add a wonderfully rich flavor to this pâté. Sauté 3 to 4 minced fresh shiitake (or reconstituted dried shiitake or Chinese black mushrooms) separately in oil, then add to the vegetable mixture after processing in food processor or blender.

INDIAN-STYLE ROASTED POTATOES
India

Roasting is a time-honored form of cooking throughout the world. This Northern Indian approach is distinguished by the exotic marinades that are used to coat the vegetables. Potatoes are seasoned with a blend of cumin and asafetida, made tart by dried mango powder and lime juice. In deference to traditional Indian style, they are cut into large pieces, which allows them to be baked until they are crisp and crunchy outside, but not dry inside. When preparing these richly browned potatoes, you needn't worry about leftovers.

For variety, use Yellow Finn or Yukon Gold potatoes.

1½ to 2 tablespoons mustard oil or canola oil

½ teaspoon asafetida powder

1½ pounds new potatoes or other all-purpose
     potatoes (5 to 6 medium), peeled or unpeeled,
     cut into 1½-inch cubes

1½ teaspoons ground cumin

¾ teaspoon salt

½ teaspoon sugar

½ teaspoon mango powder (amchoor) (if available)

2 tablespoons freshly squeezed lime juice

Ground red pepper to taste (start with a scant pinch)

1. Preheat oven to 450 degrees F. Line a large baking sheet with a piece of aluminum foil and oil it lightly.

2. Heat oil in a large steep-sided skillet over medium-low heat until sizzling. Sprinkle asafetida over the oil. Add potatoes, tossing well to coat with the oil. Add cumin. Cook potatoes for 6 to 10 minutes, or until browned in places, turning them every 2 to 3 minutes. Adjust heat as necessary to prevent burning.

3. Combine salt, pepper, sugar, mango powder, lime juice, and red pepper in a small bowl. Pour over the potatoes. Toss to coat well with the sauce. As soon as the potatoes have absorbed the sauce, remove from heat.

4. Place potatoes in a single layer on the prepared baking sheet. Bake for 12 to 15 minutes, or until tender. Preheat broiler. Broil for 2 to 3 minutes, or until lightly browned on top. Take care not to burn. Serve immediately.

Yield: 4 servings

SERVING SUGGESTIONS: As an appetizer, serve with papads (page 24) and Mint-Cilantro Chutney (page 213). For a main meal, pair with Scrambled Tempeh (page 131). Two good partners at breakfast are scrambled eggs and Maple Pears (page 241).

Korean riddle: **What is a red silk purse that contains hundreds of gold coins?** *Answer:* **A red chile pepper.**

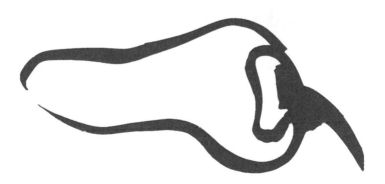

EASY BAKED POTATO CHIPS
United States/India

When I was growing up in India, we prepared our own potato chips by cutting the potatoes in thin rounds, dusting them with spices, then frying them. I didn't taste packaged potato chips until after my arrival in the West. They were oily and salty for my taste, so I continued to make my own, Indian-style. In this recipe I use some old standbys—asafetida, cumin, black salt, and red pepper, but I bake the chips instead of frying them. This not only lowers the fat content, but greatly simplifies the preparation. Make plenty, a trayful will disappear quickly.

1¼ pounds all-purpose potatoes (about 4 medium)
Black salt or regular salt
Ground red pepper to taste (start with a scant pinch)
2 tablespoons olive oil or canola oil
½ teaspoon asafetida powder
½ teaspoon ground cumin

1. Preheat oven to 425 degrees F. Line a 10 x 15-inch baking sheet with a piece of aluminum foil and oil it.

2. Cut the potatoes into slices about ¼-inch thick. Thinner slices may be crisper, but they won't brown as well. (They cook quicker than thicker pieces, which stay in the oven longer and turn brown in the process.) Pat slices on both sides with paper towels, then let rest between layers of paper towels for 5 to 10 minutes to absorb excess moisture. Remove paper towel. Place the potatoes on a large plate or in a bowl, sprinkle with salt and red pepper on both sides and toss to coat.

3. Heat oil in a small skillet until sizzling. Sprinkle asafetida over the oil. Add cumin and stir to mix well. Pour half of this mixture over the potatoes. Turn the potatoes and coat the other side with the remaining half. Arrange the potatoes in a single layer on the prepared baking sheet. Bake for about

20 minutes, or until tender. Preheat broiler. Broil for 3 to 4 minutes, or just until the tops are light to medium brown in color. Turn the potatoes and broil again to brown the other side. Check often and don't let them burn. Serve immediately. *Yield: 4 servings*

NOTE FOR THE GARDENER: My favorite variety of potatoes for this dish is Carola, a smooth-skinned, yellow-fleshed potato with a fine texture. Yellow Finn and Yukon Gold, two other yellow-fleshed potatoes, will do nearly as well and are more readily available.

SERVING SUGGESTIONS: Serve with sandwiches and burgers, as a snack, or as a side dish, alone or paired with Asian Pesto (page 215), Chile Chutney (page 212), or Cherry Tomato "Chalsa" (page 220).

VARIATION: SWEET POTATO CHIPS You can replace the potatoes entirely or in part with sweet potatoes, which produce a gentle sweet chip. Choose sweet potatoes that are similar in size and peel them before using.

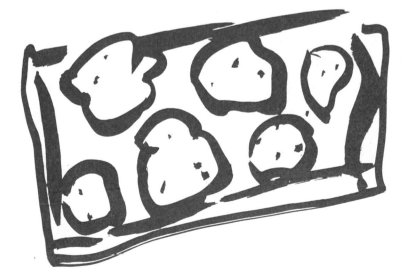

SLOW-ROASTED TOMATOES
United States/Italy

This recipe was inspired by the late Bert Greene's Long-Roasted Tomatoes. I have used this noted cook's wonderful slow-roasting technique and liberally seasoned the tomatoes with garlic, asafetida, basil, and thyme to achieve a result somewhat akin in taste to sun-dried tomatoes. In the process, the amount of oil has been greatly reduced.

Stimulate your palate before any meal with this joyous nibble.

2 tablespoons olive oil
¼ teaspoon asafetida powder
3 to 4 large garlic cloves, forced through a garlic press
2 tablespoons chopped fresh basil leaves, or
    2 teaspoons dried
2 tablespoons chopped fresh thyme, or
    2 teaspoons dried
½ teaspoon black salt or regular salt
Freshly ground black pepper to taste
1 pound Roma (plum) tomatoes (8 to 10 small)

1. Preheat oven to 450 degrees F.

2. Heat oil in a small skillet until sizzling. Sprinkle asafetida over the oil. Add garlic and sauté until golden. Remove from heat. When slightly cool, mix in basil and thyme. Add salt and pepper.

3. Cut the tomatoes in half crosswise and squeeze out the seeds. Arrange tomatoes in a single layer, cut sides up, in a large cake pan or baking dish. Spread a little of the herb-oil mixture over the top of each tomato. If any oil is remaining in the skillet, pour it over the tomatoes. Bake for about 10 minutes, or until the oil starts to sizzle. Reduce heat to 350 degrees F and continue to bake for another 1½ hours. This is best served immediately, but is also good at room temperature or chilled. Kept in the refrigerator, they

will last 1 or 2 days. If serving as a sandwich filling, keep the tomatoes in the oven for another 15 minutes after turning off the heat. This will dry them off slightly and make them easier to use as a filling.

Yield: 4 first-course or side-dish servings

SERVING SUGGESTIONS: The dish is versatile. Use it as a first course with peasant bread and a salad. Pair it at a luncheon with Wild and Brown Rice Salad (page 78). Try with baked potato and steamed vegetables for a simple supper. Fill a delightful sandwich at lunch using warm chapati, sliced tomatoes, cream cheese or plain yogurt, and these roasted tomatoes. Serve at an appetizer buffet with Indian-Style Roasted Potatoes (page 32), Spicy Roasted Chick-peas (page 24), Roasted Eggplant Relish (page 27), and some peasant bread.

MISO VARIATION: Mix in a teaspoon of red miso with the herb-oil mixture before spooning it over the tomatoes. Miso goes well with tomatoes and deepens their flavor.

VARIATION: CHERRY TOMATO CHIPS These unusual chips will be much appreciated. Use a basket (about ¾ pound) of cherry tomatoes. Slice them in half and squeeze out the seeds. Toss them gently with a dressing such as, Lime-Orange Vinaigrette (page 221) or Chile-Sesame Vinaigrette (page 223). Line a baking sheet with a piece of aluminum foil and oil it. Arrange tomatoes in a single layer on this foil with the cut sides up. Bake at 450 degrees F for 10 minutes. Reduce heat to 350 degrees F and continue to bake for another 20 minutes. Turn off heat and leave the tomatoes in the oven for another 20 to 30 minutes to dry them a bit more. Serve as above.

CURRY GYOZAS
Japan/India

Gyozas are stuffed crescent-shaped dumplings from Japan, similar to the pot-stickers offered in Chinese restaurants. These dumplings are easily made with gyoza wrappers: thin circles of dough about 3½ inches in diameter, sold in Asian markets and many supermarkets. Instead of an East Asian filling of pork and cabbage, I use a spicy sweet potato and pea mixture from India, with accents of black mustard and tamarind. These gyozas are so tasty that you can seldom stop after a few. Allow 4 or 5 per person, but it's wise to make a few extras.

You can shape gyozas by hand or use a dough press or gyoza press, a small gadget sold in kitchen stores and Asian markets. This press shapes the gyoza instantly while fluting its edges.

FILLING:

¾ pound sweet potato (1 medium), peeled and cubed
½ cup fresh or thawed frozen peas
1 tablespoon canola oil
¼ teaspoon black mustard seeds
½ to 1 teaspoon curry powder (see Note)
½ teaspoon sugar
½ teaspoon tamarind concentrate (optional)
Salt to taste
Ground red pepper to taste (start with a scant pinch)

GYOZAS:

About 25 to 30 gyoza wrappers (part of a 12-ounce
    package)
1 large egg, lightly beaten, for brushing (optional)
Oil for pan-frying

1. To prepare the filling, steam sweet potato cubes until tender, 15 to 18 minutes. Mash thoroughly. Steam the peas also until tender (5 to 8 minutes if fresh; 3 to 4 minutes if frozen). Mash the peas coarsely using a mortar and pestle or by placing them on a board and using a heavy object. They needn't be thoroughly mashed. Heat oil in a medium skillet until sizzling. Add mustard seeds and sauté until they pop and jump. (Hold the cover over the skillet to keep them from flying out.) Add curry powder and mix well. Add the reserved sweet potato, peas, and sugar and mix well. Cook, uncovered, for 2 to 3 minutes, stirring constantly. Add tamarind, salt, and red pepper. Remove from heat and allow to cool to room temperature.

2. To prepare the gyozas, remove wrappers from the package. If shaping by hand, place a wrapper on a board and spoon 1 teaspoon filling in the center. (Make sure no filling oozes out, as this will cause problems when sautéeing in the next step.) Moisten the edges with the beaten egg or water. Fold over and press firmly. If using a dough press, place a wrapper on the press. Spoon in the filling and moisten the edges as above. Bring the two handles together and press, which will fold the gyoza. Remove gyoza from the mold and place on a large plate. Repeat this process for all the wrappers.

3. Heat 1 tablespoon oil in a 10-inch skillet over moderate heat until sizzling. Reduce heat slightly and place gyozas in the skillet, folded edge on the side. You can fit about 12 gyozas at a time in this size skillet. Cook 2 to 3 minutes, or until lightly browned, then turn over to cook the other side for another minute. Check often because they burn quickly, adjusting heat as necessary. Pour ¼ cup water into the skillet and cover it to steam the gyozas. Cook for 3 to 5 minutes, or until all water is absorbed. Remove and drain in paper towels. Best if served warm.

Yield: 25 to 30 gyozas; 4 to 6 appetizer servings

NOTE: In place of storebought curry powder, you can use a mixture of ¼ teaspoon ground turmeric and ½ teaspoon each of ground cumin and ground coriander.

SERVING SUGGESTIONS: At the table, pass soy sauce and Chinese sesame oil for dipping. Continue with the Asian theme by serving Soy-Glazed Napa Cabbage (page 114) and rice. Finish with a cup of roasted barley tea and some melon or cantaloupe slices. This filling is delicious on its own and can also be served as a side dish with rice or couscous.

VARIATION: SWEET GYOZAS Turn these gyozas into a light dessert by filling them with a marmalade or preserve or any prepared fruit filling of your choice. Mince the filling finely or else it can tear the dumplings. Cook as above and, optionally, just before serving, sprinkle with some confectioner's sugar. Serve warm.

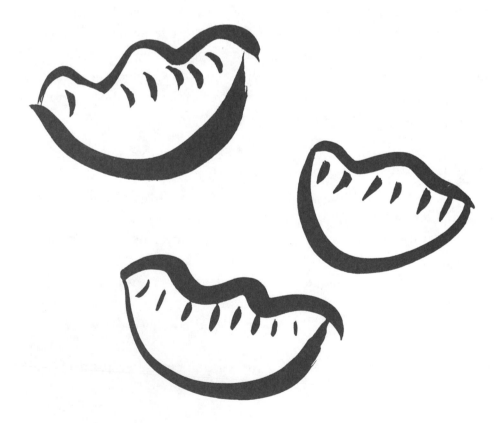

GARLIC TOAST
United States

Garlic bread is irresistible as a meal starter, but is often loaded with fat. In this recipe, the usual excess of butter has been replaced by a small amount of fine olive oil augmented by an avalanche of puréed roasted garlic.

5 whole heads garlic
1 to 2 tablespoons extra-virgin olive oil
½ teaspoon asafetida powder
1 tablespoon chopped fresh oregano or parsley
Salt to taste (optional)
1 loaf crusty sourdough or baguette bread

1. Preheat oven to 425 degrees F.

2. Arrange garlic heads on an ungreased baking sheet. Bake for 20 to 35 minutes, or just until they feel soft when pinched lightly. Remove each as it's done. Larger heads will take longer. Remove the outer skin layers and place the softened cloves in a blender or food processor container. Add the oil and asafetida and process until smooth. Remove to a small bowl. Add the oregano or parsley and salt, if desired.

3. Cut bread in half lengthwise. Spread garlic mixture evenly over the cut sides. Join the halves together, then make horizontal slashes across the bread, about 1½-inch intervals, keeping the bread intact. Place bread on a large piece of aluminum foil and cover tightly. (Up to this point the recipe can be prepared about an hour ahead.) Just before serving, bake in a pre-heated 350-degree oven for 15 minutes, or until heated through. To keep warm, remove 1 or more slices at a time from the foil pouch and serve.

Yield: 4 servings

SERVING SUGGESTIONS: Try with Corn, Potato, and Lima Bean Chowder (page 56), and a salad of Napa cabbage dressed with Lime-Peanut Vinaigrette (page 222). For luncheon, pair with Orzo and Asparagus Salad (page 83) and Kale-Apple Soup (page 68).

VARIATION: ROSEMARY-GARLIC CROUTONS Prepare through Step 2, substituting 1 tablespoon chopped fresh rosemary (or 1 teaspoon dried) for the oregano. Cut the bread into crouton-size pieces and arrange on a large ungreased baking sheet. Bake at 350 degrees F for 10 to 15 minutes, or just until the pieces are crisp and lightly browned. Using a pastry brush, spread the garlic mixture on top of each. Bake for a few minutes more to heat the topping through. These croutons are wonderful with soups, on top of green salads, and as a garnish for bean stews.

OTHER VARIATIONS: Try a dash of black salt. Consider rosemary or thyme instead of oregano.

LIGHT
AND
SUBSTANTIAL
SOUPS

The beautiful city of Qingdao in China is famous for its beer and, to me, for its fantastic soup. Returning there from a hike to the nearby Lao Shan mountain with my tour group, we stopped for lunch at a restaurant called The Mouth of Sand. Our meal was composed of rice, pickled vegetables, and several delicious stir-fries, served in courses. Just when we thought the meal was finished, the waiter brought the tastiest dish of all, an enormous tureen of plump dumplings floating in a rich, clear broth. Already pleasantly full, we helped ourselves to a bowlful and returned for seconds. We were so taken with the quality of the soup that we asked to meet the chef.

Looking a bit puzzled, the chef, a shy young man, smiled and welcomed us into a large, simple kitchen centered around a wood stove. We were amazed that the extraordinary meal we had just experienced had come from such a humble source. I wanted to tell him how wonderful his meal was, particularly the soup, but I didn't speak Mandarin well enough. So I made gestures of sipping from a bowl with a blissful expression on my face. He understood and laughed heartily.

Soups come in two widely different spectrums that range from Asian-style thin soups flecked with bits of vegetables, to Western-style thick bean and root vegetable soups. Between these two extremes lies a large selection: silken cream soups and bisques, cold gazpachos and egg-rich veloutés, dals and rice gruels. There is a soup for every mood and occasion.

If hot soups offer comfort in winter, chilled soups save us from over-heating in summer. That was my experience in Athens one scorching August day when, after sightseeing for hours, I was revived by a cooling concoction of Chilled Cucumber-Buttermilk Soup (page 66). I later found that this soup tastes good in all kinds of weather.

Soup is often the first course in a meal, and, if so, must offer a promise of things to come. This can seem intimidating, but any vegetable that one can steam or purée, can be whirled up in a blender or food processor into soup. A substantial stock helps, but isn't always necessary. When pressed for time, I prepare a soup using water as a base with garlic, gingerroot, whole spices, and vegetable bouillon to enhance the flavor.

Rice or potatoes are healthier for thickening a soup than a butter-and-flour roux. Unconventional thickeners like puréed lima beans, a handful of quinoa, or cooked and mashed sweet potatoes offer new alternatives. Besides thickening the broth, they add a special richness and nuance of flavor.

Toppings and sauces not only make a soup exciting, but allow for individual variations. When the French serve bouillabaisse, a fish soup, they put rouille, a sauce of garlic, olive oil, and bell pepper, next to it. When Asians enjoy their noodle soups, soy sauce and chile oil are standard condiments. My toppings include these standbys as well as slivers of seaweed, caramelized onions, and toasted garlic chips.

A meal centered around a hearty Western-style soup is not complete unless accompanied by a robust bread. The markets in my neighborhood sell Italian peasant bread, whole-grain and potato breads, as well as chapatis and tortillas. With such a wide variety of choices, I can always sit down to a meal of soup with pleasant anticipation.

VEGETABLE STOCK
International

A vegetable stock can be prepared in many different ways, but this recipe is my favorite. Here the vegetables are first browned in oil, then simmered in a mixture of water and wine, along with a generous amount of fresh tarragon and thyme. Sweet-tasting leeks, carrots, and parsnips add their delicate juices. I use this stock as a base for almost any soup or in place of water when cooking stews.

1 tablespoon olive oil
1 cup coarsely chopped onion
2 medium carrots (½ pound), diced
½ pound parsnips, scraped to remove root hairs
   if necessary, diced
1 red bell pepper, seeds and inner ribs removed,
   coarsely chopped
2 leeks, white parts only, thoroughly cleaned,
   coarsely chopped
2 kale leaves, coarsely chopped, stems diced
A few sprigs each of thyme, tarragon, and parsley or
   cilantro
7 cups water, or a combination of canned vegetable
   broth and water
1 cup white wine
Salt to taste (optional)

1. Heat oil in a large stockpot. Add onion, carrots, and parsnips, and cook until they are browned in places, 6 to 8 minutes. Add all the remaining ingredients except salt. Bring to a boil. Lower heat slightly and cook,

uncovered, for 30 minutes, turning the vegetables occasionally. Remove from heat. If time allows, cover and let stand for at least 15 minutes to further enrich the stock. Pour contents of the stockpot into a large colander placed over a large bowl, then press the vegetables in the colander with the back of a spoon to extract all the natural juices. (Don't press so hard that it forces them through the colander into the stock below, as it will make the stock cloudy. If this should happen, strain the cloudy stock through several layers of cheesecloth.) The clear stock that accumulates in the bowl is now ready for use. (You can prepare ahead and freeze if you like.) Add salt to taste, if desired. The vegetables remaining in the colander can be used as a purée as described below, or discarded. *Yield: 4½ cups*

MONEY-SAVING TIP: For a simple, flavorful purée that can be served as a side dish, discard thyme and tarragon sprigs, and process the rest of the vegetables in a blender or food processor until smooth, adding a little water or stock if necessary. Place in a pan and heat thoroughly. Heat 2 teaspoons oil in a small skillet. Add ½ teaspoon black mustard seeds and ½ teaspoon asafetida powder and cook until the seeds start to pop. Or you can add minced garlic and grated gingerroot and sauté until golden. Pour this mixture over the purée. Season to taste with salt and pepper.

Yield: 4 to 6 servings

ZUCCHINI VICHYSSOISE
France

The traditional vichyssoise is a thick potato purée, enriched with cream and served cold. This zucchini version, flavored with saffron and fresh herbs, is thickened with minced potatoes and skimmed milk. On top of that, it offers seasonal variations. The main recipe below is delightfully light and served chilled in summer. The warm autumn variation that follows is made substantial by the addition of golden brown chunks of potato.

1 cup coarsely chopped onion
1 small to medium potato (¼ pound), peeled and
　　finely chopped
3 cups Vegetable Stock (page 45) or canned
　　vegetable broth, or more as needed
1½ pounds zucchini or summer squash, thinly sliced
　　(see Note)
2 tablespoons fresh chopped basil or tarragon or parsley
½ cup evaporated skim milk (see Vegan Alternative)
Salt to taste
½ cup fresh corn or thawed frozen corn
½ cup fresh peas or thawed frozen peas
½ to 1 teaspoon saffron threads, soaked in 1 tablespoon
　　warm water or milk for 10 minutes (optional)
Chopped cilantro for garnish

POTATOES: (OMIT FOR THE CHILLED VERSION)
½ pound all-purpose potatoes (about 2 medium),
　　peeled and cubed
1 tablespoon olive oil
¼ teaspoon asafetida powder
Salt to taste

1. Place onion, chopped potato, and stock in a large pot and bring to a boil. Lower heat. Simmer, covered, for 5 minutes. Add zucchini and basil. Cover and simmer for 8 to 15 minutes, or until zucchini is tender. Using a slotted spoon, lift off a few zucchini pieces and set aside in a small plate to be used as a garnish. Purée the remaining mixture, in batches, in a blender or food processor. If the mixture is too thick to process, add a little more stock. Add milk and salt. Return to the pot and bring to a simmer over low heat.

2. Add corn, peas, and saffron with its soaking liquid. Cook, covered, for 5 to 8 minutes (3 to 5 minutes, if using both thawed frozen corn and peas), or until the vegetables are tender. Don't boil the soup; the texture will suffer. Taste and adjust seasoning. If serving cold, chill for at least 1 hour. Garnish chilled soup with reserved zucchini pieces and cilantro. If serving hot, keep warm until potatoes are ready in the next step.

3. Steam the cubed potatoes until tender, about 15 minutes. Heat oil in a medium skillet until sizzling. Sprinkle asafetida over the oil. Add potatoes and salt. Stirring often, cook potatoes until they turn medium brown, 5 to 10 minutes. Adjust heat as necessary to prevent burning. Add the sautéed potatoes to the warm soup. Garnish as above.

Yield: 4 entrée or 8 first-course servings

NOTE: You can use pattypan or other summer squashes. Make sure the squashes are all of the same color—either green or yellow—so the finished soup will have a uniformly pleasant color.

SERVING SUGGESTIONS: My favorite grain accompaniment is Saffron-Baked Quinoa (page 172). The salad should be light, some Bibb lettuce and toasted sunflower seeds. End the meal with a cup of hot chocolate or a slice of Chocolate-Macadamia Temptation (page 258).

VEGAN ALTERNATIVE: Substitute soy milk for regular milk or omit milk altogether. The soup will still be tasty.

FISH OR SHRIMP VARIATION: For those who eat fish or meat, a delicious alternative is to poach slivers of any firm-fleshed fish, such as salmon, cod, or tuna, raw shrimp, or scallops in this flavorful soup. Use about ½ pound seafood and add along with corn and peas in Step 2. Cook for 5 minutes, or until a toothpick inserted in the thickest part of the fish or shrimp shows an opaque color. Serve as a main course for 2.

SQUASH-RICE SOUP WITH TASTY TOPPINGS
Mexico

In Mazatlán, weary of seeing sights, I came upon a vegetarian restaurant that served this thick, smooth red-orange soup. An exercise in simplicity, it was a comforting blend of squash, rice, and seasonings. When re-creating the soup at home, I dressed it up by adding cashews and caramelized onions and topping with garlic bread crumbs. It's now a favorite first course for family dining or entertaining guests.

SOUP:

1 butternut squash (1½ pounds), unpeeled, seeded,
　　coarsely chopped (or buttercup, Delicata, or
　　Hubbard squash, peeled)
¼ pound carrots, thinly sliced (about 1 cup)
1 cup coarsely chopped onion
3 to 5 large garlic cloves, coarsely chopped
1 tablespoon coarsely chopped gingerroot
3 cups water
¼ to ½ cup low-fat milk
½ cup cooked white Basmati rice
Dash of nutmeg
Salt and freshly ground black pepper to taste

TOPPINGS:

1 tablespoon garlic chips or dehydrated garlic flakes
　　(see Note)
1 tablespoon olive oil
½ medium sweet red or other mild onion, thinly sliced
1 tablespoon unsalted raw cashew halves

GARNISH:

Chopped cilantro

1. Bring squash, carrots, onion, garlic, gingerroot, and water to a boil in a large pot. Reduce heat and simmer, covered, 20 to 25 minutes, or until the vegetables are tender. Purée in batches, along with ¼ cup milk and ¼ cup cooked rice, in a blender or food processor. If too thick, add up to ¼ cup more milk. Return to the pot along with the remaining ¼ cup rice and nutmeg and season to taste with salt and pepper. Bring to a simmer over low heat.

2. Toast the garlic chips in an ungreased skillet until lightly browned, turning them often. Transfer to a small bowl. Heat olive oil in a small skillet, and sauté onion slices and cashews until onion turns limp and cashews start to brown.

Remove from heat and transfer to a small bowl. Ladle soup into individual bowls and sprinkle with the onion-cashew mixture and garlic crumbs. Serve garnished with cilantro.   *Yield: 2 entrée or 4 first-course servings*

NOTE: Garlic flakes are available in Asian markets and garlic chips are sold in supermarkets. You can use fresh garlic instead, but dried garlic with its intense flavor and a crisper texture is better suited as a soup topping.

SERVING SUGGESTIONS: My favorite accompaniments are Savory Bean Pie (page 202), warm corn tortillas, and a salad of spinach, grapefruit sections, and sweet onions dressed with Lime-Peanut Vinaigrette (page 222). If a dessert is called for, serve some dried persimmons and dried papaya spears, or go for Almond Pear Tart (page 250).

In Assam, India, "a pot without a cover" refers to unattended business, but "a pot that has found its lid" is a Lebanese expression for a well-matched couple.

CARROT-LENTIL SOUP WITH ROSEMARY-GARLIC CROUTONS

India/United States

Lentil soup, *dal*, was my childhood favorite when growing up in India. After I came to the United States, carrot soup soon ranked alongside it. But until recently, I never considered combining them in the same dish. The resulting soup represents the best of both worlds, lentils for protein and bulk, carrots and sweet potatoes for beta-carotene and sweetness.

Two other ingredients, which further enhance this happy combination of East and West, are crispy croutons to add texture to the soup and fragrant dark green basil leaves to emphasize its deep orange color.

VEGETABLES:
¾ pound carrots (about 3 large), diced
½ pound sweet potato (1 small), peeled, cubed
1 small onion, coarsely chopped
3 large garlic cloves, coarsely chopped
1 cup Vegetable Stock (page 45) or canned
    vegetable broth
2 cups water

LENTILS:
½ cup red lentils (page 17)
1½ cups water
¼ teaspoon ground turmeric
2 whole jalapeños or other fresh chiles
Salt to taste
Ground red pepper to taste
1 tablespoon chopped fresh basil or parsley

SPICES:

1 tablespoon canola oil

¼ teaspoon black mustard seeds

¼ teaspoon kalonji seeds

1 tablespoon minced garlic

GARNISH:

Rosemary-Garlic Croutons (page 42) and chopped
 fresh basil (if available)

1. Place carrots, sweet potato, onion, garlic, stock, and 2 cups water in a large pot and bring to a boil. Lower heat and simmer, covered, until vegetables are tender, 15 to 20 minutes. Process the mixture in a blender or food processor until smooth. Return to the pot.

2. In a separate medium-size pot, bring lentils and 1½ cups water to a boil. Skim off the surface foam with a spoon and discard. Reduce heat. Add turmeric and jalapeños and simmer, covered, until lentils are tender, about 15 minutes. (When pressed between two fingers they will crumble easily.) Discard jalapeños.

3. Process the lentil mixture in a blender or food processor until smooth, and add to the carrot-sweet potato mixture. Season to taste with salt and red pepper. Add basil. Place over low heat to heat the soup through. Don't let it boil vigorously.

4. Heat oil in a small skillet until a light haze forms. Add black mustard seeds. As soon as the seeds start to pop, add kalonji. Hold the cover over the skillet if the spices start to fly out. Add minced garlic and cook until golden. Pour this oil-spice mixture over the soup. Serve garnished with the croutons and basil. *Yield: 2 entrée or 4 first-course servings*

SERVING SUGGESTIONS: To balance the color and nutritional qualities of this dish, serve with white Basmati rice and steamed Swiss chard sprinkled with Tofu Cream (page 226). Finish the meal with Lemon Mousse Surprise (page 236). For a hearty lunch, pair with Potato Koftas (page 96).

SWEET POTATO BISQUE
Caribbean

Unlike traditional cream-enriched bisques, this tasty lowfat Caribbean version is thickened with puréed sweet potato and skim milk. It is enlivened with kalonji, a blue-black seed with an onionlike flavor that is widely used in Indian cooking.

1½ pounds sweet potatoes, peeled and cubed
3 cups Vegetable Stock (page 45) or canned
    vegetable broth
½ teaspoon ground turmeric
¼ cup evaporated skim milk
1½ teaspoons sugar
Ground red pepper to taste
Salt and white pepper to taste
1½ tablespoons canola oil
½ teaspoon kalonji seeds
1 cup thinly sliced onion
1 tablespoon freshly squeezed lime juice
Finely chopped cilantro for garnish

1. In a large pot, bring sweet potatoes and stock to a boil. Add turmeric. Lower heat and simmer, covered, 15 to 18 minutes, or until potatoes are tender.

2. Process the mixture in a blender or food processor until smooth, adding a little water if the mixture is too thick. Return to the pot. Add milk, sugar, and red pepper. Season to taste with salt and white pepper. Over gentle heat, bring soup to a simmer. Keep warm over very low heat.

3. Heat oil in a small skillet until sizzling. Sauté kalonji seeds for a few seconds. Add onions and cook until richly browned, 6 to 10 minutes, stirring

often. Pour this mixture over the soup. Stir in lime juice. Taste and adjust seasoning. Serve garnished with chopped cilantro.

Yield: 4 entrée or 8 first-course servings

SERVING SUGGESTIONS: This versatile soup goes with most meals, but is especially good with Sesame-Sauced Spinach (page 125) and Indian-Style Roasted Potatoes (page 32). A platter of fresh fruits and Nutty Cream (page 264) will complete the supper. Or use it as a lunch companion to Leek-Mushroom Burgers (page 105).

VARIATIONS: For a fine fragrance, add ½ teaspoon saffron threads that have been steeped in 1 tablespoon warm water or milk for 15 minutes, along with milk and sugar in Step 2.

Seafood is delicious when poached in this soup. Once the soup is ready, add ½ pound scallops or peeled, deveined fresh shrimp and cook over gentle heat until tender, about 5 minutes. You can also add cooked crabmeat, which will only require heating through. Saffron goes particularly well with any of the above-named seafood.

CORN, POTATO, AND LIMA BEAN CHOWDER

United States

When I first came to the United States, I was fascinated by the wide variety of rich, creamy chowders. Fancy restaurants as well as simple eateries served them, each with its own unique blend of ingredients. I have come to appreciate the full feeling chowder leaves me with, and have developed my own vegetarian version. This unusual potato and corn chowder is thickened with a nutrient-dense lima bean purée and milk instead of cream, and contains fresh tarragon for a country-fresh flavor. It is wholesome, delightful, and substantial, all the things a good chowder should be.

1½ tablespoons olive oil
1 cup finely chopped onion
3 large garlic cloves, minced
1 pound potatoes (about 4 medium), peeled and diced
    (see Note)
2 cups Vegetable Stock (page 45) or canned
    vegetable broth
¾ cup bean liquid or water
1 cup home-cooked lima beans, or one 15-ounce can
    lima beans, drained, cooking or can liquid saved
1 cup whole or low-fat milk
1 medium-sized green bell pepper, coarsely chopped
1 cup fresh corn kernels or thawed frozen corn
1 tablespoon chopped fresh tarragon, or
    1 teaspoon dried
Salt and freshly ground black pepper to taste

1. Heat oil in large stockpot, and sauté onion and garlic until onion is translucent. Stir in the potatoes.

2. Add stock and bean liquid, cover, and bring to a boil. Reduce heat and cook, covered, 10 minutes, or until the potatoes are half-done.

3. Meanwhile, place lima beans and milk in a blender and purée until smooth. Add to the pot.

4. Add the bell pepper, corn (if fresh), and tarragon. Simmer, covered, 6 to 10 minutes, or until the vegetables are tender. If using thawed frozen corn, add during the last 3 minutes of cooking. Remove from heat. Process 3 cups of this soup in a blender or food processor until smooth. (This will create a textural variation in the soup, part smooth and part coarse.) Return to the pot. Season to taste with salt and pepper. Reheat gently before serving.

Yield: 2 entrée or 4 first-course servings

NOTE: If using red-skinned new potatoes, they can be left unpeeled. The red bits of skin make a lovely color pattern in the soup.

SERVING SUGGESTIONS: Garlic Toast (page 41) and Sweet Hot Swiss Chard (page 110) are lovely accompaniments. For dessert, consider ripe peach slices or frozen peach yogurt. Serve any leftovers with papads (page 24).

VARIATION: For extra richness, add 1 tablespoon half-and-half or cream to the soup at the end. If you eat seafood, toss in cooked mussels, smoked salmon or halibut while reheating in Step 4.

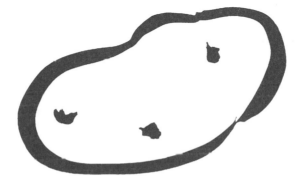

TWO-BEAN SHORBA
India

Shorba, from the cool northern part of India, is a thin, smooth lentil broth with a lime flavor. It is generally made with red lentils that turn a pleasant yellow color when cooked. This *shorba* is made more substantial by the addition of plump red kidney beans. Cumin seeds and caramelized onions are two other flavorful accents. The soup is particularly appropriate in winter, but will satisfy hearty appetites throughout the year.

1 cup red lentils (page 17)
3 cups water
¼ teaspoon ground turmeric
1 whole jalapeño or other fresh chile
¼ pound Roma (plum) tomatoes (about 2), unpeeled
    and coarsely chopped
1½ cups home-cooked or canned red kidney beans
    (one 15-ounce can), drained
Salt to taste
Ground red pepper to taste (start with a scant pinch;
    see Note)
2 tablespoons canola oil
¼ teaspoon cumin seeds
1 cup finely chopped onion
2 tablespoons freshly squeezed lime juice
Chopped cilantro for garnish
Lime wedges for garnish

1. Bring lentils and water to a boil in a large saucepan. Lower heat. Remove and discard the foam from the top. Add turmeric, jalapeño, and tomatoes. Cook, covered, until the lentils are tender, about 15 minutes. (They will crumble easily when pressed between two fingers.) Discard jalapeño.

2. Process the mixture in a blender or food processor until smooth. Return to the pot. Add kidney beans and bring to a gentle simmer. Add salt and red pepper to taste. Keep warm over very low heat.

3. Heat oil in a medium skillet until sizzling. Add cumin seeds and cook until they brown lightly. Add onion and cook until richly browned but not burned, 7 to 10 minutes, stirring often. Transfer to a plate. Remove soup from the heat and mix in lime juice. Taste and adjust seasoning. Transfer soup to a serving bowl, or ladle into individual bowls. Float the browned onions and cumin on top. Sprinkle with chopped cilantro and garnish with lime wedges. Serve piping hot.   *Yield: 2 entrée or 4 to 6 first-course servings*

NOTE: A highly recommended alternative to ground red pepper is ground chipotle pepper, available in natural food stores and specialty stores. Its pungent, smoky flavor produces a stunning effect when combined with the red lentils and kidney beans.

SERVING SUGGESTIONS: Terrific with any grain dish, such as Nut-Topped Savory Rice (page 174). For a fine accompanying sauce, try Two-Tomato Jam (page 232). A salad of spinach dressed with Lime-Orange Vinaigrette (page 221) is appropriate. For dessert, consider a platter of fresh apple or pear slices alone or with Honey-Yogurt Splash (page 225). Serve any leftovers with rice cakes for lunch.

To the Persians, an honored person may or may not be "a soup worthy of its tureen."

BEAN AND BROCCOLI SOUP
United States

A hearty soup, thickened by a navy bean and potato purée, this is a meal in itself.

1 cup finely chopped onion
3 large garlic cloves, minced
½ pound all-purpose potatoes (about 2 medium),
    peeled and cubed
3 cups Vegetable Stock (page 45) or canned
    vegetable broth
1 pound broccoli, cut into small florets, stems peeled
    and diced
1 tablespoon fresh basil, or 1 teaspoon dried
1 cup cooked navy beans or one 15-ounce can navy
    beans, drained, cooking or can liquid saved
½ cup bean liquid or water
Salt and freshly ground black pepper to taste
Garlic Bread Crumbs (page 233) and/or grated
    Parmesan or other hard cheese of choice for garnish

1. Bring onion, garlic, potatoes, stock, and broccoli stems to a boil in a large pot. Reduce heat and cook, covered, 10 minutes, or until the vegetables are almost tender. Add broccoli florets and basil and cook, covered, another 10 minutes, or until the florets are tender.

2. Remove from heat. With a slotted spoon, remove the florets and place them on a plate. Purée half of the remaining mixture along with the navy beans and bean liquid in a blender or food processor. Return to the pot. Add the reserved florets. Over gentle heat, bring soup to a simmer. Season to taste with salt and pepper. Serve with croutons and/or cheese garnishes.

Yield: 2 large entrée or 4 to 6 first-course servings

SERVING SUGGESTIONS: Try with toasted whole-grain bread and Beets and Feta Cheese in a Spinach Nest (page 86). Fresh fruit and a dipping sauce of Lemon Satin (page 263) will complete the meal. At lunchtime, it is excellent with Hazelnut-Rice Burgers (page 105).

ROASTED GARLIC SOUP
International

This recipe is a variation of the classic Spanish garlic soup. Here the garlic is roasted first to impart a robust aroma to the finished dish. Orzo, the rice-shaped pasta, swells up in the broth to become plump and mellow. The dish contains little added fat, yet has a richness commonly associated with dishes whose fat content is high.

15 large garlic cloves, peeled
Olive oil for brushing
4½ cups Vegetable Stock (page 45) or canned
    vegetable broth
1½ cups water
½ cup orzo
1 tablespoon chopped fresh thyme, or 1 teaspoon dried
½ cup fresh or thawed frozen peas
Salt and freshly ground black pepper to taste
Rosemary-Garlic Croutons (page 42) (optional)

1. Preheat oven to 450 degrees F. Lightly oil a baking sheet.

2. Brush garlic cloves with oil and arrange on a baking sheet. Bake for 10 to 15 minutes, or until soft and browned around the edges. Remove each piece as it's done. Check often and don't let them become too brown or they will impart a bitter taste to the soup. When all the cloves are done, process in a blender or food processor along with 1 cup stock until a smooth purée results. Set aside.

3. Bring the remaining 3½ cups stock and the water to a boil in a stockpot. Lower the heat slightly. Add orzo and cook, uncovered, until tender, 7 to 10 minutes. The best way to check is to taste. (It should be *al dente*.) Add thyme, the reserved garlic purée, and peas. Cook, covered, until the peas are done (3 to 5 minutes if thawed frozen; 7 to 9 minutes if fresh) and the mixture is heated through. Season to taste with salt and pepper. If allowed to stand, the orzo will absorb some of the liquid. The dish will still taste good, though the consistency will be thicker. Serve alone or accompanied by Rosemary-Garlic Croutons. *Yield: 4 to 6 first-course servings*

SERVING SUGGESTIONS: Start with Pecan Mushroom Pâté (page 30) and follow with a salad of romaine, arugula, and toasted pumpkin seeds. Plum Kuchen (page 254) will round out the meal. This is also delicious served with Tofu-Walnut Burgers (page 104).

VARIATIONS: ROASTED GARLIC AND BARLEY SOUP Substitute ¼ cup toasted pearl barley for orzo. Toast the barley by placing in an ungreased skillet over medium-low heat until lightly browned, stirring often. In Step 3, simmer covered, until barley is tender, 20 to 30 minutes.

For a more substantial soup, add leftover potato or carrot cubes in Step 3 along with peas. Alternatively, add half a 14-ounce carton of drained, rinsed, and cubed firm tofu in Step 3, along with peas.

TOMATO-PEANUT SOUP
Africa

Peanut butter can be used to make a delicious soup; however, its flavor can be overwhelming, even cloying, when used to excess. In this recipe, where tomatoes predominate, this is not a problem. To shorten the cooking time and impart a rich, roasted aroma, the tomatoes are broiled before being added to the soup. A modest amount of peanut butter, incorporated into the soup toward the end, imparts a mellow background flavor.

This is one of my year-round favorites, although it is at its best during summer when fresh Roma tomatoes and basil leaves are at the peak of flavor.

2 pounds Roma (plum) tomatoes
1 tablespoon olive oil
1 cup finely chopped onion
3 to 5 large garlic cloves, finely minced
¼ teaspoon ground turmeric
½ teaspoon salt
Freshly ground black pepper to taste
2 tablespoons peanut butter
1 large egg, lightly beaten (see Vegan Alternative)
Garlic Bread Crumbs (page 233) for garnish
Chopped fresh basil for garnish

1. Arrange the tomatoes on a baking sheet and broil them for 5 to 8 minutes, or until their skin is wrinkled and charred in places. Remove charred parts of the skin and discard. Purée the tomatoes and any accumulated juices in a blender or food processor until smooth.

2. Heat oil in a large pot. Cook onion and garlic until onion is translucent and slightly soft, 2 to 3 minutes. Stir in turmeric. Add puréed tomatoes, salt, and

pepper. Reduce heat and simmer, covered, 5 to 8 minutes. Add peanut butter and stir until dissolved. Stirring constantly, add the egg, a teaspoon at a time, until thoroughly blended. (If the heat is too high or if not stirred enough the egg will start to cook instead of forming a sauce.) Taste and adjust salt. Serve garnished with Garlic Bread Crumbs and chopped basil.

Yield: 4 first-course servings

SERVING SUGGESTIONS: Complete a simple but delicious meal with Pear Slaw with Honey Pecans (page 84), carrot sticks, and hard-boiled egg slices. On another occasion, serve with crusty rolls and a romaine and radicchio salad.

VEGAN ALTERNATIVE: The soup is good even without the egg. For more body, add ½ cup cooked white rice in place of egg in Step 2.

THAI PEA SOUP
Thailand/India

During the brief time when fresh peas are abundant, late spring through early summer, they are a delicacy. This gently sweet soup derives a hint of pungency from Thai curry paste. The spiciness is further accented by the Indian technique of sautéeing black mustard seeds in a small amount of hot oil and incorporating them into the soup at the last minute. If fresh peas aren't available, use frozen peas. The soup will still be marvelous.

4 cups shelled fresh peas, or one 20-ounce bag
    thawed frozen peas
3 cups Vegetable Stock (page 45) or canned
    vegetable broth
3 to 5 large garlic cloves, finely minced
½ to 1 teaspoon Thai green curry paste
2 tablespoons chopped fresh mint, or 2 teaspoons dried
Salt and freshly ground black pepper to taste
1 teaspoon canola oil
½ teaspoon black mustard seeds

1. Bring fresh peas and stock to a boil in a stockpot. Add garlic, curry paste, and mint, and simmer, covered, 7 to 12 minutes, or just until peas are tender. (If using thawed frozen peas, add them after the ingredients have simmered for 4 to 5 minutes. Simmer an additional 3 to 4 minutes.) Process the mixture, in batches, in a blender or food processor until smooth. Season to taste with salt and pepper.

2. Heat oil in a small skillet until sizzling. Add mustard seeds and sauté until they start to pop. Pour this oil-spice mixture over the soup.

Yield: 3 to 4 entrée or 6 first-course servings

SERVING SUGGESTIONS: Focaccia bread or breadsticks is the perfect accompaniment. Grilled Eggplant and Toasted Pecan Salad (page 78) will make this a wholesome and filling meal. Peach Flan (page 238) is a compatible dessert.

VARIATIONS: If you want a less spicy soup, omit the curry paste. For a richer flavor, fold in 2 tablespoons coconut milk along with the oil-spice mixture in Step 2. On the other hand, if you are concerned about saturated fat, omit coconut milk. For those who eat seafood, shrimp is a good addition. Cook ¼ pound (thawed frozen) shrimp in the soup at the end of Step 1, just until heated through.

CHILLED CUCUMBER-BUTTERMILK SOUP
Greece/Middle East

This is one of my favorite chilled soups, a Middle Eastern gazpacho of sorts. Traditionally, yogurt serves as the base, but I find a mixture of yogurt and buttermilk, enriched by a mayonnaise of ground walnuts and fine olive oil, greatly improves the flavor and texture of this Mediterranean classic.

2 tablespoons chopped walnuts, ground in a
    blender or food processor to a coarse powder
½ teaspoon salt
2 large garlic cloves, coarsely chopped
1½ tablespoons extra-virgin olive oil
1½ cups low-fat buttermilk
1 cup plain nonfat yogurt, lightly beaten until smooth
2 to 3 tablespoons freshly squeezed lime juice
1 cup peeled, seeded, and finely chopped cucumber
½ cup finely chopped red or other sweet onion
    (preferred; or yellow onions)
2 tablespoons dried currants, soaked in warm water
    for 15 minutes, drained
1 tablespoon chopped fresh dill or parsley for
    garnish
1 tablespoon chopped fresh mint for garnish
    (omit if not available)

In a blender or food processor, process walnuts, salt, garlic, and oil until mixture is reduced to a fine-grained purée. Transfer to a large bowl. Combine buttermilk and yogurt in a separate large bowl and stir until smooth, then add to the walnut mixture. Also add 2 tablespoons lime juice, cucumber, onion, and drained currants. Taste and adjust salt and add more lime juice if you like. Chill for at least 30 minutes. Serve garnished with chopped dill and mint.

Yield: 4 first-course servings

SERVING SUGGESTIONS: Accompany with potato salad and warm chapatis or tortillas. For a summer brunch, try with warm pita triangles, Roasted Eggplant Relish (page 27), and a salad of red-leaf lettuce and grapefruit sections. For those who eat meat, serve with lamb kabobs (or grilled chicken or fish) and Orzo and Asparagus Salad (page 83). Follow with a cup of Turkish coffee, if you like. At lunchtime enjoy with Sweet Tempeh Burgers (page 102) and perhaps some mango pickle (available in Indian groceries).

FETA CHEESE VARIATION: For extra flavor, add a dash of black salt (cutting down the amount of regular salt in this case) and crumble some feta cheese on top.

VARIATION: CHILLED JICAMA-BUTTERMILK SOUP Crispy, juicy jicama, which is available in many supermarkets, can substitute for the cucumber and makes a delightful soup. Peel the jicama and chop it finely.

OTHER VARIATIONS: Instead of olive oil, use walnut or hazelnut oil for an even more mellow and refined taste.

KALE-APPLE SOUP
United States/China

The first time I prepared a kale soup, I expected it to be a bit coarse and peasantlike. To my surprise, a few choice ingredients elevated it to a soup that is at home in fine china. One of those ingredients is Chinese black mushrooms, which provide earthiness and a succulent texture. Another is apple, which imparts a bare hint of tart-sweetness.

1 ounce dried black mushrooms (about 10), soaked
    in boiling water to cover for 15 minutes or until
    softened, drained (soaking water discarded)
¾ pound kale or a mixture of kale and spinach
    (4 firmly packed cups), thoroughly rinsed,
    stemmed
2 cups Vegetable Stock (page 45) or canned
    vegetable broth
1 teaspoon sugar
Salt to taste
1 small tart apple (6 ounces), such as Granny Smith,
    cored but not peeled, thinly sliced
    (don't use a sweet apple)
1½ tablespoons olive oil
¼ teaspoon cumin seeds
1 cup finely chopped onion
½ cup low-fat or nonfat milk
1 large egg, lightly beaten
1 tablespoon butter or ghee for drizzling (optional)

1. Slice the mushrooms, discarding the tough stems. Set mushrooms aside. In a large pot, bring kale and stock to a near boil. Reduce heat and simmer, covered, 8 to 10 minutes, or until kale is tender. Process the mixture in a

blender or food processor until smooth. Return to the pot. Add sugar and salt. Over gentle heat, bring to a simmer. Add mushrooms and apple. Cover and cook for 8 to 10 minutes. Keep warm over very low heat.

2. Heat oil in a small skillet until sizzling. Add cumin seeds and sauté until the seeds are lightly browned. Add onion and cook until medium brown in color, 5 to 7 minutes, stirring constantly. Pour this mixture over the soup. Make sure the heat is very low. Add milk and mix well. Add egg, a teaspoon at a time, stirring until it is thoroughly mixed. (If the heat is too high or if not stirred enough, the egg will scramble instead of thickening the soup.) Remove from heat. Taste and adjust salt and stir in optional butter or ghee.

Yield: 4 first-course servings

SERVING SUGGESTIONS: For a substantial meal, team with Spaghetti and Tempeh Balls (page 103), crusty French bread, and sliced tomatoes drizzled with balsamic vinegar. At lunchtime, enjoy with Peas and Potatoes in a Pocket (page 98) and shredded carrot. On another occasion, plan a soup party with Sweet Potato Bisque (page 54) and Rosemary-Garlic Croutons (page 42).

FISH VARIATION: This soup is an excellent base for poaching fish. In this case, prepare soup with fish stock instead of vegetable stock. Use salmon, halibut, cod, tuna, or your favorite firm-fleshed fish. Cut fish into 2-inch cubes and add along with mushrooms in Step 1. This will make a one-dish meal.

LEEKS, LEAFY GREENS, AND NAVY BEAN SOUP
France/United States

Leeks are known in France for the subtle sweetness and creamy quality they impart to classic potages. Here, blended with beans, they effectively take the place of milk or cream. Slivers of beet greens and a sprinkling of fresh basil and thyme, add a lively color to the soup while improving the taste.

3 leeks, white parts only, coarsely chopped
2½ cups Vegetable Stock (page 45) or canned
    vegetable broth
1 cup freshly cooked or canned navy beans (or choose
    among white beans, lima, or cannellini)
½ cup bean liquid or water
1 tablespoon fresh chopped basil, or 1 teaspoon dried
1 tablespoon fresh chopped thyme, or 1 teaspoon dried
1 cup (firmly packed) slivered beet greens, Swiss chard,
    or thoroughly rinsed spinach, stemmed
Salt to taste
2 tablespoons olive oil
½ teaspoon black mustard seeds
1 cup thinly slivered onion
A sprinkling of extra-virgin olive oil (optional)

1. Bring leeks and stock to a boil in a large saucepan. Reduce heat and cook, covered, until leeks are tender, 5 to 7 minutes.

2. With a slotted spoon, remove 2 tablespoons leeks from the soup and reserve along with 2 tablespoons beans. Process the contents of the saucepan, the remaining beans, and bean liquid, in batches, in a blender or food processor until smooth, adding a little water if necessary. Return the purée and the

reserved leeks and beans to the pot. Add basil, thyme, and greens. Over low heat, bring to a simmer. Cook until greens are tender, a few minutes. Keep warm over very low heat.

3. Heat 2 tablespoons oil in a small skillet. Sauté mustard seeds until they pop. (Hold the cover over the skillet briefly to keep the seeds from flying out.) Add onion and sauté until it is richly browned but not burnt, 7 to 10 minutes, stirring often. Pour this mixture over the soup. Ladle into individual soup bowls. At the table, sprinkle olive oil over each serving, if desired.

Yield: 4 to 6 first-course servings

NOTE: If you are not a strict vegetarian, consider substituting chicken broth for vegetable stock. Leeks go particularly well with a rich chicken broth.

SERVING SUGGESTIONS: Follow with Sweet-Spiced Millet with Cabbage and Pine Nuts (page 178) and some steamed beets alone or sprinkled with toasted, chopped hazelnuts and Spiced Ghee (page 14). A few watermelon wedges or some chilled red grapes will finish the meal nicely. At lunchtime, enjoy with Potato Koftas (page 96), some celery sticks, and Sesame-Banana Whip (page 227).

VEGETABLE BOUILLABAISSE
France

Bouillabaisse, the famed French seafood soup, is made with an ever-changing assortment of seafood based on the catch of the day, which are simmered in a richly seasoned broth. This vegetable version is brimming with tofu, potatoes, winter squash, and various other vegetables, and has a well-seasoned stock base. It is accompanied by the traditional garlic croutons and the same zesty sauce called *rouille*. It makes a hearty meal, although a mixed green salad would be welcome.

6 to 8 large garlic cloves, peeled (to taste)

4½ cups Vegetable Stock (page 45; preferred) or canned vegetable broth

½ teaspoon saffron threads, soaked in 1 tablespoon warm water for 15 minutes

½ pound all-purpose potatoes (2 medium), peeled and cut into ¾-inch cubes

¾ pound winter squash (butternut or Delicata) or sweet potato, peeled and cut into ¾-inch cubes (leave butternut unpeeled)

½ pound carrots (about 2 cups), diced

1 red bell pepper, seeds and inner ribs removed, coarsely chopped

2 leeks, white parts only, coarsely chopped

One 14-ounce carton firm tofu, drained, rinsed, cut into ¾-inch cubes

2 cups shredded savoy or regular cabbage

Salt and freshly ground black pepper to taste

Garlic Toast (page 41) or Crostini and Chutney (page 29; prepared without the chutney)

Red Rouille (recipe follows)

1. Preheat oven to 450 degrees F.

2. Arrange the garlic cloves on an ungreased baking sheet. Roast for 10 to 15 minutes, or just until tender and lightly browned around the edges. Check often and remove each clove as it's done. Don't let them turn too brown. Set aside.

3. Combine stock, saffron and its soaking water, potatoes, squash, and carrots in a large stockpot and bring to a boil. Lower heat, and simmer, covered, for 6 to 8 minutes, or until the vegetables are about half-done. Add bell pepper, leeks, tofu, cabbage, and the reserved garlic. Simmer, covered, 5 to 10 minutes, or just until the vegetables are tender. Season to taste with salt and pepper. To serve, place a toast (or crostini) in each soup bowl and ladle soup over. (If toast is too wide to fit in the soup bowl, cut it in half.) Pass Red Rouille separately.   *Yield: 3 to 4 entrée servings or 6 side-dish servings*

SERVING SUGGESTIONS: You'll need few side dishes, perhaps a salad of Bibb lettuce. Almond Pear Tart (page 250) is an appropriate dessert. Serve any leftovers for lunch with a basket of sourdough bread and Anise-Pistachio Biscotti (page 260).

RED ROUILLE

This zesty red sauce, a traditional accompaniment for a bouillabaisse, is a welcome condiment with most foods. It is excellent over baked potatoes; makes an outstanding pizza sauce; and is very good with baked or broiled fish.

3 large red bell peppers
2 large garlic cloves, coarsely chopped
1 tablespoon to ¼ cup olive oil
2 tablespoons Garlic Bread Crumbs (page 233)

1. Preheat broiler. To roast the bell peppers, place them on an ungreased baking sheet under the broiler for 10 to 15 minutes, turning them several times. They should become soft and their skins should become charred and wrinkled in places. Place them in a paper bag and close the top. Remove after 10 to 15 minutes.

2. Cut each open (saving any liquid that may have accumulated inside) and remove and discard the skin, inner ribs and seeds. Place peppers and their juices and garlic in a blender container and purée until smooth. Turn the blender to its lowest setting. Open the central cap and, with the motor running, add oil in a thin, steady stream. The mixture should acquire the consistency of mayonnaise. Transfer to a medium bowl. Add bread crumbs and mix well. Refrigerate until ready to use. It will thicken as it sits.

Yield: About 2 cups

VARIATION: GREEN ROUILLE Rouille made with red pepper is the traditional accompaniment for this soup, but Green Rouille is also delightful. For this use 3 large green bell peppers and proceed as above. Optionally, add ground chipotle pepper at the end to taste. Another variation is to add 1 or 2 roasted garlic cloves before puréeing. Serve with Garlic Toast (page 41) as an appetizer before any meal. Or spread into a pita pocket and fill with shredded red cabbage, onion slices, and grated carrot for a lovely vegetable sandwich.

SALADS
AND
SIDE VEGETABLES

Salads made from leafy green vegetables have long been popular through-out the Western World. In recent years, they have come to include a much wider variety of ingredients, both cooked and raw. This has been the case particularly in the United States. Modern salads will often incorporate mushrooms, red and yellow bell peppers, or lightly steamed broccoli. Anything goes, as long as the ingredients are compatible and nourishing. All the wealth of produce you see in a farmer's market can be used along with grains, beans, pastas, fruits, and nuts. Keep olives, pecans, and pump-kin seeds on hand to use sparingly as shapely and colorful garnishes.

A hefty salad can become a one-dish supper. One good example in this chapter is Lentil Salad in Pepper Cups (page 81). Such a dish provides the comfort of low-calorie eating, yet leaves one satisfied.

There are other advantages to a substantial salad. Once in planning for a picnic, I decided to carry plain steamed rice. Fearing it would dry out, I moistened it with a light dressing. Hours later the grains remained succulent and flavorful. Since that time, Wild and Brown Rice Salad (page 78) has become a favorite take-along to a potluck or picnic. Orzo and Asparagus Salad (page 83), another dish that can be made ahead, is elegant enough to serve at a luncheon.

In addition to salads, this chapter contains a number of vegetable side-dish recipes. I discovered one of them, Wilted Spinach Banchan (page 87) in a restaurant in Seoul, Korea. As soon as I was seated, the waiter placed small plates of vegetables, or *banchans,* on the table. This *banchan* was spinach, lightly cooked then tinged with a spicy-hot dressing to complement its bold flavor. I am sure it was originally meant to be a "good for you" dish, but it was far more than that. I happily finished my spinach before touching the entrée.

Some salads and side dishes in this chapter benefit from the grilling or roasting of vegetables to give them robustness. Glazed Carrots with Elephant Garlic (page 90) is a gorgeous dish in which elephant garlic is roasted until buttery and then, along with carrots, candied with a splash of maple syrup. They say in the Middle East, "A girl can't be married until she learns to cook eggplant in a thousand different ways." Grilling is one of the best ways, and it's evident when preparing Grilled Eggplant and Toasted Pecan Salad (page 78) that this method produces a fascinating salad without using much oil.

In Tel Aviv, a hotel owner told me that American tourists usually ask for three things: lots of towels, many cups of coffee, and a salad. I'm content with just the salad—though there are occasions when a towel is useful!

WILD AND BROWN RICE SALAD
United States

This dramatic salad has the savor of wild rice, the subtle perfume of dill, and the crunch of walnuts. It always attracts hungry picnickers, and is pretty enough for a luncheon.

> 1 cup brown Basmati (preferred) or long-grain
>   brown rice
> 1 cup wild rice
> Up to ¾ cup Chile-Sesame Vinaigrette (page 223)
> Salt and freshly ground black pepper to taste
> 2 tablespoons chopped fresh dill or parsley
> 2 tablespoons walnuts, toasted

1. Bring brown and wild rice and 4 cups water to a boil in a large pan. (To hasten cooking, you can soak brown and wild rice in 4 cups water for 4 to 6 hours. In this case, bring rice and soaking water to a boil.) Simmer, covered, until all water is absorbed and rice is tender, 35 to 45 minutes.

2. While rice is cooking, prepare Chile-Sesame Vinaigrette and set aside. When rice is ready, transfer to a large serving bowl and fluff with a fork. Add dressing, a little at a time, and mix well, stopping when the rice is moistened. Season to taste with salt and pepper. Sprinkle with dill and top with walnuts.

Yield: 6 to 8 servings

SERVING SUGGESTIONS: To complete the meal add Pecan Mushroom Pâté (page 52) and Carrot-Lentil Soup with Rosemary-Garlic Croutons (page 42). For a picnic or lunch, pair with Mango, Apple, and Blueberry Delight (page 245).

GRILLED EGGPLANT
AND TOASTED PECAN SALAD
International

Glossy and dark purple eggplants look almost like a work of art. They are incredibly tasty when grilled. The slender Japanese variety is best for this purpose, but regular eggplant will also work. In this recipe, tender smoky eggplant pieces are teamed with toasted pecans and a rich soy dressing.

THE EGGPLANT:

1½ pounds Japanese eggplants (about 5 medium),
    or 1 small regular eggplant
2 tablespoons Garlic Oil (page 231) or olive oil
1½ tablespoons rice vinegar
½ teaspoon salt
Ground red pepper to taste

SAUCE:

3 tablespoons rice vinegar
1 tablespoon low-sodium soy sauce
2 teaspoons sugar
1 teaspoon spicy prepared mustard
¼ teaspoon salt

TOPPINGS:

8 pecans, toasted
1 tablespoon chopped fresh basil or parsley
A sprinkling of Chinese sesame oil or Chinese chile oil

FOR SERVING:

Warm crusty bread

1. Preheat oven to 400 degrees F or make fire in a grill. Slice the Japanese eggplants into ½-inch-thick rounds, cutting the larger rounds in the center further in halves or quarters. If using a regular eggplant, cut into 1-inch cubes.

2. Combine Garlic Oil, 1½ tablespoons rice vinegar, salt, and red pepper in a large bowl. Brush eggplant pieces all over with this mixture until it's used up. Grill until tender. Or place the eggplant pieces in an oiled 9 × 13-inch baking pan and bake for 30 to 35 minutes, or until soft and buttery. The skin will turn pale and look shrunken. The best way to check for doneness is to taste. Remove each piece as it's ready.

3. Combine all the sauce ingredients in a large bowl. Toss eggplant pieces gently with the sauce. It can be served immediately or you can allow it to rest at room temperature, covered, for 15 minutes to develop flavor. Top with pecans and basil and sprinkle with sesame or chile oil. To serve, pile onto bread slices or place next to a basket of bread.   *Yield: 4 to 6 servings*

SERVING SUGGESTIONS: This is excellent with Roasted Garlic Soup (page 61) and Two-Tomato Jam (page 232). Carrot-Apple Halwa (page 240) is just the right dessert.

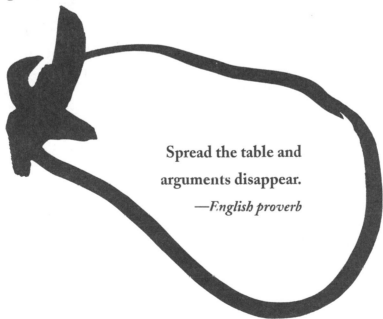

Spread the table and arguments disappear.
—*English proverb*

WARM MUSTARD GREEN SALAD
China

Traveling through Taiwan's lush green countryside, I came across a huge field of flowering mustard greens. The vivid yellow blossoms made the meadow look like a thousand suns. Once cooked, these sturdy greens soften to a tender heap. Here they are transformed into an unusual salad with turmeric-yellow onion slivers and a pungent dressing of Chinese origin.

1 tablespoon olive oil
1 cup thinly sliced onion
¼ teaspoon ground turmeric
½ teaspoon sugar
½ teaspoon salt
¾ pound mustard greens (4 firmly packed cups), thinly shredded, stems cut in 2-inch long strips (see Note)
1 tablespoon low-sodium soy sauce
½ cup white wine
¼ to ½ teaspoon Chinese sesame oil
1 tablespoon capers, drained, rinsed, and finely chopped

1. Heat oil in a 10-inch, steep-sided skillet, and sauté the onions until translucent and slightly soft, about 2 minutes. Sprinkle turmeric over onion and stir a few times. Add sugar, salt, and mustard greens and cover. Reduce heat and let the greens steam in their own juice until they are tender, 5 to 8 minutes. (During this period, uncover and turn, adding a little water if the mixture sticks to the bottom.) Don't overcook or the greens will turn darker.

2. With a slotted spoon, remove greens to a heated serving platter, leaving the juices behind in the skillet. Add soy sauce and wine and heat to boiling. Cook just until the sauce thickens slightly, a few minutes. Remove from

heat and stir in sesame oil. Pour mixture over the greens. Best served warm, but also good at room temperature. *Yield: 4 side-dish servings*

NOTE FOR THE GARDENER: One of my favorite varieties of mustard is Osaka Purple, a tender plant from Japan with showy purple and red-veined leaves.

SERVING SUGGESTIONS: Try with plain rice and Plum-Glazed Squash Rings (page 89). Follow with fresh kiwi, apples, and Nutty Cream (page 264) for dessert.

LENTIL SALAD IN PEPPER CUPS
France

While living in France, I was once invited to a French woman's house for lunch. As I walked in, she said, "I'll prepare something from your home country." A bag of greenish brown lentils sat on her kitchen counter. In the next hour, she cooked those lentils, and whipped up a vinaigrette with the ease of someone who prepares her own salad dressing daily. The combination was a lovely salad, suited for a luncheon or a light evening meal. In fact, greenish brown lentils are not available in India and that salad was a far cry from an Indian dal. No matter, I enjoyed it immensely.

In re-creating the dish, I add steamed spinach for bulk and moisten the ensemble with a dressing that exude flavors of lime and orange.

1½ cups lentils
1 cup sliced (½-inch wide rounds) carrots
1 cup thoroughly cleaned, stemmed, shredded spinach
½ sweet onion, thinly slivered
Salt and freshly ground black pepper to taste
Lime-Orange Vinaigrette (page 221; amount
    depending on taste)
2 to 3 red bell peppers, halved, cored, and seeded, or
    4 to 6 cabbage leaves
Chopped parsley for garnish
½ cup walnuts, toasted for garnish

1. In a large saucepan, bring lentils and 3½ cups water to a boil. Simmer, covered, until the lentils are tender, but not mushy, about 25 minutes. Drain, discarding the liquid. Meanwhile, steam carrots for 4 minutes. Add spinach and steam just until both vegetables are tender, another 3 to 5 minutes.

2. Combine lentils, onion, carrots, and spinach in a large bowl. Toss with half the amount of dressing that you plan to use. Season to taste with salt and pepper. Let stand in the refrigerator until ready to serve. Just before serving, steam the bell peppers (or cabbage leaves) for 4 to 5 minutes, or until slightly soft. Drain and arrange each pepper half (or a cabbage leaf) on an individual serving plate. Fold the remaining dressing into the salad. Spoon some lentil mixture onto each pepper (or cabbage) cup. Sprinkle with walnuts and parsley. *Yield: 4 servings*

SERVING SUGGESTIONS: Go Indian tonight by serving with Sun-Dried Tomato and Cucumber Raita (page 218). At lunchtime, stuff a warm pita pocket and accompany with Easy Baked Potato Chips (page 34).

VARIATION: A lovely alternative is to substitute beets for carrots and beet greens (if available) for spinach. In this case, steam beets for 10 to 12 minutes before adding beet greens. To avoid "bleeding," add beets to the lentil mixture just before serving.

ORZO AND ASPARAGUS SALAD

International

A deluxe luncheon salad, elegant and pretty. Rice-shaped orzo pasta, tinged yellow with turmeric, forms the base. Slender green asparagus spears are arranged on the top like the spokes of a wheel and sun-dried tomatoes add a splash of red to this color palette. You'll find plump softness and crunch in the same mouthful.

¼ teaspoon ground turmeric
1 cup orzo
½ to 1 cup Lime-Orange Vinaigrette (page 221)
6 to 8 sun-dried tomatoes preserved in oil, drained
    and finely chopped
¾ pound asparagus spears, tough ends trimmed,
    cut into 2½-inch pieces
Salt to taste

1. Bring 6 cups water and turmeric to a boil in a medium saucepan. Reduce heat and add orzo. Cook, uncovered 9 to 11 minutes, or until orzo is *al dente*. The best way to check is to taste. Drain and transfer to a large bowl. Immediately pour ½ cup of the Lime-Orange Vinaigrette over the orzo and stir gently to mix well. Orzo will absorb most of the sauce. Add sun-dried tomatoes and mix well.

2. Steam the asparagus 6 to 8 minutes, or just until fork-tender. Immediately plunge in cold water to stop cooking. Set aside. Add the remaining dressing to the orzo mixture, if desired. Season to taste with salt. Remove to a large serving platter. Arrange asparagus spears on top like the spokes of a wheel.

Yield: 4 side-dish servings

SERVING SUGGESTIONS: This salad goes well with Chilled Cucumber-Buttermilk Soup (page 66), Garlic Toast (page 41), and Mint-Cilantro Chutney (page 213).

PEAR SLAW
WITH
HONEY PECANS
United States/China

The classic cole slaw is good just the way it is, but the addition of juicy sweet pears improves its texture. The idea of garnishing with honey-glazed pecans came from a Chinese cook, who used them on top of his chicken entrées for elegance. To moisten the salad, try one of the two dressings suggested below.

6 cups finely shredded cabbage
1 red bell pepper, seeds and inner ribs removed,
    thinly slivered, or ¾ cup grated carrots
1 firm, ripe pear, cored but not peeled, finely chopped
Peanut Mayonnaise (page 224) or Sesame-Banana
    Whip (page 227; see Note)
Salt and white pepper to taste

GARNISHES:
1 teaspoon toasted cumin seeds
2 teaspoons toasted sesame seeds
Honey Pecans (recipe follows)
Chopped cilantro or parsley or thinly sliced
    scallions

Place cabbage, bell pepper, and pear in a large serving bowl. Add dressing and mix well. Season to taste with salt and white pepper. Refrigerate for at least 30 minutes. Just before serving, stir to combine the ingredients with juice that may have accumulated at the bottom. Taste and adjust seasoning. Garnish with cumin seeds, sesame seeds, pecans, and cilantro.

HONEY PECANS

Excellent with the slaw or alone as a snack; or with fresh fruit for dessert.

> 1 tablespoon pure maple syrup
> 1 teaspoon sugar
> 10 to 12 whole pecans

Heat maple syrup and sugar in a small skillet until it starts to bubble. Add pecans and stir gently to coat with the sugar-maple mixture. When the mixture has formed a glaze around the pecans, remove from heat. Transfer to a plate, keeping the pecans separate so they don't clump together. Allow to cool.

Yield: 4 to 6 servings

NOTE: The salad benefits from the richness of Peanut Mayonnaise, but the lower fat Sesame-Banana Whip also works well.

SERVING SUGGESTIONS: At a winter meal, team with Tomato-Peanut Soup (page 63), hard-cooked eggs, and some papads (page 24). A compatible dessert is roasted banana, sprinkled with confectioner's sugar and cinnamon. (To roast a banana, see Step 1 of Sesame-Banana Whip). During summer, enjoy with Beets and Feta Cheese in a Spinach Nest (page 86), Pecan Mushroom Pâté (page 30), and Peach Tart (page 252).

BEETS AND FETA CHEESE IN A SPINACH NEST

International

It comes as a surprise that tender, sweet beets with their brightly colored interior aren't included more often in our diet. In this attractive salad platter, ruby red beets are bordered by deep green spinach. They are complemented by a small sprinkling of milky white feta cheese with a salty taste. Suggestion: Don't throw away the nutritious beet leaves if they are still attached to the beets. Use them in preparing one of the many leafy green recipes in this book.

1 pound beets, scraped to remove root hairs, cut
    into 1-inch cubes
1 tablespoon Chinese sesame oil
1 tablespoon canola oil
2 teaspoons rice vinegar
½ teaspoon sugar
¼ teaspoon salt
2 cups spinach, firmly packed, stemmed,
    thoroughly rinsed, shredded
1 tablespoon feta cheese, crumbled

1. Steam the beets until tender, 12 to 18 minutes; set aside.

2. Whisk together the sesame and canola oils and rice vinegar in a large bowl until thick. Add sugar and salt. When beets are ready, toss with dressing, then marinate at room temperature for at least 30 minutes.

3. Just before serving, drain the beets, leaving the dressing in the bowl. Arrange beets on the center of a serving platter. Blanch spinach by dipping in boiling water for about a minute. Drain thoroughly. Combine spinach with the dressing left in the bowl, tossing to mix well. Arrange like a ring around the beets. Sprinkle feta cheese over the top. *Yield: 4 side-dish servings*

SERVING SUGGESTIONS: During summer, try with Chilled Cucumber-Buttermilk Soup (page 66) and focaccia bread. On cold days, it is good with Spicy Tofu and Pea Stew (page 140) and a baked potato drizzled with Chipotle Barbecue Sauce (page 228).

WILTED SPINACH BANCHAN
Korea

Banchan is a Korean word referring to the small side dishes or appetizers that accompany many meals there. One of the most popular is made with spinach. Here is my version.

¾ pound spinach (4 firmly packed cups), thoroughly cleaned, stemmed, shredded (see Note for the Gardener)

2 tablespoons low-sodium soy sauce

2 teaspoons Chinese sesame oil

½ teaspoon sambal oelek or red chile paste (or to taste)

¼ teaspoon garlic powder (see Note)

¼ teaspoon ground ginger (see Note)

1 tablespoon sesame seeds, toasted and ground

Salt and freshly ground black pepper

Toasted sesame seeds for garnish (optional)

1. Steam spinach for 3 to 4 minutes, or just until wilted. Take care not to overcook or spinach will lose its color and texture. Drain off excess water and set aside.

2. Combine soy sauce, sesame oil, sambal oelek, garlic powder, ground ginger, ground sesame seeds, salt, and pepper in a large bowl and stir to mix well.

Toss spinach gently in this mixture. Let stand at room temperature for 5 to 15 minutes. Taste and adjust seasoning. Best served freshly prepared, but can also be made ahead and refrigerated. In this case, bring to room temperature before serving. To serve, lift spinach off with a slotted spoon and place on individual serving plates. Sprinkle with sesame seeds, if desired.

Yield: 4 side-dish servings

NOTE: You can use 1 tablespoon each of minced fresh garlic and gingerroot instead. Since they are not cooked, they may overpower the other ingredients in the sauce.

Grind garlic chips or dehydrated garlic flakes in a blender or food processor until reduced to a coarse powder. This powder is more flavorful than commercial garlic powder.

NOTE FOR THE GARDENER: You can also use thinnings of mustard, chard, or beet greens in this dish instead of throwing them away. Cook them slightly less.

SERVING SUGGESTIONS: This banchan can accompany most meals as a side dish or take the place of a salad. It is especially delicious with brown rice, Gingery Squash Quiche (page 200), and some honeydew melon slices.

PLUM-GLAZED
SQUASH RINGS
China/United States

I celebrate the arrival of winter squash in the marketplace with this dish. There are many new varieties to choose from besides the familiar acorn: Delicata, Honey Delight, Red Kuri, for instance. My favorite for this dish is Delicata, a squash with a sweet orange-red flesh and tubular shape that lends itself well to cutting into rings. The dish requires little more than brushing a glaze over the rings before baking.

> 2 pounds acorn, Delicata, or butternut squash
> 1½ cups Chinese plum sauce (or apricot preserves),
>   thoroughly mixed with ½ cup water (see Note)

1. Preheat oven to 350 degrees F. Line a large baking sheet with aluminum foil.

2. Cut squash into ½-inch-thick rings. With the tip of a vegetable peeler or a blunt knife, scoop out the seeds and strings from each ring, leaving the middle hollow with smooth edges. Arrange squash rings on the baking sheet. Bake for 20 to 30 minutes, or until tender.

3. About 10 minutes before squash is ready, heat the plum sauce and water mixture to boiling. Lower heat and cook, uncovered, for a few minutes to thicken the sauce, stirring to break up any lumps. Remove from the heat. When the squash rings are out of the oven, spread generously with this sauce. Preheat broiler. Broil for a few minutes, just until lightly browned on top. Serve immediately. Serve any leftover sauce on the side.

Yield: 4 to 6 side-dish servings

NOTE: If using apricot jam or preserves, which are not as spicy as plum sauce, add 1 teaspoon grated gingerroot to it before cooking.

SERVING SUGGESTIONS: This goes well with most meals, but is particularly good with Sesame-Sauced Spinach (page 125) and Nut-Topped Savory Rice (page 174). My dessert of choice is Poppy Seed Fruit Ring (page 246).

GLAZED CARROTS
WITH ELEPHANT GARLIC
United States

Candied carrots are an American classic. In this contemporary version, buttery smooth elephant garlic provides a counterpoint to the crunchy carrots. An easy, lovely dish for entertaining guests or family.

½ pound carrots, scraped, cut into 2-inch long strips, halved or quartered
½ pound elephant garlic (about 2 heads), peeled, cloves separated
1 tablespoon olive oil, ghee, or butter
2 tablespoons maple syrup
¼ cup white wine
2 teaspoons fresh tarragon, chopped, or ½ teaspoon dried
Salt and freshly ground black pepper to taste

1. Preheat oven to 350 degrees F.

2. Steam carrots until tender-crisp, 8 to 10 minutes. Set aside. Place the garlic cloves on a lightly oiled baking sheet. Bake for 15 to 20 minutes, or until soft and lightly browned in places. If overcooked, juices will start to ooze out of the cloves. Different size cloves will finish cooking at different times; remove each as it's done. Handle them gently from this point; they will be fragile.

3. In a large skillet heat oil and cook the carrots and garlic cloves until lightly browned, 2 to 3 minutes. Add maple syrup. In a few minutes, when the syrup starts to form a glaze around the vegetables, add wine and tarragon. Cook, uncovered, until most of the liquid evaporates, a few minutes. Remove from heat. Preheat broiler. Transfer to a broiler pan and broil just until the tops of the vegetables are medium brown in color. Don't let them burn. Season to taste with salt and pepper. *Yield: 4 servings*

SERVING SUGGESTIONS: Zucchini Vichyssoise (page 47; served hot) is a refreshing choice for soup. To complete the meal, add a salad of spinach and orange sections and a dessert of chilled green grapes.

SANDWICHES
AND
BURGERS

Because I grew up in a sandwichless culture, I had to live in the West for a few years before I acquired a taste for them. Later, while living in Iran, I realized I had come to appreciate sandwiches, and found myself missing them. I visited Iranian homes and restaurants, sampling a cuisine with a well-deserved reputation as one of the world's finest, yet I craved a sandwich.

One day in a market displaying all manner of goods, I smelled dough baking. I asked a thin bearded shop owner for the source of this wonderful aroma, and if I could get a sandwich nearby. "Saandvich," he replied, "I don't know what it is." Then he asked, "But would you like to see my beautiful Isfahani rugs?"

Sandwiches invaded my dreams. Sleeping, I would sit in clean, quaint coffee shops, enjoying double-deckers and cheese melts. Then one day, an inspiration came to me as I bought some freshly baked *barbari* bread from a bakery. My first sandwich in Teheran was warm, fragrant *barbari*, piled high with shredded carrot, lettuce, cucumbers, and a thick, spicy dressing, then rolled up like a burrito. It was splendid.

That experience led me to think differently about sandwiches. I learned to fashion them using whatever bread is available, from Western-style rye and wheat to tortillas or chapatis. Today I brush the bread lightly with a dash of olive oil, or spread it with almond butter, mashed avocado, or puréed roasted garlic. For fillings, I am partial to Indian-style vegetables, crumbled tempeh, or grilled vegetables. For condiments, I typically use chutneys, salsas, Szechwan pickles, and raw vegetables. I have discovered that the world of sandwiches offers endless variety; one need never be bored.

Thinking back, I realize that even India, with its spicy mashed potato patties and stuffed breads, is not without its sandwiches and burgers. In fact, most cultures have something similar to a sandwich, an easy way to carry food to the field or workplace, or to eat out of hand on the streets. They have been used since ancient times in many countries. The Vietnamese, for example, roll vegetables in transparent rice wrappers for a delicate meal-on-the-go; the Mexican taco is as common as burgers in America.

And then there are European open-face sandwiches. In Copenhagen, I arrived for lunch in a jam-packed restaurant, anticipating a long, dreary wait. A server passed my table, pushing a trolley loaded with tiny sandwiches made with crustless bread and a variety of tasty toppings. One was made with a robust rye bread and was adorned with pickled vegetables; another was a colorful creation of brown bread, bright yellow cheese, and leafy greens. All were dainty and appealing. I made an enjoyable meal out of those delicious tidbits.

Burgers are another lunchtime treat that allow for innumerable variations. I prepare vegetarian burgers by grinding wild and brown rice, beans, shredded vegetables—almost any leftovers. Shaped into patties and spiced imaginatively, these burgers add a new dimension to dining. The resulting combinations of taste and texture, where no single ingredient is readily identifiable, are not just sumptuous, they offer a healthy alternative to their animal forebears. This is probably why these vegetarian burgers are becoming popular in an increasingly health-conscious America. Then again, it may be that the attraction is more rooted in the traditional appearance of the bun, its accompanying pickles, and the thick slices of sweet onions.

Celebrate sandwiches and burgers by enjoying them with all the trimmings.

SANDWICH SAVVY

You needn't confine your vegetable sandwich repertoire to avocado, sprouts, and cream cheese. Leftover spicy vegetables, mashed beans, and whole grains with a chewy texture, such as brown rice can be combined to make tasty, nutritious sandwiches in a matter of minutes.

A WORD ABOUT BREADS. Any type of bread will suffice for most fillings. If the filling is juicy or runny, try using a firm, dense bread. Experiment with different types of bread and fillings for the best match.

TO ADD ZEST AND VARIETY. Consider a flavorful spread, such as olive paste, sun-dried tomato paste, and almond or other nut butters, as substitutes for mayonnaise.

TO KEEP SANDWICH FROM GETTING SOGGY. Fillings and spreads penetrate bread and make it soggy. To avoid this, assemble your sandwich just before serving. If sandwich is to be prepared ahead and carried to a picnic or workplace, consider the following technique: on top of a piece of bread, place a piece of wax paper larger than the bread. Place a lettuce leaf (cut to the size of the bread) on top of the wax paper and lay the filling on the lettuce. Top with another lettuce leaf of the same size and a second piece of wax paper. Place the second piece of bread on top. Before eating, remove wax papers. An alternative is to put the filling in a sealed container, and use a spoon to assemble the sandwich at the picnic or workplace.

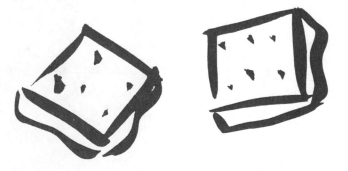

PEAR AND CHEESE
TEA SANDWICHES
United States

These delicate open-faced sandwiches are tasty and attractive and will be a welcome surprise in the lunch box or picnic basket. They require little effort.

1 to 1½ tablespoons honey
½ cup part-skim or low-fat ricotta cheese
8 slices white or whole wheat bread, crust removed
    (or banana bread or other sweet bread)
2 ripe Bosc pears or sweet apples, cored but
    not peeled, cut into thin slices, then into
    semi-circles
2 tablespoons chopped crystallized ginger (optional)
2 tablespoons walnuts, toasted and chopped

1. Combine honey and cheese thoroughly in a bowl. Taste and adjust the amount of honey; the mixture should be gently sweet.

2. Cut each slice of bread into 4 nearly equal triangles. Spread thinly with honey-ricotta mixture. Place a pear slice over each and sprinkle the top of the pear with ginger bits and toasted walnuts.   *Yield: 16 small sandwiches*

TWO-CHEESE VARIATION: If you prefer a salty rather than a sweet flavor, substitute up to 1 ounce creamy goat cheese for the honey. Add goat cheese to ricotta gradually, according to taste.

POTATO KOFTAS
India

Koftas generally refer to ground meat patties that are threaded on skewers and grilled. In India, with its large vegetarian population, koftas are made with vegetables and are often stuffed imaginatively before grilling. Once I watched an aunt fill each with a whole hard-boiled egg. Another cook stuffed them with minced beets. The recipe below is a quick version that requires no grilling, uses stuffing only as an option, and is as delicious as the Indian original.

1½ pounds all-purpose potatoes (about 6 medium), peeled and cubed
2 tablespoons canola oil
1 cup minced onion
1 teaspoon ground cumin
1 teaspoon ground coriander seeds
1 teaspoon seeded, minced jalapeño or other fresh green chile, or to taste
Dash black salt (optional)
Salt to taste
1 tablespoon chopped fresh mint, or 1 teaspoon dried
1 tablespoon freshly squeezed lime juice
2 large eggs, lightly beaten
¾ cup Garlic Bread Crumbs (page 233; or more if needed)

1. Steam the potatoes until tender, 15 to 18 minutes. Mash thoroughly with a fork.

2. Preheat oven to 350 degrees F.

3. Heat oil in a large skillet until sizzling. Sauté onion until limp, 3 to 5 minutes. Stir in cumin, coriander, jalapeño, black salt, and regular salt and

stir to distribute evenly. Add reserved potatoes. Cook, uncovered, for about 5 minutes, stirring often, to heat mixture through. Remove from heat, transfer to a large bowl, and allow to cool.

4. Add mint, lime juice, adjust salt, and add eggs along with ¾ cup bread crumbs; mix well. Scoop out a portion, slightly bigger than a walnut, and roll between the palms of your hands to make a smooth ball. Flatten to a patty, about 3 inches in diameter. If the mixture is too sticky, add a little more bread crumbs. Arrange on a large, lightly oiled baking sheet. Continue making patties until you use up the mixture. (Up to this point the dish can be made a day ahead and refrigerated.) Bake for 10 to 15 minutes, or until thoroughly heated. Preheat broiler. Place under the broiler for a few minutes to brown the top lightly. Serve warm. *Yield: 10 to 12 koftas; 4 side-dish servings*

SERVING SUGGESTIONS: Serve on a bun or stuff into a pita pocket with sweet onion rings, chopped cilantro, and fresh chile slivers. Serve an Indian version of eggs Benedict by layering these koftas on a toasted English muffin, placing a poached egg on top, and sprinkling with salsa. These koftas also go well as a side dish with Mint-Cilantro Chutney (page 213).

STUFFED VARIATION: For a taste treat, stuff these koftas as described below. Some suggestions for fillings are commercial mango or lime pickle, chopped hard-cooked eggs, or Asian Pesto (page 215). You can also use Marinated Carrot Chutney (page 214) or the filling from the recipe Peas and Carrots in a Pastry Nest (page 204). Make a hollow in the ball in Step 4, and place a small amount of your choice of filling. Close it carefully and roll it a few more times between the palms of your hands to smooth it. You need not flatten it to a patty in this case. Cook the balls the same way as above.

PEAS AND POTATOES IN A POCKET
India/Middle East

Potatoes are not generally considered a sandwich filler in the West, but in India, spiced potatoes accompanied by chapatis are a popular meal. An Indian cook once told me that she always prepared this combination for picnics because it tasted delicious even at room temperature. With that inspiration from my homeland, I have taken to stuffing the more readily available pita bread with a delectable Indian-style peas-and-potatoes mixture, as in the recipe below.

1 pound all-purpose potatoes (about 4 medium),
      peeled and cubed
¾ cup fresh peas or thawed frozen peas
2 tablespoons chopped cilantro
2 tablespoons minced sweet red or other mild onion
½ teaspoon sugar
½ teaspoon salt
Ground red pepper to taste (start with a scant pinch;
      best if slightly hot)
1 tablespoon mustard oil or canola oil
¼ teaspoon black mustard seeds
¼ teaspoon ground turmeric
2 pita breads (preferably whole wheat)
Sweet onion rings
Alfalfa sprouts
Chopped hard-cooked eggs

1. Steam the potatoes until very tender, 15 to 20 minutes. Mash thoroughly. Steam peas until tender, 6 to 10 minutes if fresh and 3 to 5 minutes if using thawed frozen. Mash them thoroughly using a mortar and pestle or a food

mill. Or place peas on a board and mash with a heavy object. Combine potatoes, peas, cilantro, minced onion, sugar, salt, and red pepper in a large bowl.

2. Heat oil in a large skillet over moderate heat until sizzling. Add mustard seeds and sauté until the seeds start to pop. Stir in turmeric. Add the potato-pea mixture. Stirring often, cook for a few minutes to brown the potatoes lightly and to heat the mixture through. Remove from heat. Taste and adjust seasoning.

3. Cut pita bread in halves. Divide potato mixture to fill the pockets, and insert onion rings, alfalfa sprouts, and chopped egg.   *Yield: 2 servings*

SERVING SUGGESTIONS: All you'll need to complete the lunch is a mixed green salad and a cup of Indian-Style Tea (page 262). On another occasion, accompany with Kale-Apple Soup (page 68); together they make a satisfying meal. Consider the pretty yellow filling, flecked with bits of bright green cilantro for a light main dish and serve with warm chapatis, carrot sticks, and Red Lentils in Coconut Cream (page 158). Better still, double the recipe and serve the leftovers the next day.

ADDITIONAL SANDWICH IDEAS

Create exciting new sandwiches using recipes from other chapters of this book. Sandwiches are a great way to use leftovers.

Roasted Eggplant Burritos

Use Roasted Eggplant Relish (page 27) as a filling and create your own international burrito with chapati or whole wheat tortilla. For condiments, consider sliced tomatoes, sautéed mushrooms, scallions, and green-leaf lettuce. Top this burrito with Ancho and Red Pepper Salsa (page 216) and pop into a 350-degree oven for 10 to 12 minutes to make a new, exciting enchilada. It goes great with plain rice and a mixed green salad.

Sweet-Sour Carrot Roll-ups

Top a few spoonsful of Marinated Carrot Chutney (page 214) with chopped scallions, cilantro, blanched mung bean sprouts, and a sprinkling of freshly squeezed lime juice. Fill a warm chapati or flour tortilla with this mixture and roll into a cigar shape.

Curried Vegetables in Tortilla Rolls

Prepare the carrot-pea filling in the recipe Peas and Carrots in a Pastry Nest (page 204). Fill 2 to 3 warm tortillas and sprinkle with chopped scallions, cilantro, and freshly squeezed lime juice.

Seven Little Veggies in a "Pillow"

If you have any leftover Seven Vegetables Stew (page 138), use it to make these lovely "pillows." Fold 2 opposite sides of the chapati over the top of the vegetables (garnished with sweet onion rings, green chile slivers, and chopped cilantro), then fold the remaining 2 sides over the top to form a rectangular pillow. Hold in place with a toothpick inserted vertically in the center.

Roasted Tomatoes in Baguette

Slow-Roasted Tomatoes (page 36) or Cherry Tomato Chips (page 37) make excellent sandwich fillings. Use a baguette or sourdough bread and brush lightly with extra-virgin olive oil, black salt (if available), and regular salt. Add the prepared tomatoes, pitted and sliced olives, capers, chopped fresh basil leaves, and a sprinkling of your favorite hard cheese. Broil until the filling bubbles.

BURGER TIPS

This chapter contains a number of vegetarian burger recipes. After trying them, you may be inspired to create your own. You'll need a base, such as cooked vegetables, grains, beans, soy products (tofu, tempeh); flavorings such as onions, garlic, sautéed mushrooms; liquids for moistening, such as milk, stock, or a prepared sauce; and "binders," such as crushed nuts or bread crumbs.

• If the burgers have been refrigerated, bring them to room temperature before grilling or broiling.

• Burgers should be shaped as evenly as possible for consistent cooking. A thickness of about ¾-inch is ideal. Don't make them too thin or they may dry out.

• If you are grilling, you can prepare the bread along with the burgers. Oil (or butter) and season the bread if you like, then wrap it in foil. Grill bread for 4 to 10 minutes, according to your preference or its thickness. You can also grill vegetable accompaniments—zucchini slices, corn on the cob, thickly cut onion rings—along with the burger.

• You needn't always serve these burgers on buns. Offer them alone as a main course accompanied by salsa, guacamole, or chutney, and a carbohydrate source, such as rice pilaf or baked potato.

SWEET TEMPEH BURGERS
International

This is one of my favorite vegetarian burgers. The unlikely combination of strongly flavored kasha and tempeh are transformed almost magically, by savory Chinese sauces into a gourmet treat. These burgers are gently sweet with a pleasant nutlike flavor and are filling.

One 8-ounce package soy tempeh, cubed
1 tablespoon canola oil or olive oil
½ cup minced onion
3 to 4 garlic cloves, forced through a garlic press
1 tablespoon grated gingerroot
1 teaspoon seeded, minced jalapeño or other fresh chile of choice, or to taste
½ pound Roma (plum) tomatoes (2 large), peeled, seeded, and chopped
1 teaspoon black bean sauce
2 tablespoons plum sauce
½ cup whole kasha
1 cup Vegetable Stock (page 45) or canned vegetable broth
¼ teaspoon salt
6 to 8 whole pecans, lightly toasted, ground in a blender or food processor to a coarse powder
1 large egg, lightly beaten

1. To prepare tempeh, steam for about 10 minutes until it puffs and acquires a spongy texture. Allow to cool slightly, then crumble using a fork. Set aside. In hot oil in a large skillet, sauté onion and garlic until onion is lightly browned. Add gingerroot, jalapeño, and tomatoes. Simmer, covered, 10 minutes, or until the tomatoes break down in a thick sauce. During this

period, uncover once or twice and mash the tomatoes with the back of a spoon to help the process along. Add a teaspoon of water if the mixture begins to stick. Stir in tempeh, black bean sauce, and plum sauce. Cook, uncovered, for a few minutes until thoroughly heated. Transfer to a large bowl and set aside.

2. To prepare kasha, toast it by placing in a skillet over low to medium-low heat. Stir often. When kasha darkens slightly and a nutty brown aroma emanates, remove from heat and transfer to a small bowl. Bring broth to a boil. Reduce heat and add kasha and salt. Cover and cook for 10 minutes, or until all liquid is absorbed and kasha is tender and fluffy. Allow to cool slightly, then add to the tempeh mixture.

3. When the mixture is cool enough to handle, add ground pecans and egg and mix well. Shape into patties, about 3 inches in diameter. Handle them gently from this point; they will be tender. Grill or broil 3 to 5 minutes per side, or just until medium brown in color.   *Yield: 10 burgers*

SERVING SUGGESTIONS: Serve on sourdough bread with onion rings, salsa, and red-leaf lettuce. Or try as an entrée with Chipotle Barbecue Sauce (page 228), mashed potatoes, and Pear Slaw with Honey Pecans (page 84). For dessert Plum Kuchen (page 254) and a cup of oolong tea would be a good choice.

VARIATION: SPAGHETTI AND TEMPEH BALLS A vegetarian alternative to the popular spaghetti and meatballs dish. In Step 3, shape the kasha-tempeh mixture into balls, 1 inch in diameter. Grill or broil the balls as above. Because of their smaller size, they will cook quicker. Cook 1 pound spaghetti according to package directions; drain. Place spaghetti on individual serving plates. Pour Peppery Tomato Sauce (page 230) or your favorite tomato sauce over it, and serve topped with tempeh balls.

TOFU-WALNUT BURGERS
East Asia

Burgers made with tofu are more tender than those made with grains or vegetables. Served as an entrée accompanied by a grain dish and one or more vegetable side dishes, they make a most satisfying meal. For an extra zing, I include a fiery chutney or pickle.

One 14-ounce carton firm tofu, drained and rinsed
1 cup finely chopped onion
2 to 3 large garlic cloves, minced
1 tablespoon canola oil or olive oil
2 tablespoons bottled chili sauce
¼ to ½ teaspoon sambal oelek (optional)
1 teaspoon Worcestershire sauce
2 teaspoons low-sodium soy sauce
1 teaspoon ground cumin
¼ cup walnuts, ground to a coarse powder in a blender
    or food processor
1 cup Garlic Bread Crumbs (page 233)
Salt and freshly ground black pepper to taste

1. Press water out of tofu: Wrap tofu in a kitchen towel or several layers of paper towel. Place on a cutting board and put a heavy object, such as an iron skillet, on top. Let rest for 30 to 45 minutes. Remove towel or paper towels and transfer tofu to a large bowl. Using a fork, mash thoroughly.

2. Meanwhile, sauté onion and garlic in oil until onion is limp and slightly brown around the edges. When tofu is ready, combine with onion-garlic mixture. Add chili sauce, sambal oelek, if desired, Worcestershire sauce, soy sauce, cumin, and walnuts. Place in a food processor and pulse several times so that a mealy consistency results. Add bread crumbs and mix well with a spoon. Season to taste with salt and pepper. Divide into 8 equal portions and

shape into patties about 3 inches in diameter. Handle the patties gently from this point; they will be delicate. Grill or broil for 5 to 7 minutes, or until the top is lightly browned. Turn the patties and cook the other sides the same way until lightly browned.   *Yield: 8 burgers*

SERVING SUGGESTIONS: Try with brown rice, sliced tomatoes, cole slaw, and either mango pickle or Chile Chutney (page 212). Stuff into a pita pocket or use as a main ingredient in a submarine sandwich. Or enjoy on a toasted whole wheat bun with the works.

LEEK-MUSHROOM BURGERS
United States

Leeks, less well-known than the onion, their strongly flavored cousin, enhance the flavor of a dish without overwhelming it. Here they are slowly sautéed to draw out their essence, then combined with fresh mushrooms and potatoes to form moist, tender patties. These tasty patties can be served on a bun, or, more formally, as an entrée. Instead of mustard and ketchup, try them with an herb chutney, tomato salsa, or a roasted chile salsa.

½ pound all-purpose potatoes (about 4 medium),
    peeled and cubed (½-inch cubes)
½ pound parsnips, scraped to remove root hairs if any,
    cubed (½-inch cubes)
1½ tablespoons olive oil
3 large garlic cloves, minced
6 ounces fresh mushrooms (about 15), thinly sliced
1 cup coarsely chopped leeks (whites and 2 inches of
    greens only)
Salt and freshly ground black pepper to taste
½ cup unsalted raw cashews, ground to a coarse powder
    in a blender or food processor
1 cup Garlic Bread Crumbs (page 233)

1. Steam potatoes and parsnips until tender, 15 to 18 minutes. Set both aside. Heat oil in a large skillet until a light haze forms. Sauté garlic, mushrooms, and leeks until the vegetables are limp, 5 to 7 minutes, stirring often. Remove from heat and drain off the liquid that has accumulated at the bottom. (Retain this liquid for soups, stocks, or cooking grains.)

2. Place potatoes, parsnips, and the drained mushroom mixture in the container of a food processor. Pulse several times until a mealy consistency results. Transfer to a large bowl and allow to cool. Season to taste with salt and pepper. Combine ground cashews and bread crumbs, and add to the vegetable mixture. Shape into 8 patties, each about 3 inches in diameter.

3. Grill or broil 6 to 8 minutes, or until lightly browned. Turn the patties and cook the other side the same way.   *Yield: 8 burgers*

SERVING SUGGESTIONS: Serve on a whole wheat bun with Mint-Cilantro Chutney (page 213) or Ancho and Red Pepper Salsa (page 216). The toppings can consist of chopped sweet onions and shredded romaine lettuce. Or try as an entrée accompanied by Peppery Tomato Sauce (page 230).

HAZELNUT-RICE BURGERS
United States

Rice is not generally thought of as burger material, but I have found that a hearty, chewy mixture of wild and brown rice, when combined with other ingredients, makes an excellent base for burgers. Toasted hazelnuts improve the taste, sautéed fresh mushrooms provide a rich, meaty flavor and texture, and an Asian-style chili sauce adds bite.

¾ cup brown Basmati rice (available in natural
    food stores)
½ cup wild rice
1 tablespoon olive oil
3 large garlic cloves, minced
¼ pound fresh mushrooms, sliced
¼ cup chili sauce (see Note)
3 tablespoons hazelnuts, toasted and chopped
1 large egg, or 2 egg whites
Salt and freshly ground black pepper to taste
¾ cup Garlic Bread Crumbs (page 233)
Olive oil for brushing

1. Bring Basmati rice, wild rice, and 2½ cups water to a boil. Simmer, covered, until all water is absorbed and rice is tender, 25 to 35 minutes. Allow to cool. Measure 2 cups rice and set aside. (Retain any leftover rice for thickening soups.)

2. Heat oil in a small skillet until sizzling. Sauté garlic until golden. Add mushrooms and cook, uncovered, for a few minutes, stirring often. Remove from heat. Combine 2 cups rice, garlic-mushroom mixture, chili sauce, hazelnuts, and egg or egg whites in the container of a food processor. Pulse several times until a meal-like consistency results. Transfer to a large bowl

and add salt and pepper to taste. (Up to this point the recipe can be made several hours ahead and refrigerated.) Add bread crumbs and mix. Shape mixture into patties, each 2½ to 3 inches in diameter.

2. Cover a large cookie sheet with a piece of aluminum foil and brush thoroughly with oil. (These patties tend to stick.) Place the patties on this sheet and brush the tops lightly with oil. Grill or broil 4 to 6 minutes, or just until light to medium brown in color. Turn, brush other sides with oil, and broil for another 4 to 6 minutes, until brown. Watch carefully; they tend to burn quickly. *Yields: 7 to 8 burgers*

NOTE: For a taste treat, use sweet chili sauce sold in Asian markets instead of the supermarket variety. The sweet chili sauce, with a sharp, sweet-hot flavor, goes well in this dish.

SERVING SUGGESTIONS: Serve on sourdough bread, spread lightly with almond butter and top with lettuce and onion rings. These patties can make a full meal when teamed with Two-Tomato Jam (page 232), Sesame-Sauced Spinach (page 125), and a salad of red-leaf lettuce, celery, and cucumber. For dessert I would recommend Chocolate-Glazed Banana Cake (page 242). Enjoy any leftovers as a snack with a bowl of plain or lightly sweetened yogurt.

> **According to a Malay proverb, "The fuller the ear, the lower rice bends; empty and it grows taller and taller."**

STIR-FRIES
AND
QUICK ENTRÉES

Stir-frying is a technique used in many parts of Asia, but Chinese cooks are the masters. I once watched a Chinese chef stir-fry some vegetables. He began by swirling a little oil in his preheated iron wok. As the oil sizzled over a high flame, he sautéed crushed garlic, tossing and turning it for a few seconds. Next he added the harder vegetables: carrots, cut diagonally to expose a wider surface area, and broccoli florets, split in half. The hot oil coated the vegetables, sealing in their juices. Within minutes the vegetables softened and the chef pushed them to one side to keep them crisp. Then he added some tender green pea pods. As the pods danced in the hot oil and began to turn a deeper shade of green, he sprinkled the dish with a ladle of broth, a pinch of salt, and a dash of soy sauce. These seasonings produced an intensely flavored glaze to coat everything. The chef served the dish immediately and the glistening vegetables, tender-crisp and crunchy, were utterly delicious.

What made the dish a success was that he had cooked each vegetable for precisely the right amount of time over high heat; a technique simple enough in theory, but one that requires an understanding of the characteristics of each vegetable. And a bit of practice.

I save stir-fry dishes for days when I have limited time. My stir-fries tend to be international. Vegetables complement each other in color and texture and may include such atypical items as Brussels sprouts and parboiled sweet potato. For a rich flavor, I frequently sprinkle asafetida powder in the oil, as Indian cooks traditionally do. And I vary my sauces. One day, it's a standard mix of soy sauce, Chinese cooking wine, and dark sesame oil. Another time it's a blend of the deeper flavors of tamarind and hoisin sauces.

With these recipes in this chapter you can spread your table with a tempting dinner in minutes.

SWEET HOT SWISS CHARD
China/Italy

Swiss chard is one of the tastiest of all hearty greens and is nearly a staple for me during summer and autumn. The sturdy firm-textured leaves take well to bold seasonings, particularly Asian. In this recipe, the earthy flavor of Chinese plum and hoisin sauces complement the sour, salty flavor of the chard. Italian balsamic vinegar adds a hint of mellow sweetness.

1½ tablespoons olive oil or Garlic Oil (page 231)
1 cup finely chopped onion
3 to 4 large garlic cloves, minced
12 large Swiss chard leaves, coarsely chopped,
     stems diced (see Note for the Gardener)
2 tablespoons hoisin sauce
2 teaspoons plum sauce
2 teaspoons balsamic vinegar
Salt to taste
Rosemary-Garlic Croutons (page 42) or
     commercial garlic croutons for garnish

1. In hot oil in a wok or large skillet, sauté onion until richly browned, 8 to 10 minutes. Add garlic and stir several times. Add Swiss chard. Lower the heat slightly. Cover and cook until the greens are wilted and tender to the bite, 5 to 7 minutes. Overcooking will destroy their color.

2. Combine hoisin and plum sauces and the vinegar in a small bowl, and pour over the greens. Toss gently. Remove from heat and let sit, covered, for a few minutes. Serve garnished with the croutons.

Yield: 2 entrée or 4 side-dish servings

NOTE FOR THE GARDENER: The high-yielding Swiss chard provides large quantities of leafy greens throughout the season from one sowing. Harvest the leaves and more will grow in their place.

SERVING SUGGESTIONS: You could serve this with either brown rice or baked potato, accompanied by Sun-Dried Tomato and Cucumber Raita (page 218) and Chile Chutney (page 212). Finish with some mandarin or regular orange segments and perhaps some Honey Pecans (page 85) for a most pleasant meal.

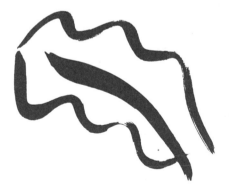

Russian riddle: **What reduces one to tears without pain or grief?** *Answer:* **Chopping onions.**

SNOW PEA-MUSHROOM STIR-FRY

China

By using different combinations of vegetables and sauces, you can create an infinite variety of stir-fries. This particular recipe calls for snow peas and mushrooms. An intriguing mix of Chinese hoisin sauce and Indonesian chile paste, called sambal oelek, coats the vegetables. A number of other sauce suggestions are given below; they can be prepared ahead of time, making your weeknight meal preparation a cinch. Before beginning, cut and arrange all vegetables and keep them within easy reach.

Sauce:

2 tablespoons canned vegetable broth
1 teaspoon hoisin sauce
¼ teaspoon sambal oelek, or to taste

Vegetables:

2 teaspoons canola oil
3 to 5 large garlic cloves, forced through
    a garlic press
1 tablespoon grated gingerroot
¾ pound fresh mushrooms, thinly sliced
¼ pound snow peas, stems and strings removed
Salt to taste (optional)

1. Combine all the sauce ingredients in a small bowl; set aside.

2. Heat oil in wok or large steep-sided skillet until sizzling. Add garlic and gingerroot and stir-fry until golden. Add mushrooms and cook for a few seconds. Stir in sauce. Cook, uncovered, for 2 minutes. Add snow peas. Reduce heat slightly. Cover and cook for 3 to 4 minutes, or just until vegetables are tender. Add salt to taste, if desired. Best served immediately. If

allowed to stand, the snow peas will lose their bright color, although the dish will still taste good. *Yield: 2 entrée or 4 side-dish servings*

SERVING SUGGESTIONS: Plain white or brown rice is the best accompaniment, but quinoa, couscous, or pasta also go well. If you need a more substantial meal, add Scrambled Tempeh (page 131). Finish with oolong tea and some orange sections.

OTHER STIR-FRY SAUCES

Sauces are combinations of intensely flavored ingredients used to complement and enhance the flavor of main ingredients in a stir-fry. They are generally added to the dish after the main ingredients have been briefly sautéed. The standard Cantonese combination of soy sauce, rice vinegar, and Chinese cooking wine works well in most stir-fries, but for variety try the sauces below. You can prepare them ahead and refrigerate.

Hot and Spicy Sauce

This sauce has a good chile bite and a hint of sweetness. It goes particularly well with leafy greens such as Mizuna mustard or regular mustard greens.

2 tablespoons sambal oelek
½ cup rice vinegar or mild white wine vinegar
2 tablespoons plus 2 teaspoons sugar
Salt to taste

Combine all ingredients in a screw-top jar and shake thoroughly. Refrigerate until ready to use. *Yield: 1 cup*

Soy-Orange Sauce

This delicate sweet and salty sauce enhances such vegetables as cauliflower, bell pepper, and green beans.

½ cup freshly squeezed orange juice
1 tablespoon sugar
2 tablespoons plus 2 teaspoons low-sodium soy sauce
¼ cup rice vinegar
4 teaspoons Japanese cooking wine (mirin)
Dash of Chinese sesame oil
Salt to taste

Combine all ingredients in a screw-top jar and shake thoroughly. Refrigerate until ready to use.

Yield: 1 cup

SOY-GLAZED NAPA CABBAGE
Japan

The tender Napa or Chinese cabbage is popular all over Asia, especially in Japan. Japanese love to snack on the raw, crisp leaves, dipping them in a bit of salt. They also glaze this cabbage during cooking with a mixture of soy sauce and mirin, then top it with crunchy sesame seeds. Napa cabbage prepared this way is oil-free, yet has a rich, satisfying taste.

1 cup Vegetable Stock (page 45) or canned
    vegetable broth
2 teaspoons low-sodium soy sauce
2 teaspoons sugar
1 teaspoon Japanese cooking wine (mirin)
Salt to taste
1 head Napa cabbage (about 1½ pounds) or
    ½ medium-size regular cabbage, cut diagonally
    into ¾-inch strips
1 tablespoon toasted sesame seeds

1. Place stock, soy sauce, sugar, mirin, and salt in a large steep-sided pot and bring to a boil. Reduce heat and add cabbage. Simmer, covered, 3 to 5 minutes, or just until cabbage is wilted. (If using regular cabbage, cook 5 to 10 minutes.) Remove cabbage with a slotted spoon to a large heated platter. Keep warm.

2. Cook the sauce, uncovered, for 3 to 5 minutes, or until thick and reduced in volume. Taste and adjust seasoning. Pour over the cabbage. Sprinkle with sesame seeds. *Yield: 2 entrée or 4 side-dish servings*

SERVING SUGGESTIONS: For a light meal, serve with white Basmati rice and papads (page 24). It is also delightful when accompanied by Saffron-Baked Quinoa (page 172) and Red Rouille (page 73). A cup of green tea and ripe mango or peach slices make a satisfying ending. If there are any leftovers, roll them with some blanched bean sprouts in a warm chapati or tortilla at lunchtime.

BRUSSELS SPROUTS, GARLIC, AND SWEET PEPPER STIR-FRY

International

Brussels sprouts might seem an unlikely vegetable for a stir-fry, but these "little cabbages" cook quickly when an X is made at the bottom with a knife. They are delicious when combined with garlic, spinach, and bell pepper. Garlic is added whole, rather than minced or pressed, and it becomes tender and buttery when simmered in broth. This unusual dish will soon become a favorite.

1 tablespoon olive oil
5 to 10 large garlic cloves
¼ cup Vegetable Stock (page 45) or canned
     vegetable broth
¼ teaspoon black bean sauce with chile (see Note)
2 teaspoons hoisin sauce
½ pound medium-size Brussels sprouts, larger ones
     cut in half, bottoms with an X (about
     ⅛-inch deep) (see Note for the Gardener)
1 red bell pepper, seeds and inner ribs removed,
     thinly slivered
4 cups firmly packed thoroughly cleaned, stemmed,
     coarsely shredded spinach, Swiss chard, or beet greens
Salt and freshly ground black pepper to taste
2 hard-cooked eggs, chopped, for garnish

1. In hot oil in a large skillet or wok, stir-fry garlic until golden. Add Brussels sprouts and stir to coat with the oil. Add stock, black bean sauce, and hoisin sauce and bring to a boil. Reduce heat. Simmer, covered, about 7 to 9 minutes, or until Brussels sprouts are about half-done.

2. Add bell pepper and spinach. Cook, covered, for 3 to 5 minutes, or until spinach is just wilted and the Brussels sprouts are tender. Don't overcook or the Brussels sprouts will develop an odor. Season to taste with salt and pepper. Remove from heat. Serve garnished with eggs.

Yield: 2 entrée or 4 side-dish servings

NOTE: If black bean sauce with chile is not available, use black bean sauce, which is sold in Asian groceries, supermarkets, and natural food stores. Add ground red pepper to taste in this case.

NOTE FOR THE GARDENER: Baby Brussels sprouts are especially tasty prepared this way. Suggestion: Don't throw away the tender leaves at the top of a Brussels sprout plant. These leaves are delicious after a frost or two, when they turn sweet. They can take the place of Swiss chard or mustard greens in most recipes, and are also delicious sautéed in oil with garlic and onions as a dish in their own right.

SERVING SUGGESTIONS: This stir-fry is luscious with brown rice and grilled butternut or acorn squash topped with Green Rouille (page 74). My dessert of choice is Plum Kuchen (page 254).

SWEET-AND-SOUR POMEGRANATE TOFU

Middle East/China

"**A** cook is known by her *fesenjan*," Iranians say of their famous game stew, prized for its tantalizing sauce. The base for this sauce is smooth, fruity pomegranate syrup, thickened with ground walnuts. Here tofu is cooked *fesenjan*-style and the result is delicious.

SAUCE:

1½ to 2 tablespoons canola oil
1 cup finely chopped onion
3 large garlic cloves, minced
1 tablespoon minced gingerroot
¼ teaspoon ground turmeric
2 teaspoons ground cumin
½ cup walnuts, ground to a coarse powder in a blender
     or food processor
2 teaspoons sugar
2½ teaspoons pomegranate syrup
½ teaspoon salt
Ground red pepper to taste

TOFU:

One 14-ounce carton firm tofu, drained, rinsed, and
     cut into 1-inch cubes
½ cup fresh peas or thawed frozen peas

GARNISHES:

Chopped fresh cilantro
Red bell pepper strips

1. In hot oil in a large skillet, sauté onion until richly browned, but not burned, 8 to 12 minutes, stirring often. (If necessary sprinkle a little water to keep the onions from burning. If the onions burn, the sauce will turn bitter.) Stir in garlic and gingerroot. Add turmeric, cumin, and ¼ cup water. Cover and cook 3 to 5 minutes. Remove from heat. (Up to this point, the dish can be made ahead and refrigerated.)

2. Process onion-garlic mixture, walnuts, and ½ cup water in a blender or food processor until thick and creamy, adding a little extra water if the mixture is too thick to process. Remove to a medium bowl and add sugar, pomegranate syrup, salt, and red pepper. Mix well and transfer to the same skillet.

3. Bring the mixture to a simmer. Add tofu and fresh peas (if using). Simmer, covered, 5 to 7 minutes. During this period, uncover once and gently turn the tofu pieces. If using thawed frozen peas, add during the last 2 to 3 minutes of cooking. Taste and adjust the amount of salt and red pepper. Serve garnished with cilantro and pepper strips, for contrast with the dark sauce.

Yield: 2 entrée or 4 side-dish servings

SERVING SUGGESTIONS: This dish is best served with plain steamed Basmati rice, but it also goes well with potatoes. Two suggestions are Indian-Style Roasted Potatoes (page 32) and Potato Koftas (page 96). Other possible accompaniments are Green Beans and Red Pepper Gratin (page 142) and Beets and Feta Cheese in a Spinach Nest (page 86). A compatible dessert is Peach Tart (page 252) or some ripe peach slices.

PESTO-LACED BROCCOLI
Italy/East Asia

Broccoli can be prepared in innumerable ways, but steaming is one of the quickest and tastiest. To complement this succulent vegetable, all you need is a light Asian-style pesto for a lower-fat treat.

1½ tablespoons Garlic Oil (page 231) or olive oil
¼ teaspoon asafetida powder
1 cup thinly sliced onion
¼ cup Vegetable Stock (page 45) or canned vegetable
   broth, or more as required
1 pound broccoli florets
Salt and freshly ground black pepper to taste
Asian Pesto (page 215)
6 pecans, toasted and chopped for garnish

Heat oil in a large skillet until sizzling. Sprinkle asafetida over the oil. Add onion and sauté until it is translucent. Add stock and bring to a boil. Add broccoli. Cover and simmer 7 to 10 minutes, or until broccoli is fork-tender. Don't overcook. Season to taste with salt and pepper. Serve topped with pesto and garnished with pecans.   *Yield: 2 entrée or 4 side-dish servings*

SERVING SUGGESTIONS: I like to serve this with Nut-Topped Savory Rice (page 174) and Two-Tomato Jam (page 232). Maple Pears (page 241) or some Asian pear slices served as a dessert make this a perfect meal.

BOK CHOY IN
MISO-TAMARIND SAUCE
China/India

Bok choy, a graceful leafy vegetable with milky white stalks similar in appearance to Swiss chard, is available in Asian food shops and many supermarkets. Mixed with earthy black mushrooms, it makes a wonderful dish. The miso-tamarind sauce is rich and complex with a hint of tartness. Puréed mushrooms, used to thicken the sauce and intensify its flavor, take this dish a step beyond the usual stir-fry.

1 teaspoon red miso (akamiso)

1 teaspoon tamarind concentrate

1 teaspoon sugar

1 teaspoon cornstarch or sweet rice flour

2 to 3 tablespoons mushroom soaking liquid

1 tablespoon canola oil

3 to 4 large garlic cloves, forced through a
    garlic press

2 tablespoons finely minced gingerroot

2 ounces dried black mushrooms (about 15), soaked
    in boiling water for 15 minutes or until softened,
    drained, tough stems removed; soaking liquid
    retained (see Note)

½ cup plus 2 tablespoons Vegetable Stock (page 45)
    or canned vegetable broth

1 pound bok choy, coarsely shredded, stems diced
    (see Note for the Gardener)

Toasted pecans for garnish

1. Combine miso, tamarind, sugar, cornstarch, and 1 tablespoon mushroom soaking liquid in a small bowl and stir with a fork until smooth. Set aside.

2. In hot oil in a large nonstick skillet, sauté garlic and gingerroot for 2 to 3 minutes, or until lightly browned. Add mushrooms and stir to coat with the oil. Add broth and bring to a boil. Lower heat, cover, and cook 3 to 5 minutes. Remove from heat.

3. With a slotted spoon, remove 3 black mushrooms. Using a little mushroom soaking liquid, process these in a blender or food processor to a smooth purée. Add purée to the skillet and return to heat. Add reserved sauce and stir until it begins to thicken. Add bok choy. Simmer, covered, 6 to 9 minutes, or until bok choy is wilted but still retains its color. Don't overcook. Serve garnished with toasted pecans.

Yield: 2 entrée or 4 side-dish servings

NOTE: If there is not enough time to soak black mushrooms, use fresh mushrooms (shiitake, if possible), which also work well in this dish. In this case, substitute canned vegetable broth or water for mushroom-soaking liquid.

NOTE FOR THE GARDENER: An alternative to bok choy is joi choi, an improved hybrid version which has crunchy, spicy-sweet stalks and deep green leaves.

SERVING SUGGESTIONS: All you'll need to complete the meal are Orzo-Stuffed Maple Squash (page 167) and a shredded cabbage salad. My dessert of choice would be Chocolate-Macadamia Temptation (page 258), although fresh strawberries in season alone or sprinkled lightly with balsamic vinegar will also go nicely.

GREEN BEANS AND DRIED TOFU FOOGATH
India/China

*F*oogath, a spicy-hot South Indian dish, is typically made with green beans or cabbage, black mustard, curry leaves, and fresh coconut. I had thought *foogath* could not be improved upon until I added Chinese dried tofu and found it not only made the dish more substantial, but enhanced the taste as well. This precooked tofu, sold in Asian markets, has a deliciously chewy skin with a soft, tender, custardlike interior. The combination of bright green beans, turmeric-tinted yellow-brown tofu pieces, and yellow mustard sauce make this dish colorful as well.

3 to 5 large garlic cloves, coarsely chopped

2 tablespoons coarsely chopped gingerroot

2 teaspoons seeded, minced jalapeño or other fresh
    chile (see Notes)

1 tablespoon mustard oil or canola oil

6 to 8 fresh or dried curry leaves

¼ teaspoon ground turmeric

A scant ½ teaspoon salt

½ teaspoon sugar

1 tablespoon black mustard seeds, ground to a powder,
    mixed with 2 tablespoons water and allowed to
    rest 10 minutes

¾ cup Vegetable Stock (page 45) or canned vegetable
    broth

¾ pound green beans, ends trimmed, cut into
    3-inch strips

One 8- to 10-ounce package dried tofu (see Notes)

1 tablespoon dried sweetened flaked coconut

1. Using a food processor, mini chopper, or mortar and pestle, process garlic, gingerroot, and jalapeño to a smooth paste. If you don't have any of these gadgets, mince all three finely.

2. Heat oil in a large skillet over moderate heat until a light haze forms. Add curry leaves and cook for a few seconds. Add garlic-ginger mixture. Sauté for 1 to 2 minutes, or until lightly browned. Stir in turmeric. Add salt, sugar, black mustard paste, and broth. Do this carefully and have a lid handy to cover the skillet, as the mixture will sizzle and may spatter a bit. Bring to a boil. Reduce heat, cover, and simmer for 5 minutes.

3. Add green beans and simmer, covered, for 6 to 8 minutes, or until the beans are almost fork-tender. During this period, uncover and sprinkle a little broth or water over the mixture if it sticks. Add tofu and coconut, reserving a teaspoon of coconut for garnish, and mix well. Continue to cook, covered, until the mixture is heated through, another 2 to 4 minutes. Remove from stove. Taste and adjust salt if necessary. Sprinkle lightly with reserved coconut.

Yield: 2 to 3 entrée or 4 to 6 side-dish servings

NOTES: A ripe red jalapeño, if available, will enhance the visual appeal of the dish.

Dried tofu (sometimes labeled as fried tofu) is a solid brownish square usually with a shrivelled skin. It is sold refrigerated or canned in Asian markets. Don't confuse this either with a puffy variety also sold refrigerated, or the brittle, almost flat sheets of tofu that are sold in packages and found on shelves. If you don't fancy tofu, you can omit it entirely.

SERVING SUGGESTIONS: *Foogath* is traditionally served with plain white rice, but I've found that a mixture of brown Basmati and wild rice is a delicious, and more nutritious, alternative. To complete the meal, add steamed or grilled winter squash, such as acorn or butternut, and steamed cauliflower lightly sprinkled with Spiced Ghee (page 13). Peach Flan (page 238) is an appropriate dessert.

VARIATIONS: Try this wonderful cabbage variation using savoy cabbage, if available. You'll need 6 firmly packed cups of cabbage. Because of the quantity of cabbage, use a 12-inch steep-sided skillet. Those who eat seafood can substitute ½ pound cooked shrimp for tofu.

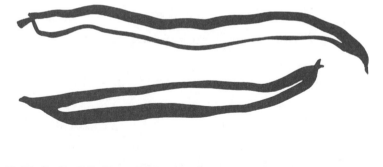

SESAME-SAUCED SPINACH
Middle East/China

So popular is the sesame seed in the Middle East that people there refer to it as "a food, not a spice." In this dish, ground sesame seeds are used to thicken an intensely flavored base of garlic, onions, tomatoes, and soy sauce.

1 tablespoon olive oil
1 cup thinly sliced onion
3 large garlic cloves, minced
½ pound Roma (plum) tomatoes, peeled, seeded,
    and sliced
2 teaspoons low-sodium soy sauce
½ teaspoon sugar
Salt to taste
2 tablespoons water
6 firmly packed cups spinach, thoroughly rinsed,
    stemmed, and coarsely shredded, or mustard greens,
    beet greens, or Swiss chard, stems diced
2 tablespoons sesame seeds, roasted and ground
1 hard-cooked egg for garnish
Chopped cilantro for garnish

In hot oil in large skillet, sauté onion and garlic until onion is translucent. Add tomatoes, soy sauce, sugar, salt, and water. Bring to a boil. Reduce heat slightly, cover, and simmer 5 to 7 minutes, or until the tomatoes begin to break down. With the back of a spoon, mash any tomatoes that still hold their shape. Add sesame powder and mix well. Cover and simmer 3 to 5 minutes, or until the sauce thickens. Add spinach. Cover and cook another 2 to 3 minutes, or just until spinach is wilted but still retains its color. (If using mustard greens or chard, cook for 5 to 7 minutes.) Taste and adjust salt if necessary. Sieve egg over the greens. Serve garnished with cilantro.

Yield: 2 entrée or 4 side-dish servings

SERVING SUGGESTIONS: My favorite accompaniments are brown Basmati rice, steamed beets, and Chile-Ginger Parsnips (page 128). On another occasion, serve Asian-style with brown rice and condiments—chopped peanuts, raisins, browned onion rings, and plain yogurt.

COOL-HOT CABBAGE
India

Cabbage and coconut have a special affinity for each other. In South India, where coconut grows in abundance, coconut milk is often used as a flavoring. The amount of coconut milk used in this recipe is small, but it gives the cabbage a delicate, sweet coating. Fresh green chile, another ingredient that goes well with both cabbage and coconut, provides a spicy background hotness.

1 tablespoon canola oil

1 cup thinly sliced onion

2 tablespoons grated gingerroot

1 to 2 small jalapeños or other green chiles,
    seeded and minced (to taste)

½ teaspoon ground turmeric

1½ teaspoons ground cumin

1½ pounds cabbage (1 medium head), coarsely
    shredded

Salt to taste

3 tablespoons to ¼ cup canned coconut milk (stir to
    mix the thin and thick parts before measuring)

1 hard-boiled egg, finely chopped, for garnish

Chopped cilantro for garnish

1. Heat oil in a 12-inch steep-sided skillet over moderate heat until a light haze forms. Sauté onion until slightly browned around the edges, 3 to 5 minutes. Stir in gingerroot, jalapeño, and turmeric. Add cumin, cabbage, and salt to taste. Lower heat and simmer, covered, about 10 minutes, or just until cabbage is limp.

2. Turn heat to very low. Stir in coconut milk; as soon as it is incorporated into the sauce, remove from the stove. Serve garnished with egg and cilantro.

Yield: 2 to 3 entrée or 4 to 6 side-dish servings

SERVING SUGGESTIONS: This dish goes well with Wild and Brown Rice Salad (page 77) and a baked sweet potato topped with Red Rouille (page 73). Conclude the meal with Anise-Pistachio Biscotti (page 260).

"The most important duty of a host," they say in the Middle East, "is cheerfulness."

CHILE-GINGER PARSNIPS
Thailand/India

The often-neglected parsnip tastes delicious when treated with herbs and spices from the East, as in this dish. Perhaps the most interesting aspect here is the use of gingerroot as a vegetable. Instead of being grated or minced, it is cut in slices, forming an unusual contrast with the sweetness of the parsnip. These juicy ginger morsels stimulate the palate with their warm pungency. Fresh hot chiles complement the effect of ginger nicely, and dried kaffir lime leaves, a common ingredient in Thai cooking, add a fragrant hint of tartness. This unique combination of hot, sweet, and sour flavors will bring your guests back for seconds every time.

1 tablespoon canola oil

2 whole dried red chiles

5 to 6 dried lime leaves (omit, if not available)

1 teaspoon grated gingerroot

A 1-inch piece gingerroot, peeled, thinly sliced

½ teaspoon sambal oelek, or 1 teaspoon seeded, minced
    jalapeño or other fresh chile of choice, or to taste
    (best if slightly hot)

¼ teaspoon ground turmeric

½ teaspoon sugar

½ teaspoon salt

1 cup Vegetable Stock (page 45) or canned
    vegetable broth

1 pound parsnips, scraped to remove root hairs
    if any, cut into ¼-inch-thick slices

1 red bell pepper, seeded, inner ribs removed,
    cut into 1-inch strips

1. Heat oil in large skillet over moderate heat until sizzling. Sauté dried red chiles until they blacken. Add lime leaves, grated gingerroot, sliced gingerroot, sambal oelek, and turmeric and stir a few times. Add sugar, salt, and broth and bring to a boil. Lower heat. Add parsnips and bell pepper, cover, and cook for 6 to 10 minutes, or until parsnips are tender and bell pepper is tender-crisp.

2. If the dish is still watery, reduce sauce. To do so, remove vegetables with a slotted spoon to a large platter and keep covered. Raise heat to medium and cook for 3 to 5 minutes, or until sauce thickens, stirring constantly. Remove from heat. Return vegetables to the skillet and stir thoroughly. Taste and adjust seasoning. Discard red chiles and lime leaves. Gingerroot slices can be left in or taken out, as desired. *Yield: 2 entrée or 4 side-dish servings*

SERVING SUGGESTIONS: Excellent with any grain dish such as Saffron-Baked Quinoa (page 172). Another side dish that shows off this sauté is Sesame-Sauced Spinach (page 125) or Cool-Hot Cabbage (page 126). Try Carrot-Apple Halwa (page 240) for dessert.

VARIATION: For a richer taste, add 2 to 3 tablespoons canned coconut milk (stirred to mix the thin and thick parts before measuring). Just after reducing the sauce, remove skillet from the heat and allow the sauce to cool for a minute. Add coconut milk and the reserved vegetables and stir thoroughly.

If too much salt, pour water. If too much water, put salt.

—Tamil proverb

CHINESE BROCCOLI WITH SHIITAKE MUSHROOMS
International

Strictly speaking, this is a stir-fry of succulent gai lan, also known as Chinese broccoli, with rich, meaty shiitake mushrooms. This unusual dish involves an added ingredient, garlic cloves roasted to a fragrant, buttery consistency. These soft, richly flavored morsels serve not only as a vegetable, but also enhance the smoky quality of the mushrooms. The small extra effort is rewarded by a unique dish of many flavors and textures.

1 whole garlic head

1 tablespoon olive oil

6 to 8 fresh shiitake mushrooms, or ¼ pound dried
     reconstituted shiitake or other Asian mushrooms,
     tough ends trimmed, slivered

2 to 3 tablespoons canned vegetable broth

1 medium-sized red bell pepper, seeds and inner ribs
     removed, thinly sliced

2 teaspoons regular or vegetarian oyster sauce
     (see Note)

1 bunch gai lan (about 1 pound), or 8 firmly packed
     cups shredded Swiss chard, stems diced
     (see page 12)

Raw sweet onion rings for garnish

1. Preheat oven to 400 degrees F.

2. Carefully remove the outer layers of skin of the garlic bulb, and gently separate the cloves. Peel cloves. Arrange on an ungreased baking sheet and bake for 10 to 15 minutes, or until the cloves are tender and browned around the edges. Larger cloves will take longer. Remove each clove as it's done. Allow to cool.

3. Heat oil in a wok or large skillet. Add mushrooms and sauté gently for 1 or 2 minutes. Add 2 tablespoons broth and bring to a boil. Add oyster sauce and stir well. Add gai lan. Reduce heat and simmer, covered, for 6 to 10 minutes, or just until gai lan is tender-crisp. (The cut ends will turn pale green.) Overcooking will destroy the texture of this vegetable. During this period, uncover and add a little more stock if the mixture is beginning to stick. If substituting Swiss chard, cook for about 5 minutes, or just until chard is wilted. Add roasted garlic during the last 3 to 5 minutes of cooking. Transfer to a heated platter and garnish with onion rings.

Yield: 2 entrée or 4 side-dish servings

NOTE: Asian markets carry oyster sauce, also known as oyster-flavored sauce. If you are a strict vegetarian, use vegetarian oyster sauce, which is now sold in many Asian markets.

SERVING SUGGESTIONS: Curry Gyozas (page 38) accompanied by brown Basmati rice and a mixed green salad will make this a memorable meal. Finish with frozen yogurt or almond cookies sold in Asian markets and, if you like, a cup of oolong tea.

SCRAMBLED TEMPEH
Indonesia/China

Cooking with tempeh is often a challenge for Western cooks. This protein-rich fermented soy product has a bold flavor and requires a little ingenuity to make it tasty. Here tempeh is steamed and crumbled, then cooked with a reduced amount of eggs in a richly flavored sauce of onion, garlic, basil, and turmeric. The result is a nutritious, lower-cholesterol version of scrambled eggs with an Asian accent.

One 6-ounce package soy tempeh, cut into cubes
2 large eggs, lightly beaten
1 tablespoon canola oil
1 cup finely chopped onion
3 to 5 large garlic cloves, minced
¼ teaspoon ground turmeric
2 tablespoons fresh chopped basil, or 2 teaspoons dried
2 tablespoons regular or vegetarian oyster sauce
    (see Note on page 131)
Salt to taste

1. Steam tempeh about 10 minutes, or until it puffs up. Using a fork, crumble tempeh thoroughly. Add eggs and mix well. Set aside.

2. In hot oil in large skillet, sauté onion and garlic until onion is translucent and slightly soft, 2 to 3 minutes. Stir in turmeric. Add tempeh mixture and basil and cook, uncovered, for about 5 minutes, stirring constantly. Add oyster sauce and mix well. Season to taste with salt. Remove from heat and let stand, covered, for a few minutes before serving.

Yield: 2 entrée servings

SERVING SUGGESTIONS: For a full meal, accompany with crusty rolls and Sweet Hot Swiss Chard (page 110). At brunchtime, enjoy with Maple Pears (page 241) and perhaps a cup of roasted barley tea. Serve leftovers anytime, rolled in a warm tortilla or chapati or stuffed in a pita pocket, garnished with shredded lettuce and chopped tomatoes.

CASSEROLES, STEWS, AND STUFFED VEGETABLES

The tantalizing aroma of cumin and bay leaf welcomed me into a friend's kitchen. As I entered, she stood over a pot of fragrant beans and vegetables, which she slowly stirred with a wooden spoon. "A pinch more cumin and it's done." She smiled at me. It was obvious that a good hour had gone into preparing this stew—cooking the presoaked beans, chopping the vegetables, and simmering them together with fresh herbs and spices. She was a picture of contentment.

We ate in the kitchen, enjoying a hearty brown stew with just a crisp green salad and warm crusty bread. I told her how good the meal made me feel. She replied that this from-scratch recipe was handed down from her grandmother, and preparing it gave her a feeling of great satisfaction.

Old-fashioned casseroles, stews, and stuffed vegetables frequently appear on my table. For convenience, I simmer the beans in a Crockpot while I attend to other chores. When contrasted with the hectic pace of our lives, these one-pot meals have an appealing, earthy quality. Their scent evokes time spent in a country inn or in the kitchen of a favorite aunt. I eat slowly and savor every spoonful, believing that a long, slow simmer not only develops the flavor, but also extracts the maximum nutrition from each ingredient.

Although it seems to be a jumble of things, the best stew contains carefully selected ingredients. In India, where such stew-type dishes as Seven Vegetable Stew (page 138) are common, skilled cooks select vegetables to complement each other in taste, texture, shape, and color. Cooks often add a member of the protein-rich legume family: dried peas, beans, and lentils, perhaps, and serve the finished dish with rice or whole-grain bread. An excellent example is Split Pea and Sweet Potato Sambhar (page 148), a thick, chile-hot stew of lentils and vegetables, popular in South India. It is served with plain rice or rice dumplings.

Another standard in my kitchen is bean loaf. It has a dense, chewy texture reminiscent of meat loaf and is appropriate as the centerpiece for a meal, as an appetizer, or for filling a sandwich. A bean loaf satisfies our cravings when we need extra energy and is easy to carry to the workplace or on a hike. A friend observed, "It tastes even better at four thousand feet."

Because good stews and casseroles contain an assortment of vegetables, they require few accompaniments other than a salad and carbohydrates. On top of the stew or casserole, I sprinkle an assortment of condiments—chopped peanuts, pickles, Ancho and Red Pepper Salsa (page 216), or Mint-Cilantro Chutney (page 213). Occasionally I include such compatible side dishes as chapatis or tortillas, sautéed mushrooms, or steamed Swiss chard. Any of these adds a nice touch, but the essence of the meal is always the stew.

SWEET-AND-SOUR CABBAGE WITH PEANUT SAUCE
Germany/India

Cabbage is considered simple to prepare, but this often-underestimated vegetable becomes positively alluring when treated with the respect it deserves. This recipe owes its inspiration to both the world-famous German sweet-and-sour cabbage and an equally fine method from western India, where cabbage is smothered in a peanut sauce.

1 tablespoon canola oil
½ teaspoon black mustard seeds
1 tablespoon grated gingerroot
1 to 2 teaspoons seeded, minced jalapeños or other
    green chile (see Note)
½ teaspoon ground turmeric
1 tablespoon ground cumin
1 tablespoon ground coriander seeds
¼ cup water
¾ teaspoon salt
2½ pounds red cabbage, shredded (about 8 cups)
1 tablespoon sugar
¼ cup rice vinegar or mild white wine vinegar
1 tablespoon peanut butter thoroughly mixed with
    1 tablespoon water
2 tablespoons freshly squeezed lime juice
Crushed peanuts for garnish

1. Heat oil in a large saucepan until a light haze forms. Add mustard seeds and sauté until they start to pop. (Hold the cover over the pan to prevent the seeds from flying out.) Add gingerroot, jalapeño, turmeric, cumin, and

coriander and stir until evenly distributed. Add water and bring to a boil. Add salt and cabbage, lower heat, and simmer, covered, until cabbage is tender but still retains some color, 10 to 15 minutes.

2. Add sugar, vinegar, and the peanut butter mixture; stir. Cook, uncovered, until thoroughly heated. Remove from heat. Add lime juice and mix well. Taste and adjust the amount of salt, sugar, and vinegar; the dish should have a gentle sweet-and-sour taste. Serve garnished with crushed peanuts.

Yield: 4 entrée or 8 side-dish servings

NOTE: This dish tastes best if slightly chile-hot. If jalapeños are not hot enough, add ground red pepper, a scant pinch at a time, until the flavor is satisfactory.

SERVING SUGGESTIONS: This is attractive served over Red and Green Polenta (page 176). You can eschew a green salad and serve, instead, steamed beets, grated carrots, grated daikon radish, and blanched mung bean sprouts on the side. In season, a fresh fruit platter with a bowl of Nutty Cream (page 264) would be an excellent finale.

EAST-WEST EGGPLANT STEW
International

It's my aunt who said that every vegetarian cook should have a good eggplant stew recipe in her repertoire. Eggplant tends to soak up oil, which presents a challenge: how to create a tasty dish that is low in fat. One possibility is this spectacular stew, which derives its flavor mostly from herbs and spices. It combines elements of a ratatouille, caponata, and Indian eggplant stew all in one. East-West Eggplant Stew has a rich hearty taste and is simple to prepare.

2 tablespoons olive oil

1 cup finely chopped onion

3 to 5 large garlic cloves, minced

1 tablespoon ground cumin

½ teaspoon ground turmeric

1½ pounds Japanese eggplant, or 1 medium-sized
    regular eggplant, cut into 1-inch cubes

2 Roma (plum) tomatoes, unpeeled, seeded, and
    coarsely chopped

1 large green bell pepper, coarsely chopped

One 16-ounce can tomato sauce

2 tablespoons chopped fresh basil, or 2 teaspoons dried

1 teaspoon tamarind concentrate

2 teaspoons sugar

Salt to taste

Chopped cilantro for garnish

1. In hot oil in a large saucepan, sauté onion until it is richly browned, 8 to 10 minutes. Add garlic, cumin, and turmeric and stir until evenly distributed in the oil. Add eggplant, tomatoes, green pepper, and tomato sauce. Bring to a boil. Lower heat and simmer, covered, 20 to 30 minutes, or until eggplants are almost tender. During this period, uncover occasionally and stir; add a little water if the mixture sticks to the bottom.

2. Add basil, tamarind, sugar, and salt. Simmer, covered, another 10 minutes. Let stand a few minutes before serving to help develop flavor. Serve garnished with cilantro. *Yield: 4 entrée or 6 side-dish servings*

SERVING SUGGESTIONS: This is especially good with Saffron-Baked Quinoa (page 172) or plain brown rice, and steamed Brussels sprouts. Plum Kuchen (page 254) is a terrific dessert to follow. Serve with warm chapatis for a light lunch, or stuff (after draining) in pita pockets along with shredded cabbage and cucumber slices.

SEVEN VEGETABLE STEW
India

There's something about this stew that satisfies the heart and the palate. Perhaps it's the wide variety of nutrient-dense vegetables or the rich, buttery cashew-sesame thickener. It may be the slow simmering that extracts the natural juices from the vegetables and blends them into a flavorful sauce. Served with grains such as rice, quinoa, millet, or couscous, this stew brightens any meal.

2 tablespoons mustard oil or canola oil

2 to 3 large garlic cloves, forced through a garlic press

2 tablespoons grated gingerroot

¼ teaspoon ground turmeric

1½ teaspoons ground cumin

½ pound Roma (plum) tomatoes (about 5), coarsely
  chopped

2 teaspoons jalapeño or other green chile of choice,
  seeded and minced, or to taste

1 tablespoon sesame seeds, toasted, ground to a
  powder, and thoroughly mixed with 2 tablespoons
  water

3 tablespoons unsalted raw cashew halves, ground
  to a coarse powder in a blender or food processor

1½ cups water

½ teaspoon salt

2 tablespoons finely chopped cilantro

½ pound all-purpose potatoes (about 2 medium),
  peeled or unpeeled, cut into 1-inch cubes

½ pound sweet potatoes (about 2 cups), peeled and cut
  into 1-inch cubes

½ pound cauliflower (½ medium head), cut into small
  florets

1 pound eggplant (1 small), unpeeled, cut into
    1-inch cubes
½ pound kohlrabi or turnip (about 2 cups), scraped to
    remove root hairs, cut into 1-inch cubes
1 large red bell pepper, seeds and inner ribs removed,
    coarsely chopped
½ cup fresh or thawed frozen peas
Hard-boiled egg slices or toasted cashew halves
    for garnish

1. In hot oil in a 12-inch steep-sided skillet, sauté garlic and gingerroot until garlic is golden, about 1 minute. Add turmeric and cumin and stir until evenly distributed. Add tomatoes, jalapeño, sesame paste, ground cashews, water, and salt and bring to a boil. Reduce heat and simmer, covered, 8 to 10 minutes, or until the tomatoes have broken down. With the back of a spoon, mash those that still hold their shape.

2. Add cilantro, potatoes, sweet potatoes, cauliflower, eggplant, kohlrabi, bell pepper, and fresh peas. Simmer, covered, 20 to 25 minutes, or until the vegetables are tender. If using thawed frozen peas, add them now and cook for another 1 or 2 minutes. Taste and adjust seasoning. Remove from heat and garnish with egg slices or cashew halves.

Yield: 4 entrée or 8 side-dish servings

SERVING SUGGESTIONS: All that is needed to complement this substantial stew are Nut-Topped Savory Rice (page 174) or plain jasmine rice, and a condiment such as Asian Pesto (page 215). Any accompanying salad should be light, perhaps some Bibb lettuce lightly dressed with extra-virgin olive oil and balsamic vinegar. Follow with fresh ripe peach slices or grilled peach halves.

SPICY TOFU AND PEA STEW
India

This dish takes its inspiration from *mattar panir,* the rich, saucy dish made with peas (*mattar*) and fresh Indian cheese (*panir*). Fresh Indian cheese takes time to prepare and is not readily available in Indian groceries in the West. An American friend once suggested that I come up with a recipe that substituted tofu for fresh cheese. To my surprise it worked very well.

The original recipe required some modification because tofu differs from Indian cheese in both taste and cooking properties. Nonetheless, tofu blends well with Indian spices and produces a protein-rich dish that is just as attractive and tasty as the original and is easier to prepare.

1½ to 2 tablespoons canola oil or mustard oil (see Notes)
½ cup shallots, made into a paste (see Notes)
3 large garlic cloves, forced through a garlic press
1 tablespoon grated gingerroot
2 tablespoons canned vegetable broth, or more
    as needed
1 teaspoon seeded, minced jalapeño or other fresh
    chile, or to taste
¾ pound Roma (plum) tomatoes (about 6), unpeeled,
    seeded, and finely chopped
2 teaspoons ground cumin
½ teaspoon salt
¾ teaspoon sugar
Ground red pepper to taste
One 14-ounce carton firm tofu, drained and rinsed
½ cup thawed frozen peas
2 tablespoons to ¼ cup part-skim or low-fat ricotta
    cheese (see Notes)
Chopped cilantro for garnish

1. Press water out of tofu by placing it between layers of kitchen towel or paper towels on a cutting board and by resting a heavy weight, such as an iron skillet, on top for 30 minutes. Remove tofu and cut it into small cubes. Set aside.

2. In hot oil in large skillet, sauté shallot, garlic, and gingerroot until the mixture is light brown in color, 2 to 3 minutes, stirring constantly. Lower heat. Add broth and cook, covered, for 6 to 8 minutes to remove the raw taste of these aromatics. Sprinkle in a little extra broth if the mixture sticks to the bottom. Add jalapeño, tomatoes, cumin, salt, sugar, and red pepper. Bring to a boil. Reduce heat and simmer, covered, until the mixture has formed a thick sauce, 10 to 15 minutes.

3. Add tofu and peas. Simmer, covered, 5 minutes more to heat the mixture through. Turn heat to very low. Add ricotta cheese. As soon as cheese has been incorporated into the sauce, in 2 to 3 minutes, remove from heat. Adjust seasoning and taste for hotness, adding a bit more red pepper if necessary. Serve garnished with cilantro. *Yield: 2 entrée or 4 side-dish servings*

NOTES: For a richer dish, substitute butter or ghee for part of the oil.

Place shallot in a mini chopper or food processor and process to a smooth purée. Or use a mortar and pestle. You can also process garlic and gingerroot along with shallot to a smooth paste instead of preparing them separately. Because of its milder flavor, shallot blends better with the sauce, but onion can be substituted.

For a special occasion, add 1 tablespoon half-and-half along with the cheese to make the sauce creamier.

SERVING SUGGESTIONS: For a main meal, this stew is great with almost any rice, quinoa, or millet dish, a baked sweet potato, and Pesto-Laced Broccoli (page 120). A simple dessert would be kiwi and fresh papaya slices, but for a special occasion, try Carrot-Apple Halwa (page 240).

GREEN BEANS AND RED PEPPER GRATIN

France

This French-style gratin is a lovely mixture of green beans, red bell pepper, and spices, and is topped with garlic bread crumbs. As with any gratin dish, it is baked until the top is richly browned. The traditional cheese is absent, but you won't miss it because of the spicy note of paprika, red pepper, and asafetida.

1½ tablespoons olive oil
¼ teaspoon asafetida powder
3 to 4 large garlic cloves, forced through a garlic press
¾ pound green beans, cut into 1½-inch strips
1 medium red bell pepper, seeds and inner ribs
    removed, cut into strips 1½ inches long
    (see Note for the Gardener)
¼ cup Vegetable Stock (page 45) or canned
    vegetable broth
2 tablespoons fresh chopped basil, or 2 teaspoons
    dried (see Note)
½ teaspoon sweet Hungarian paprika
Ground red pepper to taste
Salt to taste
¼ cup Garlic Bread Crumbs (page 233)

1. Preheat broiler. Oil an 8-inch-square cake pan or 1½-quart gratin dish.

2. Heat oil in a large skillet until sizzling. Sprinkle asafetida over oil. Add garlic and sauté until golden. Add green beans, bell pepper, stock, basil, paprika, and ground red pepper and bring to a boil. Lower heat and simmer,

covered, 8 to 12 minutes, or until the vegetables are tender. Add salt. Taste for hotness and add a bit more red pepper if necessary. Remove from heat.

3. Transfer vegetables to prepared pan. Spread bread crumbs evenly over the vegetables. Broil for 3 to 5 minutes, or just until the top is lightly browned in places. Check often and don't let the gratin burn.

Yield: 4 side-dish servings

NOTE: In season, you can also use a combination of fresh basil, thyme, and oregano in this dish.

NOTE FOR THE GARDENER: Bulls Horn, or *Corno di toro,* are sweet Italian peppers perfect for this dish. The long *corno* peppers are thin-skinned and more delicate than regular peppers. They are also delicious in salads.

SERVING SUGGESTIONS: Precede with Carrot-Lentil Soup with Rosemary-Garlic Croutons (page 52) and a salad of spinach, toasted walnuts, and orange segments dressed with Lime-Orange Vinaigrette (page 221). Follow with a fresh fruit platter alone or accompanied by Lemon Satin (page 263).

YAM MASALA
India/Italy

In Northern India, the word *masala* refers to a spice or mixture of spices, which is why well-seasoned recipes are called *masalas*. "Add a little more *masala*," my mother and aunt would say when asked how to improve a dish. The *masalas* in this international Indian dish are tamarind and black mustard seeds from India and sun-dried tomatoes from Italy. The complex tartness of tamarind and the rich, intense flavor of sun-dried tomatoes provide a counterpoint for the smooth sweetness of the yams. The colorful garnish of onions, tomatoes, and cilantro gives the dish a bright, cheery look.

1 pound yams, fresh pumpkin, peeled and cut into
　　1½-inch cubes, or butternut squash (unpeeled)
1 tablespoon canola oil
2 whole dried red chiles
¼ teaspoon kalonji seeds
2 to 5 large garlic cloves, forced through a garlic press
¼ teaspoon ground turmeric
1 teaspoon ground cumin
¾ teaspoon sugar
Ground red pepper to taste
½ teaspoon salt
1 ounce sun-dried tomatoes (about 10), soaked in
　　boiling water to cover for 5 to 15 minutes, or until
　　thoroughly softened (reserve soaking liquid)
¾ teaspoon tamarind concentrate
Red or other sweet onion rings for garnish
Seeded, chopped tomatoes for garnish
Chopped cilantro for garnish

1. Steam yams until very tender, 15 to 18 minutes. Mash thoroughly.

2. Heat oil in a wok or large skillet until a light haze forms. Sauté dried chiles until they blacken, turning them once. Add kalonji seeds and garlic and cook until golden. Stir in turmeric, cumin, sugar, red pepper, and salt. Add the drained sun-dried tomatoes and ½ cup soaking liquid. Cook, uncovered, until the tomatoes have formed a sauce, 5 to 7 minutes. During this period, mash the tomatoes occasionally with the back of a spoon to help break them down. Add mashed yams and mix well. Cover and cook for 3 to 5 minutes to heat the mixture through. Add tamarind and stir until it dissolves into the sauce. Remove from heat. Taste and adjust salt. Serve garnished with onion rings, tomatoes, and cilantro.

Yield: 4 side-dish servings

SERVING SUGGESTIONS: Try with white or brown rice or quinoa, steamed Brussels sprouts drizzed with Lime-Peanut Vinaigrette (page 222), papads (page 24), and Mint-Cilantro Chutney (page 213). Also good served as an appetizer with crackers or chips.

VARIATION: YAM AND CHICK-PEA MASALA Chick-peas add protein and make the dish more substantial. Use ½ to ¾ cup cooked or canned chick-peas and add in Step 2 along with the yam. Serve this as an entrée for 2 or 3 people accompanied by a large romaine and chicory salad, warm chapatis, and Peanut Mayonnaise (page 224).

BEANS
WITH FANCY TOPPINGS
International

This recipe takes you beyond bean soups and baked beans. An easy recipe, it works well for most types of canned beans, allowing you to prepare the dish with a minimum of hassle. You can vary the finished dish by choosing from a variety of exotic toppings such as Asian Pesto, Garlic Bread Crumbs, or Mint-Cilantro Chutney.

BEANS:

2 tablespoons olive oil or canola oil

1 cup finely chopped onion

2 large garlic cloves, forced through a garlic press

¼ teaspoon ground turmeric

2 teaspoons ground cumin

¾ pound Roma (plum) tomatoes, peeled, seeded, and finely chopped

1 large red or green bell pepper, cored, seeded, and finely chopped

1 teaspoon seeded, chopped jalapeño or other fresh chile of choice, or to taste

¼ cup bean liquid or water

2 cups cooked or canned beans (black beans, lima beans, chick-peas, or other beans), cooking or can liquid saved (see Note)

Salt to taste

Ground red pepper to taste

FINAL SPICING:

1 teaspoon olive oil

1 large garlic clove, minced

1 teaspoon fresh basil or a mixture of basil and
   tarragon or cilantro

TOPPINGS (OPTIONAL; CHOOSE ONE):

Asian Pesto (page 215) or any pesto sauce

Mint-Cilantro Chutney (page 213)

Chipotle Barbecue Sauce (page 228)

Garlic Bread Crumbs (page 233) mixed with a
   sprinkling of grated Parmesan cheese

1. Heat 2 tablespoons oil in a large skillet. Sauté onion until it is richly browned, but not burnt, 7 to 10 minutes. Add garlic, turmeric, and cumin and stir until evenly distributed. Add tomatoes, bell pepper, jalapeño, and bean liquid and bring to a boil. Lower heat and simmer, covered, 10 to 12 minutes, or until a sauce has formed. With the back of a spoon, mash those tomatoes that still hold their shape, to mix in with the sauce. Add beans. Simmer, covered, 5 to 8 minutes to blend the flavors. Add salt and red pepper. Remove from heat and keep warm.

2. Heat 1 teaspoon oil in a small skillet. Add minced garlic and sauté until golden. Stir in basil. Pour this oil-herb mixture over the beans. Just before serving, sprinkle with one of the toppings.

Yield: 2 entrée or 4 side-dish servings

NOTE: To fresh-cook beans, soak them overnight in three times their volume of water. Next day, bring to boil in a large pot in the soaking water. Simmer, covered, until tender, adding more water during cooking if water level falls below the beans. Most beans will triple in volume when cooked.

Beans can also be cooked in Crockpots. First, bring them to a boil on top of stove, then transfer them to a Crockpot. Leave on "High" until they start to bubble, then cook on "Low" until tender.

SERVING SUGGESTIONS: Accompany with small bowls containing finely chopped sweet onion, gingerroot, garlic, and jalapeño that each diner can add according to their taste. Goes well with Basmati rice or cracked wheat, Plum-Glazed Squash Rings (page 89), and mixed green salad, dressed with Chile-Sesame Vinaigrette (page 223). For a fancy finish, serve Mango-Apricot Bread Pudding (page 247).

SPLIT PEA
AND
SWEET POTATO SAMBHAR
South India

A folk saying in South India is, "No wedding is possible without a dish of lentils." One popular version is sambhar, a richly spiced, soupy stew made with *toor dal,* split pigeon peas. It is served not only at weddings, but in the humblest of homes on a daily basis. Here I substitute the more familiar yellow split peas for pigeon peas with excellent results. Sambhar is actually a style of cooking that can be applied to many peas and beans. It always uses sambhar powder, a mixture of coriander, fenugreek, turmeric, black mustard seeds, red chiles, and at least two vegetables. Almost any vegetable is appropriate, but South Indian cooks always add a few pieces of eggplant because of its ability to absorb flavors. In this recipe, I also use green beans and sweet potatoes. Green beans add a touch of color and sweet potatoes impart an appealing sweet taste. Both contrast nicely with the spicy hotness of the stew.

¾ cup yellow split peas

5½ cups water

½ teaspoon ground turmeric

1 pound sweet potato (1 medium), peeled, cut into
    1-inch cubes

½ to 1 teaspoon sambhar powder (see Note)

½ pound eggplant (½ small), cut into 1-inch cubes

¼ pound green beans, cut into 1-inch pieces

2 teaspoons tamarind concentrate

Salt to taste

1½ tablespoons canola oil or mustard oil

2 whole dried red chiles

½ teaspoon asafetida powder

½ teaspoon black mustard seeds

8 to 10 fresh or dried curry leaves

1 cup diced onion

Chopped cilantro for garnish

1. If possible, soak split peas in 5½ cups water for 6 hours or overnight. Whether soaked or not, bring split peas and soaking water or 5½ cups fresh water to a boil in a large steep-sided pan. Skim off foam from the top of the surface and discard it or let it subside in the liquid. Lower heat slightly. Add turmeric and simmer, covered, 20 minutes (30 to 35 minutes, if they haven't been soaked). At this point the peas will not be completely cooked. Add sweet potato and ½ teaspoon sambhar powder. Simmer, covered, another 6 to 8 minutes. Add eggplant and green beans. Simmer, covered, an additional 10 to 12 minutes, or until the peas have disintegrated into the sauce and the vegetables are tender. Taste and add the remaining ½ teaspoon sambhar powder if you like. Add tamarind and mix well. Season to taste with salt. Keep warm.

2. Heat oil in a small skillet until a light haze forms. Add dried chiles and sauté until they turn black, turning once. Sprinkle asafetida over the oil.

Add mustard seeds and sauté until the seeds start to pop. (Hold the cover over the skillet to keep the seeds from flying out.) Add curry leaves and cook until they darken slightly, a few seconds. Add onion and cook until it is medium brown in color, 5 to 8 minutes. Discard chile or leave it as a garnish. (Be sure to warn the guests not to bite into it.) Pour this oil-spice mixture over the stew and mix well. Serve garnished with cilantro.

Yield: 2 to 3 entrée or 4 to 6 side-dish servings

NOTE: Some brands of sambhar powder can be very hot. It's best to start with ½ teaspoon, adding more later during cooking, according to taste.

SERVING SUGGESTIONS: My favorite grain accompaniment is brown rice, although white rice, baked potato, or mashed potato goes perfectly well. As sambhar already contains many vegetables, you'll need fewer side dishes, perhaps sliced cucumber, sweet onion rings, and Chile Chutney (page 212). Offer some sherbet or ripe pineapple slices for dessert.

CHIPOTLE CHICK-PEAS
Mexico/India

This spectacular stew is a blending of techniques from India and Mexico, two bean-loving traditions. Plump, robust chick-peas are slowly simmered in a pungent, smoky sauce of roasted sweet peppers, Mexican chipotle chiles, and fresh and sun-dried tomatoes. The Indian seasonings of cumin, turmeric, and asafetida powder finish the dish. Although the ingredient list may seem long, this exciting dish is not difficult to prepare. Try it for a leisurely weekend meal or when entertaining guests.

4 large red bell peppers

1 ounce sun-dried tomatoes (about 10), soaked in boiling water to cover for 5 to 15 minutes, or until softened, soaking water retained

3 cups cooked or canned chick-peas, cooking or can liquid saved (see Notes)

¾ cup chick-pea liquid or water

1½ to 2 tablespoons olive oil or canola oil

½ teaspoon asafetida powder

1 cup finely chopped onion

2 to 4 large garlic cloves, minced

¼ teaspoon ground turmeric

1 teaspoon ground cumin

Ground chipotle pepper or canned chipotle sauce to taste (start with a scant pinch) (see Notes)

½ teaspoon ground ancho pepper or sweet paprika

¾ pound Roma (plum) tomatoes (about 5), unpeeled, finely chopped

¼ cup finely chopped cilantro

Salt to taste

1 to 2 tablespoons tomato soaking water

Chopped cilantro for garnish

1. Preheat broiler. Roast the bell peppers by placing them on an ungreased baking sheet under the broiler for 10 to 15 minutes, turning them several times. They should become soft and their skins should become charred and wrinkled in places. Remove from the broiler. Place them in a paper bag and close the top. After 10 to 15 minutes or when cool, cut each open (saving any liquid that may have accumulated inside). Remove and discard the skin, inner ribs and seeds. Process the flesh and any accumulated juices in a blender or food processor until smooth. Measure 1½ cups. (Retain excess, if any, to serve over boiled or roasted potatoes.)

2. Process the sun-dried tomatoes with enough soaking water in a blender or food processor until smooth; set aside. Purée ½ cup chick-peas with ¼ cup chick-pea liquid or water in a blender or food processor; set aside.

3. Heat oil in a 12-inch skillet until sizzling. Sprinkle asafetida over the oil. Add onion and cook until it is richly browned, but not burned, 7 to 10 minutes, stirring often. Add garlic, turmeric, cumin, ground chipotle, and ancho pepper; stir until evenly distributed. Add the remaining ½ cup chick-pea liquid or water and bring to a boil. Add chick-pea purée, fresh tomatoes, blended sun-dried tomatoes, cilantro, and salt. Lower the heat and cook, uncovered, until a thick sauce forms, 12 to 15 minutes. Stir often, adding a little tomato soaking water if sticking to the bottom.

4. With the back of a spoon, mash those tomatoes that still hold their shape. Add the reserved bell pepper purée. Cook, uncovered, for a few minutes to bring the mixture to a simmer. Add the remaining 2½ cups chick-peas. Cook, covered, to heat the mixture through. Taste and adjust seasoning. Serve garnished with chopped cilantro.

Yield: 4 entrée servings or 8 side-dish servings

NOTES: Ground chipotle pepper is available in specialty shops and natural food stores. Canned chipotle sauce is sold in Latin American groceries. Use small amounts, adjusting according to taste.

Other beans that work well here are navy, white, or black beans.

SERVING SUGGESTIONS: All you'll need is baked or mashed potatoes and crusty bread to sop up the sauce. Pear Slaw with Honey Pecans (page 84) would be an appropriate salad. My dessert of choice is Peach Flan (page 238) or roasted bananas (Step 1, page 227) sprinkled with confectioners' sugar and powdered crystallized ginger.

BROWNED POTATO VARIATION: These pan-roasted potatoes add a roasted aroma, bulk, and texture. Use ½ pound all-purpose potatoes, peeled or unpeeled, cut into ½ inch cubes. To brown the potatoes, steam them until tender, about 15 minutes. Heat 1 tablespoon olive oil in a medium skillet until sizzling. Sprinkle ¼ teaspoon asafetida over the oil. Add potatoes and salt, if desired, and cook over medium heat until browned in places, 5 to 8 minutes, turning them often. Remove from heat. Add them to the dish along with chick-peas in Step 4.

GARLICKY CHARD
AND
CHICK-PEAS
International

Chick-peas and dark leafy greens make a delightful combination. A blend of dark, rich miso and sweet, garlicky hoisin sauce produces a depth of flavor that one associates with long, slow cooking. This dish is fast and easy to prepare.

1 tablespoon canola oil

3 to 4 large garlic cloves, forced through a garlic press

1 tablespoon grated gingerroot

1 teaspoon seeded, minced jalapeño or other fresh chile, or to taste

½ pound Roma (plum) tomatoes, peeled and coarsely chopped

¼ cup bean liquid or water

1 teaspoon red miso paste (akamiso)

1 teaspoon hoisin sauce

1½ cups cooked chick-peas, or one 15-ounce can chick-peas, drained (cooking or can liquid saved)

½ pound red chard or Swiss chard or mustard greens, coarsely shredded, stems diced

Salt to taste

Sweet raw onion rings for garnish

1. In hot oil in a large skillet, sauté garlic and gingerroot until golden. Add jalapeño, tomatoes, and bean liquid or water, and bring to a boil. Lower heat and cook, uncovered, until a thick sauce has formed, 7 to 12 minutes. With the back of a spoon, mash any tomato that still hold its shape.

2. Add miso and hoisin sauce and mix well. Add chick-peas and chard. Simmer, covered, 6 to 8 minutes, or just until chard is tender. Season to taste with salt. Don't overcook or you will destroy the color and texture of chard. Serve garnished with onion rings.   *Yield: 2 entrée or 4 side-dish servings*

SERVING SUGGESTIONS: Wonderful with any plain-cooked grain, especially rice or millet. Sweet Potato Bisque (page 54) and Pear Slaw with Honey Pecans (page 84) are two other excellent accompaniments. A compatible dessert is Chocolate-Glazed Banana Cake (page 242). For a light lunch, team with warm chapatis and crisp carrot sticks.

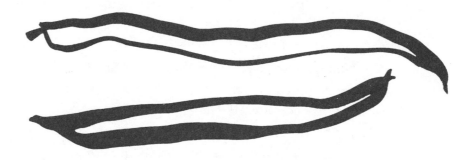

SUPER TOMATOEY GREEN BEANS
Spain/Italy

Green beans and tomatoes are a popular combination in Spain. This recipe doubles the flavor by using two types of tomatoes: fresh and sun-dried. Another Spanish technique is to use garlic in two different ways in the same dish. First whole garlic cloves are browned in oil to impart flavor and then discarded. Afterward, minced garlic is sautéed lightly in the same oil and it becomes a part of the sauce.

12 sun-dried tomatoes, soaked in boiling water
    to cover for 5 to 15 minutes, or until tender
    (reserve soaking liquid)
1½ tablespoons olive oil
3 large whole garlic cloves, halved lengthwise
1 cup thinly sliced onion
3 to 4 large garlic cloves, forced through a garlic press
¾ pound Roma (plum) tomatoes, peeled, seeded, and
    coarsely chopped
1 teaspoon seeded, minced jalapeño or other fresh chile,
    or to taste (use a red one, if available)
½ teaspoon hot Hungarian paprika, or to taste
½ teaspoon salt
Freshly ground black pepper to taste
1 pound green beans, cut into 2-inch-long strips
Raw sweet onion rings for garnish

1. Process the softened sun-dried tomatoes in a blender or food processor with enough soaking water to produce a smooth purée. Reserve the rest of the soaking water.

2. In hot oil in large skillet, sauté garlic cloves until they are browned. Using a slotted spoon remove the garlic cloves and discard. Add onion and pressed garlic and sauté until onion is softened, 2 to 3 minutes. Add sun-dried tomato purée, Roma tomatoes and any accumulated juices, jalapeño, paprika, salt, and pepper. When the mixture comes to a boil, lower heat slightly. Simmer, covered, 8 to 10 minutes, or just until green beans are fork-tender. During this period, uncover and add a little tomato soaking water if the mixture sticks to the bottom. Don't overcook. Taste and adjust seasoning. Serve garnished with onion rings.   *Yield: 4 to 6 side-dish servings*

SERVING SUGGESTIONS: Some of the many possible accompaniments are Corn, Potato, and Lima Bean Chowder (page 56), Italian peasant bread, and Chile-Basil Dip (page 229). Other choices are Pecan Mushroom Pâté (page 30) and plain couscous.

BEAN BARS
WITH ANCHO SALSA
AND HERB CHUTNEY
International

My husband says that he has never met a bean he didn't like, so cooking different beans has always been a pleasurable challenge for me. Kidney beans are one of the most versatile. Mashed and seasoned with cumin and gingerroot, they bake well in a square pan or in loaf form. Topped with a rich brown salsa and a green chutney, these versatile bean bars serve equally well as a tasty main course or an appetizer. They will also be a welcome treat in a lunch box.

¼ pound carrots, thickly sliced (1 cup)

1½ cups cooked or canned red kidney or black beans,
   cooking or can liquid saved

1 cup coarsely chopped onion

4 large garlic cloves, coarsely chopped

1 tablespoon coarsely chopped gingerroot

2 teaspoons ground cumin

1 teaspoon seeded, chopped jalapeño or other fresh
   chile of choice, or to taste

1 cup minced celery

½ cup chopped raw, unsalted cashew halves

2 large eggs plus 2 egg whites

½ cup cornmeal

1 tablespoon chopped fresh oregano, or 1 teaspoon dried

1¾ cup Garlic Bread Crumbs (page 233)

Salt to taste

Ground chipotle pepper or freshly ground black pepper
   to taste

Ancho and Red Pepper Salsa (page 216) for topping

Mint-Cilantro Chutney (page 213) for topping

Cilantro or Italian parsley sprigs (about 8) for garnish

1. Preheat oven to 350 degrees F. Oil an 8-inch-square pan or a 9 × 5 × 3-inch loaf pan.

2. Place all ingredients except bread crumbs, salt and pepper, toppings, and garnish in the container of a food processor. Pulse, in batches, for a few seconds until a meal-like consistency results. Transfer to a large bowl. Add bread crumbs, salt, and pepper; mix well.

3. Spoon mixture into prepared pan. Bake for 30 to 40 minutes, or until firm to the touch. Let rest until cool enough to hande. Then slice carefully to avoid breaking the pieces. Serve topped with salsa and chutney, and garnish with cilantro sprigs. Note: Immediately after baking, the bars will be tender and difficult to slice. This is especially true when baking in the loaf pan, as it has a smaller surface area. You can bake several hours ahead and refrigerate in the baking pan. This will make the bars firm. Before serving, reheat in a 350-degree oven for 10 to 12 minutes, or just until heated through.

Yield: 4 entrée or 6 to 8 appetizer servings

SERVING SUGGESTIONS: Alternatives to the above salsa and chutney are Chipotle Barbecue Sauce (page 228) and Asian Pesto (page 215). These squares are especially good accompanied by Saffron-Baked Quinoa (page 172) and a cooling side dish of Sun-Dried Tomato and Cucumber Raita (page 218). Ripe mango or cantaloupe is a possible fresh fruit choice to round out the meal. At lunchtime, stuff in a pita pocket, or roll in a chapati or tortilla along with chopped sweet onions, chopped tomato, shredded romaine, and the above salsa and chutney.

RED LENTILS
IN COCONUT CREAM
Sri Lanka

I thought I had eaten red lentils prepared in every possible way while growing up in India. I was pleasantly surprised when a Sri Lankan friend served me an unfamiliar red lentil dish, one that used coconut milk. Even a small amount of coconut milk enhances the taste of this dish, which is infused with the fragrance of cumin and caramelized onions. These delicious lentils can be served either as a soup or over the grain of your choice.

3 cups water
1 cup red lentils (see Note)
¼ teaspoon ground turmeric
1 whole jalapeño or other fresh chile
1 tablespoon grated gingerroot
2 tablespoons to ¼ cup coconut milk, stirred to
    mix the thin and thick parts before measuring
2 tablespoons freshly squeezed lime juice
Salt to taste
Ground red pepper to taste
1½ tablespoons canola oil or mustard oil
½ teaspoon cumin seeds
1 cup finely chopped onion
A sprinkling of ghee or melted butter (optional)
Lime wedges for garnish

1. Bring water to a boil in a saucepan. Add red lentils and return to a boil. Lower the heat. With a spoon, remove and discard foam from the top. Add turmeric and jalapeño. Simmer, covered, until lentils are very soft and have almost dissolved in the liquid, about 15 minutes. (When pressed between the thumb and the index finger, they will squash easily.) Discard jalapeño.

2. Purée the mixture in a blender or food processor until smooth. Return to the heat, add ginger and bring to a simmer. Before adding the coconut milk, which will curdle at a boil, make sure the heat is low and the soup is at a gentle simmer. Add coconut milk and mix well. Remove from heat and add lime juice. Season to taste with salt and red pepper.

3. In hot oil in a small skillet, sauté cumin seeds until they are medium brown. Add onion and cook until it is medium brown, 5 to 8 minutes, stirring constantly. Pour onion mixture over the soup, or ladle soup into individual serving bowls and top with a portion of the onion mixture. Sprinkle with ghee, if desired. Serve garnished with lime wedges. (If this dish needs reheating, do so over low heat until it comes to a simmer to keep coconut milk from separating.) *Yield: 4 side-dish servings*

NOTE: Red or Egyptian lentils are available in Indian food shops and specialty stores. Don't substitute supermarket greenish brown lentils; they will not work in this recipe. The color of red lentils will change to yellow during cooking.

SERVING SUGGESTIONS: Perfect as a prelude to Red Rice with Five Vegetables (page 171) and a romaine and arugula salad. Papads (page 24) and Ancho and Red Pepper Salsa (page 216) would go nicely with this meal. Some chilled red grapes or, if you want a more special dessert, Peach Tart (page 252) would bring this supper to a delightful conclusion.

SPUDS AND BLACK BEAN CASSEROLE

United States

One day, when my pantry was nearly bare, I put together a simplified version of the following recipe from a can of beans and a few potatoes. This dish is great for days when you crave something filling and flavorful.

POTATOES:

1½ pounds all-purpose potatoes (5 to 6 medium)
   (see Notes)
2 tablespoons olive oil (see Notes)
2 to 5 large garlic cloves, slivered (optional)

SAUCE:

1 tablespoon olive oil
3 large garlic cloves, minced
1 teaspoon seeded, minced jalapeño or other
   fresh chile (see Notes)
2 medium-sized green bell peppers, cored, seeded,
   and coarsely chopped
1 pound Roma (plum) tomatoes (about 5 medium),
   peeled and seeded
¼ cup Vegetable Stock (page 45) or canned
   vegetable broth
1 tablespoon fresh chopped tarragon, or 1 teaspoon dried
½ teaspoon sugar
1½ cups cooked black beans, or one 15-ounce can
   black beans, drained
Salt and freshly ground black pepper to taste
¾ cup Garlic Bread Crumbs (page 233)
½ cup grated Parmesan or other hard cheese of choice
   (optional)

1. To prepare the potatoes, halve them crosswise, and cook in boiling salted water for 15 to 18 minutes, or until tender. Drain, cool, and slice into ¼-inch-thick rounds.

2. Heat 2 tablespoons oil in a large nonstick skillet over medium heat. Sauté potato rounds and slivered garlic until potatoes are richly browned and garlic is golden, 7 to 10 minutes, turning occasionally. Transfer to a large bowl.

3. Preheat oven to 400 degrees F. Oil a 1½-quart baking dish or a 7 × 11-inch cake pan.

4. Add 1 tablespoon oil to the same skillet and heat until sizzling. Sauté minced garlic until golden. Add jalapeño, bell peppers, tomatoes and their juice, stock, tarragon, sugar, and black beans. Bring to a boil. Lower heat slightly and cook, uncovered, until a thick sauce forms, about 5 minutes. The tomatoes need not break down completely. Season to taste with salt and pepper. Remove from heat and mix in gently with the potatoes.

5. Pour the potato-bean mixture into the prepared pan. Sprinkle evenly with bread crumbs. Cover with a piece of aluminum foil and bake for 15 to 20 minutes, or until thoroughly heated. Sprinkle with cheese, if you like.

Yield: 2 entrée or 4 side-dish servings

NOTES: One exceptional variety of potato is Yellow Finn, which is now sold in many supermarkets. It's referred to as "butterless potato" because the tender flesh with a rich yellow color tastes buttery when prepared. This potato cooks well both on top of stove and in the oven.

If available, use serrano or habanero chiles, either of which goes particularly well with beans. Use very small amounts of these hot chiles, adding more later, if desired.

To reduce the amount of oil even more, don't sauté the potatoes in Step 2. Instead lightly brush the rounds with oil and bake in a 400-degree oven for 15 minutes, or just until browned in places, turning them once halfway through. To eliminate oil altogether, omit this initial baking as well as Step 2. In this case, the potatoes will not have a roasted flavor, but will still taste good. Don't use slivered garlic in this case.

SERVING SUGGESTIONS: Two notable suggestions are Sesame-Sauced Spinach (page 125) and grilled or roasted acorn or butternut squash. Chocolate-Glazed Banana Cake (page 242) or fresh strawberries in season would be a pleasant way to finish.

VARIATIONS: Other beans that work well in this dish are kidney, pinto, lima, and navy beans. If using lima beans, which are buttery and have a compatible color, purée ½ cup of the beans and ¾ cup or more of bean liquid in a blender or food processor until smooth. Add this mixture to the skillet in Step 4, after the tomatoes have formed a sauce. Cook for a few extra minutes to heat the mixture through.

NEW TOUCH TO STUFFED PEPPERS
Eastern Europe

This recipe uses a braising technique common in the former Yugoslavia, but the combination of stuffing ingredients is new. This bold mixture of kasha, black beans, cashews, and raisins is so tasty that it can also be served on its own in place of a richly spiced pilaf. Rolled in a chapati, burrito-style, it can serve nicely as an entrée for a light meal. A good tomato sauce, such as Peppery Tomato Sauce, is absolutely essential when making stuffed peppers.

Much of the preparation can be done ahead of time, which adds to the appeal of the dish.

STUFFING:
½ cup whole kasha
1 cup Vegetable Stock (page 45) or canned
    vegetable broth
1 tablespoon olive oil
1 cup finely chopped onion

3 large garlic cloves, minced

1 teaspoon seeded, minced jalapeño or other
   fresh green chile of choice

3 to 4 cups Peppery Tomato Sauce (page 230,
   preferred) or your favorite tomato sauce

1 tablespoon chopped fresh tarragon, or 1 teaspoon
   dried

½ cup cooked or canned black beans, drained

¼ cup unsalted raw cashew halves

¼ cup raisins

Salt and freshly ground black pepper to taste

PEPPERS:

8 medium to large bell peppers (green, red, or yellow,
   or a mixture)

½ cup grated Cheddar or other hard cheese of choice
   (optional; see Note)

1. To prepare stuffing, bring kasha and stock to a boil in a medium saucepan. Cover and simmer 5 to 8 minutes, or until all liquid is absorbed. Remove from heat and set aside. In hot oil in large skillet, sauté onion and garlic until onion is translucent and slightly soft, about 2 minutes. Stir in jalapeño and ½ cup tomato sauce. Add cooked kasha, tarragon, black beans, cashews, and raisins. Cook, uncovered, for a few minutes to heat the mixture through, stirring often. Season to taste with salt and pepper. Remove from heat.

2. Preheat oven to 375 degrees F.

3. Cut peppers in half lengthwise and remove stems and inner ribs. Plunge them into boiling water; boil, uncovered, 2 to 3 minutes. The peppers will remain firm. Immediately drop them into cold water to stop cooking. Drain out any water that accumulates in the cavities.

4. To stuff the peppers, place them, single-layered, in a large nonmetallic baking pan or an ovenproof casserole. Divide stuffing among peppers, fill-

ing slightly below the top. Spread 1 or 2 tablespoons tomato sauce over the top of each, making sure the sauce does not run down the sides. Bake, uncovered, for 30 to 35 minutes, or just until the filling is heated through. If using cheese, sprinkle over tops at this point, then broil for a few minutes just until the cheese melts. Reheat the remaining tomato sauce. Arrange peppers on individual serving plates and pour sauce over. Pass any extra sauce at the table.   *Yield: 4 entrée servings*

NOTES: Because the filling is spicy, the traditional cheese topping is optional.

You can make the tomato sauce and the stuffing the day before. Prepare the peppers earlier in the day and stuff them as described in Step 3, but don't spoon sauce over them. About 45 minutes before serving, top the peppers with sauce and bake.

SERVING SUGGESTIONS: All that is needed to complement these peppers is a mixed green salad, some crusty French bread, and Asian Pesto (page 215) for dipping. My dessert of choice would be apple slices and gjetost cheese, or for a real treat, Poppy Seed Fruit Ring (page 246).

POTATOES ANANDA
International

This dish is based on a French classic called Potatoes Anna, a baked casserole of butter-drenched, scalloped potatoes. In my version, the potatoes are drizzled with a mixture of olive oil, lemon juice, and puréed roasted garlic. It is spiked with green chiles and fresh tarragon and has sweet onion slices sandwiched in between the layers. I call this happy, healthy combination *ananda*, which is an ancient Sanskrit word meaning joy.

5 to 7 large garlic cloves, unpeeled
3 tablespoons olive oil
3 tablespoons freshly squeezed lemon juice
1 teaspoon seeded, minced jalapeño or other fresh chile
    of choice, or to taste
1 tablespoon chopped fresh tarragon or dill, or
    1 teaspoon dried
¾ teaspoon salt
1½ pounds all-purpose potatoes (about 6 medium)
    (see Note)
1 cup thinly sliced red or other sweet onion
Chopped scallions for garnish

1. Preheat oven to 450 degrees F. Oil an 8-inch-square baking pan or a 1½-quart casserole.

2. Bake the garlic cloves in preheated oven for 8 to 10 minutes, or just until tender. If overcooked, juice will ooze out of the cloves.

3. Peel and discard the skins. Place the cloves, oil, and lemon juice in a blender or food processor and purée until smooth. Transfer to a small bowl. Add jalapeño, tarragon, and salt and mix well.

4. Slice the potatoes in ¼-inch-thick rounds; peeling is optional. As you slice each potato, arrange the rounds in the prepared baking pan with edges overlapping by about ¼ inch. When you have completed a layer, drizzle with some oil-herb mixture and use a pastry brush to distribute evenly so that the tops are well coated. Next add a layer of onions. Repeat the process with the rest of the potatoes, onions, and oil-herb mixture, finishing with a potato layer on top.

5. Bake, tightly covered with a piece of aluminum foil, for 25 to 35 minutes, or until a fork inserted in the center goes through easily. Preheat broiler. Remove foil and broil for 4 to 8 minutes, or until the potatoes are browned in places. Don't overbroil or this will make the potatoes dry and hard. Serve garnished with scallions.   *Yield: 2 entrée or 4 side-dish servings*

NOTE: One delicious potato variety is Yukon Gold, available in many supermarkets. The yellow-skinned Yukons are excellent all-purpose potatoes with a butterlike taste.

SERVING SUGGESTIONS: Accompanied by Kale-Apple Soup (page 68) and Sun-Dried Tomato and Cucumber Raita (page 218), these potatoes make for a colorful and nourishing meal. Fresh pineapple slices or a platter of dried pineapple, persimmon, and nectarines will be a nice way to finish. The oil-herb mixture in Step 3 is excellent alone on top of baked potatoes or mixed with mashed potatoes.

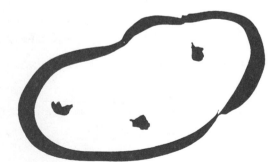

ORZO-STUFFED MAPLE SQUASH
Greece/United States

In autumn when the leaves turn rust and birds start migrating South, I have a desire to roast vegetables, especially winter squash. They are at the peak of flavor and nutritional value at this time of the year. A few drops of maple syrup, drizzled over a squash before baking, enhances its natural sweetness. One of my favorite methods is to bake a squash, then stuff it with orzo—plump, rice-shaped Greek pasta. I top the finished dish with a tomato jam, a thick, sweet tomato sauce intensely flavored with fresh and sun-dried tomatoes. The ensemble makes a perfect entrée for a vegetarian meal.

THE SQUASH:
2 to 3 pounds butternut, acorn, Delicata, or
 kabocha squashes, cut in half horizontally,
 seeded, and cleaned (see Note)
1 to 2 tablespoons pure maple syrup

THE STUFFING:
2 tablespoons olive oil
1 cup minced onion
3 garlic cloves, minced
¼ cup slivered almonds
1 tablespoon golden raisins, soaked in hot water
 for 30 minutes or until softened, drained
1½ cups cooked orzo
¼ cup ½-inch cubes cooked carrots
¼ cup ½-inch strips cooked green beans
Salt and freshly ground black pepper to taste

GARNISHES:
Chopped fresh mint
Two-Tomato Jam (page 232)

1. Preheat oven to 450 degrees F.

2. Trim the bottom of the squash a bit so they will lie flat on a baking sheet. Drizzle maple syrup on the cut surface of each squash. Arrange them on an ungreased baking sheet and cover loosely with a piece of aluminum foil. Bake for 15 to 25 minutes, or until tender (a toothpick inserted in the middle goes through easily).

3. Meanwhile, heat oil in a large skillet, and sauté onion and garlic until onion wilts. Add almonds and drained raisins and stir to mix well. Add orzo, carrots, and green beans. Cook, stirring, until the mixture is heated through. Season to taste with salt and pepper. Keep warm until squash is ready.

3. Fill the squash cavities with equal amounts of the orzo mixture. Drizzle Two-Tomato Jam on top and decorate with mint. Serve any leftover orzo mixture on the side.   *Yield: 4 entrée servings*

NOTE: Squashes that weigh 1 to 1½ pounds a piece are best; a filled half will serve 1 person. Kabocha squashes are also known as Honey Delight and are increasingly becoming available in supermarkets. Acorn and kabocha halves have a good-sized cavity. Butternut squash halves don't, so you'll need to scrape off some flesh surrounding the cavity to make room for the stuffing.

SERVING SUGGESTIONS: Start with Kale-Apple Soup (page 68) and serve the stuffed squash with Grilled Eggplant and Toasted Pecan Salad (page 78). Follow with Anise-Pistachio Biscotti (page 260) and Indian-Style Tea (page 262).

GRAINS
AND
PASTA DISHES

Once on a picnic in San Francisco, I watched an Eastern European acquaintance look for bread. There were casseroles and gratins, pickles and desserts, but he cried out unhappily, "Where's the bread?" As an Asian might have complained, "There is no rice!" with a table full of food in front of him.

A grain or pasta dish supplies the carbohydrates and a feeling of fullness essential to any meal. Our connection with grains begins early in life. I once saw a boy, two years old, eating rice in a restaurant in Taiwan with a pair of chopsticks. He popped the pearly white grains into his mouth from a bowl held close to his chest and didn't miss one of them. The boy ate the rice with the same relish that a Western child licks an ice cream cone.

While growing up in northern India, I too ate rice with a legume or *dal* dish everyday. South India is widely known for its rice specialties. When I asked a South Indian to describe his typical meal, he replied, "We begin with *dal* and rice. Then we have vegetables and lentils with rice." Just when I thought he was done, he chirped, "And we always finish the meal with yogurt and rice."

Since moving to the West, I have begun experimenting with a number of different grains. Kasha, the grainlike seeds of the buckwheat plant, is one of my favorites. I like Old-Fashioned Kasha (page 177) best. In this recipe, kasha turns a nutty brown during its initial roasting, before it is simmered with onions in vegetable broth. Then it's tossed with bow-tie pasta to form a savory Eastern European version of pilaf. I serve this kasha dish with Peach Salsa (page 219). They make unconventional but refreshing partners.

Then there's polenta, that marvelous Italian staple made with yellow cornmeal. Normally polenta has a puddinglike consistency, which makes it excellent as a tender bed for vegetables. Mixed with bell pepper bits and chopped cilantro, Red and Green Polenta (page 176) becomes a colorful border for hearty stew. When baked until firm and cut into squares, the same polenta takes the place of bread.

Quinoa, a tasty import from Peru, is becoming popular in the United States. The grainlike seeds cook quickly into a feathery mass. A backpacker told me that he began by carrying bulgur with him on hikes, but since discovering quinoa, he prefers it for its faster preparation, higher protein content, and lighter taste.

Pasta goes places too, and has been on the move since Marco Polo reportedly brought it to Italy from China. I am always fascinated by the new shapes and flavors that appear in the market each year—saffron ribbons, spinach shells, tomato wheels. The list is endless and I combine each type with a constantly changing repertoire of international sauces. Pasta cooking will be a lifetime study for me.

With so many grains and pastas to choose from, selection can be a pleasant dilemma. When in doubt or when I need comfort, I rely on the plain, boiled rice of my childhood.

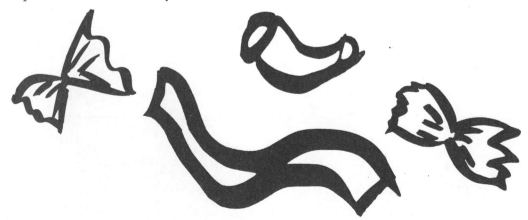

RED RICE WITH
FIVE VEGETABLES
Mexico/Sri Lanka

The technique for cooking rice varies in different cultures. Mexicans often add tomatoes for a touch of red color and rich flavor. Sri Lankans lavish a mixture of whole spices, cashews, raisins, and vegetables on their rice. This recipe combines elements of both these techniques to produce a center-stage dish.

¾ pound cauliflower (½ medium head), cut
    into small florets
¼ pound carrot (1 medium), diced
2 tablespoons olive oil
¼ teaspoon cumin seeds
3 large garlic cloves, minced
1 white of leek, thinly sliced
½ pound Roma (plum) tomatoes (about 2), unpeeled,
    seeded, and diced
½ cup thawed frozen peas
3 cups cooked and cooled Basmati, jasmine, or
    long-grain white rice (see Note)
¾ pound Roma (plum) tomatoes (about 3),
    coarsely chopped and whirled in a blender or food
    processor to a smooth purée (¾ cup)
1 teaspoon sugar
¼ to ½ cup unsalted raw cashew halves,
    lightly toasted
¼ cup golden raisins, soaked in hot water for
    30 minutes, or until plump
Salt to taste

1. Steam cauliflower and carrot together till both are fork-tender, 8 to 10 minutes. Set aside.

2. Heat oil in a large steep-sided pan over moderate heat until sizzling. Add cumin seeds and sauté until the seeds are lightly browned. Add garlic and cook until golden. Add the reserved cauliflower and carrots, leeks, and diced tomatoes; cook for 3 to 4 minutes, stirring constantly.

3. Stir in rice, puréed tomatoes, and sugar, and cook, uncovered, for another few minutes, until all liquid is absorbed and the mixture is heated through. Add peas, cashews, raisins, and salt and cook for a few more minutes. Remove from heat. Serve immediately or keep covered. It will stay warm for 20 minutes. *Yield: 6 side-dish servings*

NOTE: Long-grain brown rice is a good substitute for white rice, and makes a heartier dish. Enjoy this as a main dish for 3 at supper, along with hard-boiled egg wedges and Mint-Cilantro Chutney (page 213).

SERVING SUGGESTIONS: Especially good with Chilled Cucumber-Buttermilk Soup (page 66) and Mint-Cilantro Chutney. Almost any green salad will go with this supper. One suggestion is lightly dressed green-leaf lettuce and some sliced apples. A few wedges of cantalope or watermelon will finish the meal nicely.

SAFFRON-BAKED QUINOA
Middle East/South America

Quinoa becomes light and fluffy when cooked. The highly nutritious grain is one of my favorites. In this recipe, bright yellow saffron threads, plump chick-peas, and roasted sweet red pepper combine to produce a tasty and colorful meal. I frequently make this dish on busy days because it's easy to prepare.

1 tablespoon canola oil, butter, or ghee

3 to 4 large garlic cloves, finely minced

1 cup quinoa, rinsed several times, drained thoroughly
   (see Note)

½ teaspoon saffron threads, soaked in 1 tablespoon
   warm water for 10 to 15 minutes

½ cup slivered almonds

½ cup golden raisins

½ teaspoon salt

2 cups boiling water

½ cup cooked or canned chick-peas

1 roasted red bell pepper, seeded, thinly sliced (page 4),
   or a 2-ounce jar diced pimiento, drained

1. Preheat oven to 350 degrees F.

2. In hot oil in a large skillet, sauté garlic until it is golden. Add quinoa and mix well. Remove from heat and transfer to an ungreased 1-quart baking dish or a 9-inch glass pie pan (preferably one that can double as a serving dish). Add saffron and the soaking water, almonds, raisins, and salt. Pour in boiling water. Cover tightly with a piece of aluminum foil. Bake for 20 to 25 minutes, or until all water is absorbed and quinoa is tender and fluffy. Arrange chick-peas and pepper strips on top. Cover and bake for 3 to 5 minutes more, to heat the mixture through. Serve directly from the baking dish. *Yield: 2 entrée or 4 side-dish servings*

NOTE: An excellent alternative is couscous. Cook couscous for 5 to 10 minutes, or until all water is absorbed before adding chick-peas and peppers. Other grains that work well are Basmati rice and millet.

SERVING SUGGESTIONS: This quinoa dish teams well with most vegetable and bean dishes. It is especially good served with Cherry Tomato Chips (page 37) and a cabbage salad. A platter of fresh fruit and Honey Pecans (page 85) will round out the meal.

SHRIMP VARIATION: Substitute ½ pound cooked, shelled shrimp for chick-peas.

NUT-TOPPED SAVORY RICE
India

Rice is rarely left over from a meal in an Indian home. But if there is any uneaten rice, it often becomes a dish like this. Chiles, cashews, cumin, lime juice, and sesame oil turn even plain rice into a special feast. In this recipe, I use an exotic combination of brown Basmati and wild rice. Light Indian sesame or canola oil is my medium for cooking, but just before serving I sprinkle stronger Chinese sesame oil on the dish for improved flavor.

¾ cup brown Basmati rice

½ cup wild rice

2 tablespoons canola oil

1 whole dried red chile

½ teaspoon cumin seeds

2 teaspoons seeded, minced jalapeño or other fresh
    green chile, or to taste

¼ to ½ cup unsalted raw cashew halves

2 tablespoons freshly squeezed lime juice

Salt to taste

2 teaspoons sesame seeds, toasted

½ teaspoon Chinese sesame oil for sprinkling, or
    more to taste

1. The dish will be better if the rice is cooked several hours before continuing with the recipes. Bring Basmati rice, wild rice, and 2½ cups water to a boil. Lower heat and simmer, covered, until all water is absorbed and rice is tender, 30 to 35 minutes. Set aside.

2. Heat oil in a large skillet until sizzling. Add red chile and cook until it blackens. Add cumin seeds and cook until the seeds are medium brown in color. Add jalapeño and cashews. Cook until cashews are lightly browned, stirring constantly. Watch carefully and don't let the cashews burn. Lower the heat. Add reserved rice. Cook, stirring often, until the mixture is heated through, about 5 minutes. Remove from the heat. Discard red chile.

3. Mix in lime juice, season to taste with salt, and fluff with a fork. Sprinkle with sesame seeds and sesame oil.   *Yield: 4 side-dish servings*

SERVING SUGGESTIONS: This savory rice complements most vegetable dishes. It is especially good with Vegetable Bouillabaisse (page 72) and Chile-Coconut Parsnips (page 128). The salad should be plain—romaine lettuce dressed with Lime-Peanut Vinaigrette (page 222). For a light and elegant finish, try Lemon Mousse Surprise (page 236).

WHITE RICE VARIATION: You can substitute 1¼ cups of white Basmati, jasmine, or long-grain white rice for brown Basmati and wild rice.

When something is easily understood, the Chinese liken it to "rice dropped in clear water."

RED AND GREEN POLENTA
Italy

In this recipe, cilantro and red bell pepper brighten the yellow cornmeal. Add this savory mixture as a border to your stew or casserole to make the meal more inviting.

1 cup polenta (see Note)
½ cup finely chopped green bell pepper
½ cup finely chopped red bell pepper
2 tablespoons finely chopped cilantro
Salt to taste

Bring 4 cups water to a boil in a large steep-sided saucepan. Add polenta gradually, stirring constantly. Cook, uncovered, stirring often for 10 minutes. Add red and green bell peppers. Continue cooking until the mixture becomes thick and forms a lump around the spoon, another 5 to 15 minutes. At this point, the grains will swell and become tender and the peppers will be tender-crisp. (The timing will vary with the type of polenta.) Remove from heat, season to taste with salt, and stir in cilantro. Serve immediately.

Yield: 6 side-dish servings

NOTE: Instant polenta cooks faster, in about 5 minutes, but has a soft, mushy quality. Use regular polenta or yellow corn grits for a more solid texture.

SERVING SUGGESTIONS: Excellent as a bed for Seven Vegetable Stew (page 138) or as a border for Garlicky Chard and Chick-peas (page 153). The dish is also perfect with Warm Mustard Green Salad (page 80) and Beans with Fancy Toppings (page 146). Peach Flan (page 238) will finish an exciting meal.

OLD-FASHIONED KASHA
WITH PEACH SALSA
Eastern Europe/Mexico

Kasha cooks quickly and requires few added ingredients. This well-known Jewish dish is a traditional meal accompaniment in Eastern European countries.

1 cup whole kasha
1 large egg, lightly beaten
1 cup finely chopped onion
1 to 2 tablespoons butter
½ teaspoon salt
¼ pound bow-tie pasta
Peach Salsa (page 219)

1. Toast kasha in a large, ungreased skillet over medium-low heat for a few minutes, stirring constantly. When it is lightly browned, lower the heat slightly and pour in egg. Stirring quickly, coat the kasha kernels with the egg. If the heat is too high or if not stirred enough, the egg will remain separate from kasha and will start to scramble. Add onion, 2 cups hot water, butter, and salt. Bring to a boil. Lower the heat, and cook, covered, for 15 minutes, or until all water is absorbed and kasha is light and fluffy. Remove from heat. Let stand a few minutes to develop flavor.

2. Meanwhile, cook pasta according to package directions; drain. Add pasta to kasha. Taste and adjust seasoning. Serve with Peach Salsa on the side.

Yield: 2 entrée or 4 side-dish servings

SERVING SUGGESTIONS: Try this Eastern European specialty with Caramelized Garlic (page 26) from Spain as an appetizer, and the German-inspired Cool-Hot Cabbage (page 126) as a side dish. Peach Tart (page 252) from France can be a delightful conclusion.

SWEET-SPICED MILLET WITH CABBAGE AND PINE NUTS

Middle East

Millet is a tiny, round, whole grain that cooks quickly and is easy to digest. It is tasty, has a soft, fluffy texture, and blends well with a wide range of ingredients. Cooked like a Middle Eastern pilaf, it acquires a lilting sweetness from a touch of honey and is further enhanced by nutmeg and cardamom. These two sweet spices permeate the yellow grains as they burst during cooking.

1 tablespoon olive oil
3 large garlic cloves, minced
¼ teaspoon ground turmeric
1 cup millet (see Note)
1 tablespoon honey or brown rice syrup
½ teaspoon ground nutmeg
Dash of ground cardamom
Salt to taste
1 cup shredded cabbage
1 red bell pepper, thinly sliced
1 tablespoon toasted pine nuts

1. Heat oil in a large steep-sided skillet over moderate heat until a light haze forms. Add garlic and cook until golden. Sprinkle turmeric over the garlic and stir briefly. Add millet. Stirring often, cook for a few minutes, until millet is lightly browned. Adjust the heat as necessary so that millet doesn't turn too dark. Add 2½ cups hot water, honey, nutmeg, cardamom, and salt and heat to boiling. Cover and simmer 12 to 15 minutes, or until all water is absorbed.

2. Arrange cabbage, bell pepper, and pine nuts over the millet, without stirring millet. Cover and simmer another 8 to 10 minutes, or until the grain and

the vegetables are tender. (There will be enough residual moisture in the grains of millet to finish cooking both it and the vegetables. If the grains seem too dry, sprinkle with a tablespoon of water.) Remove from heat. Let stand, covered, for a few minutes to help develop the flavor. Before serving, fluff with a fork and taste and adjust seasoning.

Yield: 2 entrée or 4 side-dish servings

NOTE: Both couscous and Basmati rice are good alternatives. With couscous, the dish is particularly pretty. Cook couscous only for 5 to 8 minutes in Step 1.

SERVING SUGGESTIONS: Great with an eggplant dish such as Grilled Eggplant and Toasted Pecan Salad (page 78). Another lovely accompaniment at the same meal will be Beets and Feta Cheese in a Spinach Nest (page 86). Warm slices of Peach Tart (page 252) will complete an unforgettable supper.

He who fears a sparrow will never sow millet.

—Russian proverb

SESAME EGGPLANT AND SPAGHETTI
India/Italy

The city of Hyderabad in India is venerated for its cuisine. One of the specialties of this city is *bahare baingan,* an eggplant stew richly spiced with coconut, tamarind, and sesame seeds. While this dish is typically paired with a mound of fragrant rice or silky thin flat bread, I find it goes equally well with pasta. This marvelous sauce turns plain spaghetti into an exotic mystery. No wonder it's said that the Muslim kings, centuries ago, demanded eggplant in their royal dinners.

1½ pounds eggplant (1 large), cut in half lengthwise

SPICE PASTE:
3 large garlic cloves, forced through a garlic press
1 teaspoon sambal oelek or red chile paste, or to taste
2 tablespoons sesame seeds, roasted and ground
2 tablespoons sweetened flaked coconut, ground in a
    blender or food processor to a coarse powder
1½ teaspoons ground cumin
½ teaspoon sugar
½ teaspoon salt
1 tablespoon water

SAUCE:
1 to 1½ tablespoons canola oil
½ teaspoon cumin seeds
½ cup finely chopped onion
½ cup water
1 teaspoon tamarind concentrate

PASTA:

8 ounces regular spaghetti or quinoa spaghetti
(see Note)

GARNISHES:

Chopped cilantro
Chopped red bell pepper
Chopped sweet onion

1. Preheat broiler. To roast the eggplant, place it, cut side down, on a baking sheet lined with a piece of aluminum foil. Broil for 12 to 20 minutes or until the eggplant is soft to the touch and the skin is wrinkled. Allow to cool. With a fork, carefully extract the pulp (saving the shell, if necessary, for the stuffing variation below). Chop the pulp coarsely and place in a large bowl along with accumulated juice.

2. Combine all spice paste ingredients in a small bowl and mix well. Set aside.

3. Heat oil in a large skillet until a light haze forms. Add cumin seeds and sauté until they are lightly browned. Add onion and cook until it is richly browned but not burnt, 6 to 10 minutes, stirring constantly. Add spice paste and stir to distribute it evenly. Add ½ cup water and bring to a boil. Lower heat, cover, and simmer for 15 minutes. During this period, uncover a few times, stir, and add a little water if the bottom of the skillet is too dry. Stir in eggplant pulp. Cover and cook for 15 minutes to blend in flavors. Add tamarind concentrate and stir until dissolved. Taste and adjust salt. Remove from heat. Let sit, covered, for a few minutes to develop flavors.

4. Cook pasta according to package directions; drain. Divide between 2 individual serving plates and pour sauce over. To complement the dark color of the sauce, garnish generously with cilantro, bell pepper, and onion rings.

Yield: 2 entrée or 4 side-dish servings

NOTE: For a change of taste or if you are allergic to wheat, use quinoa pasta, which is a wheat-free, high-protein pasta sold in natural food stores. Note that this pasta breaks into inch-long pieces during cooking, which does not pose a problem in presenting it. After cooking drain the pasta; rinsing is not necessary.

SERVING SUGGESTIONS: Grilled or roasted vegetables blend well with this dish, so serve grilled radicchio, summer squash, or tomatoes along with a mixed green salad. Another alternative is bright-colored steamed vegetables such as beets, carrots or sweet potato. My dessert of choice is Plum Kuchen (page 254).

STUFFED EGGPLANT VARIATION: Prepare up to Step 3. Stuff the eggplant into the reserved shells. Omit pasta in this case. Serve as a side dish for 2 people.

LINGUINE WITH TOMATO CURRY
India/Italy

A friend who had tried recipes from my book, *The Healthy Cuisine of India*, asked why I didn't include a recipe for tomato sauce. I explained that plain tomato sauce is not traditionally used in India, only realizing later that I could easily come up with a flavorful tomato sauce spiced Indian-style. Vine-ripened tomatoes were in abundance at that moment, and all I needed to enhance their mellow sweetness was a dried red chile, some turmeric, and asafetida powder.

The sauce is delicately sweet with a pungent background note. In the tradition of Indian cooks, I don't use a standard curry powder mix; I call the recipe a "tomato curry" simply to indicate its Indian influence.

1 tablespoon olive oil

2 dried red chiles

½ teaspoon asafetida powder

2 tablespoons minced garlic

½ teaspoon ground turmeric

3 pounds Roma (plum) tomatoes, peeled, seeded, and
   coarsely chopped

1½ teaspoons sugar

½ teaspoon black salt (if available)

Salt to taste

1 pound linguine

1 tablespoon pitted, chopped, Kalamata (black) olives

1 tablespoon crumbled feta cheese

1. Heat oil in a large steep-sided skillet until sizzling. Add chiles and cook until they turn black, 1 to 2 minutes. Sprinkle asafetida over the oil. Add garlic and cook until golden. Stir in turmeric. Add ½ of the tomatoes and accumulated juices. Stirring constantly, cook, uncovered, for about 2 minutes to blend the flavors. Add the remaining tomatoes and accumulated juices, and sugar. Cook, uncovered, for about 5 minutes, or until the mixture is heated through. Season to taste with salt. Cover and keep warm until pasta is ready.

2. Cook and drain linguine according to package directions. Serve sauce over linguine, garnished with olives. Scatter feta cheese on top.

Yield: 4 entrée servings

SERVING SUGGESTIONS: Serve with a side dish of Glazed Carrots with Elephant Garlic (page 90) and a salad of red-leaf lettuce, arugula, and toasted pecans drizzled with Lime-Orange Vinaigrette (page 221). Chocolate-Macadamia Temptation (page 258) would follow it well as a dessert.

SOBA NOODLES AND SMOKED PEPPER FANTASY
International

Soba, the hearty, nutritious buckwheat noodle from Japan, is a culinary gem. In this recipe, the tasty noodles are topped with an intensely flavored sauce of ripe Greek olives and Italian sun-dried tomatoes, accented by smoky Mexican chipotle chile peppers. The result is an international treat. This bright red sauce makes an especially attractive topping for the brownish-gray noodles.

6 medium to large red bell peppers

4 to 5 sun-dried tomatoes, soaked in boiling
water to cover for 5 to 15 minutes, or until
softened, drained

1 tablespoon olive oil

2 to 4 large garlic cloves, forced through a garlic press

¼ teaspoon plus chipotle sauce, or ground
chipotle pepper to taste (see Note)

8 Kalamata (black) olives, pitted and thinly sliced

1 teaspoon capers, drained, minced

1 teaspoon sugar

Salt and white pepper to taste

½ pound soba noodles

A sprinkling of Chinese sesame oil or ghee or both

2 tablespoons thinly sliced scallions

Chopped mild red or other sweet onion and/or
roasted garlic cloves (see Step 2, page 41)

1. To roast bell peppers, see page 3. Place the flesh and any accumulated juice in a blender or food processor and process to a smooth purée. Set aside. Chop the drained sun-dried tomatoes very finely.

2. Heat oil in large skillet, and sauté garlic until golden. Add pepper purée and gently bring it to a near boil. Lower heat and add sun-dried tomatoes, chipotle sauce, olives, capers, and sugar. Simmer, covered, 3 to 5 minutes to heat the mixture through and blend the flavors. Season to taste with salt and white pepper. Remove from heat. (Optionally, transfer about 3 table-spoons sauce to a small bowl. Add ½ teaspoon or more of chipotle sauce to this bowl. Pass this hot sauce at the table for each diner to adjust the amount of heat individually.)

3. Cook and drain soba noodles according to package directions. Place on individual serving plates and pour equal amounts of sauce over. Sprinkle with sesame oil and/or ghee and scatter scallions over the top. At the table, sprinkle with chopped onion and/or roasted garlic according to taste.

Yield: 2 entrée servings

NOTE: Chipotle sauce is available in cans in Latin American food shops. Ground chipotle powder is sold in natural food stores and specialty shops. An alternative is to soak 1 to 2 dried chipotle chiles in boiling water until soft. Remove seeds and stems and discard them. Process the flesh in a blender or food processor with a little water or orange juice until smooth. As this chile can be very hot, add a little at a time to the pepper purée in Step 2, taste, and add more if you like.

SERVING SUGGESTIONS: It is luscious with grilled zucchini and a spinach salad. Finish with Hazelnut Lime Bars (page 257) and a cup of green tea. The versatile smoked pepper sauce is excellent over grains, such as rice, kasha, or cracked wheat; can be spread over baked potato; and can serve as a pizza sauce. Enjoy a colorful summer meal by serving this red-orange sauce and the green colored Asian Pesto (page 215) with grilled vegetables of choice.

SQUASH-FILLED MANICOTTI
Italy/China

Round, attractive, large manicotti shells are a welcome break from common pastas. Traditionally, such shells are stuffed with ricotta cheese, but here they are filled with a sweet mixture of squash and cheese, accented by soy sauce. Once stuffed, they are baked in a pool of tomato sauce spiked with cumin. As the plump warm shells bake in the oven, a rich aroma fills the kitchen.

This recipe may appear to be time consuming, but it isn't. The tasty filling can stand alone as a side dish.

FILLING:
1 pound butternut squash (unpeeled) or sweet potatoes, peeled and cubed
1 tablespoon canola oil
1 cup finely chopped onion
3 large garlic cloves, minced
¼ to ½ cup Vegetable Stock (page 45) or canned vegetable broth
1 cup thinly shredded cabbage
1½ teaspoons sugar
3 tablespoons ricotta cheese (preferably part-skim or low-fat)
1 tablespoon low-sodium soy sauce (see Note)
Salt to taste

PASTA:
8 ounces manicotti (14 large shells)
2 cups Peppery Tomato Sauce (page 230) or a tomato sauce of your choice (see Note)
2 teaspoons ground cumin
¼ cup shredded low-fat mozzarella or other cheese of choice (optional)

1. To prepare filling, steam the squash or sweet potatoes until tender, 15 to 18 minutes. Mash thoroughly.

2. Heat oil in a large skillet and sauté onion and garlic just until onion is translucent and slightly soft, about 2 minutes. Add stock and heat to boiling. Add cabbage and sugar. Lower heat, cover, and cook for 3 to 5 minutes, or just until cabbage is wilted. During this period, uncover once and add a little more stock if the bottom of the skillet is dry. Add the mashed squash or sweet potatoes and cook, uncovered, for another 5 to 6 minutes to heat the mixture through and blend the flavors. Add ricotta cheese and soy sauce. As soon as the cheese is mixed with the sauce, remove from heat. Season to taste with salt. Set aside to cool.

3. Preheat oven to 350 degrees F.

4. Follow package directions to cook manicotti, then drain. Fill cooked shells with the vegetable mixture using a teaspoon, being careful not to tear the shells.

5. Combine tomato sauce and cumin. Place half the sauce in a small saucepan and bring to a boil. Cover bottom of a 13 × 9-inch baking pan with the sauce. Arrange filled manicotti shells in a single layer over the sauce. Pour remaining sauce over the center of the shells in a straight line across the pan. Bake, covered with foil, for 12 to 15 minutes, or just until the sauce at the bottom is bubbly. Overcooking will toughen the shells. Uncover and sprinkle with cheese. *Yield: 3 to 4 entrée servings*

NOTES: If you are not a strict vegetarian, substitute fish sauce for soy sauce. Fish sauce blends well with either butternut squash or sweet potato.

If using canned sauce, try one of the chunky varieties.

SERVING SUGGESTIONS: Perfect with crusty bread and Wilted Spinach Banchan (page 87). Almond Pear Tart (page 250) is a worthy companion as dessert. If serving the tasty filling alone as a side dish, don't mash the squash; leave it as cubes.

FUSILLI IN CHICK-PEA–WALNUT CREAM

Middle East/Italy

A Middle Easterner who loved chick-peas told me that his uncle ate them every day and lived to be a hundred. Whether or not chick-peas had any influence on his longevity, this recipe explains why one might wish to eat them daily. Here chick-peas are simmered in a rich mixture of walnuts and pomegranate syrup. The meatlike flavor of the sauce is particularly appealing to those who are switching to a vegetarian diet. Combining it with pasta creates a hearty, substantial meal.

1½ to 2 tablespoons canola oil
1 cup finely chopped onion
2 tablespoons minced garlic
¼ teaspoon ground turmeric
2 teaspoons ground cumin
Ground red pepper to taste (start with a scant pinch)
1½ cups cooked chick-peas, or one 15-ounce can chick-peas, cooking or can liquid saved
1 cup chick-pea liquid
½ cup walnuts (or pecans), lightly toasted, ground in a blender or food processor to a coarse powder
½ pound broccoli, cut into small florets, stems peeled and diced
1 Roma (plum) tomato, unpeeled, seeded, and diced
1½ teaspoons pomegranate syrup
Salt to taste
1 pound fusilli or linguine

1. In hot oil over moderate heat, sauté onion until it is richly browned but not burned, 8 to 12 minutes, stirring constantly. (Watch carefully and don't

let the onions burn, as this will make the finished dish bitter.) Add turmeric, ground cumin, and red pepper, and stir until evenly distributed. Add 1 cup plus 2 tablespoons water and bring to a boil. Lower heat, cover, and cook for 5 minutes. Place this mixture along with chick-peas, chick-pea liquid, and ground walnuts in a blender or food processor and process to a smooth purée. Return to heat. Add broccoli stems, cover, and simmer gently for 2 to 3 minutes. Now add broccoli florets, tomato, and pomegranate syrup. Cover and simmer for 5 to 7 minutes until broccoli is tender-crisp. Remove from heat. Season to taste with salt. Keep warm until pasta is ready.

2. Cook and drain pasta according to package directions. Pour sauce over and serve.   *Yield: 2 entrée servings*

SERVING SUGGESTIONS: Kale-Apple Soup (page 68) and Roasted Eggplant Relish (page 27) combine well with this pasta dish. The sauce is good on its own as a topping for grains or baked potato, and as a dip for steamed vegetables. For dessert consider Mango, Apple, and Blueberry Delight (page 245) or the more elaborate Mango-Apricot Bread Pudding (page 247).

THAI TORTELLINI
Thailand/Italy

Tortellini, plump Italian cheese-filled dumplings, blend amazingly well with a sauce of Thai curry paste and coconut milk. Even a small amount of coconut milk enhances the tenderness of tortellini. Broccoli and bell peppers add color accents. This is a dish to prepare on days you long for a spicy Thai taste, or when you wish to dazzle your dinner guests.

1 to 1½ tablespoons canola oil
1 cup thinly sliced onion
½ to ¾ teaspoon Thai yellow curry paste
1 large red bell pepper, coarsely chopped
½ pound broccoli, cut into florets
½ to ¾ cup coconut milk, stirred to mix the thin
    and thick parts before measuring
8-ounces spinach cheese tortellini or any tortellini
Chopped cilantro for garnish

1. In hot oil in large skillet, sauté onion until it is translucent, about 2 minutes. Add curry paste and stir until evenly distributed. Add ¼ cup water and bring to a boil. Add bell pepper and broccoli. Lower heat and simmer, covered, 5 to 7 minutes, or just until the vegetables are tender-crisp. Don't let them get too soft. Remove from heat and keep warm.

2. Cook tortellini according to package directions. While it is draining, add coconut milk to the vegetables in skillet and return to very low heat. (The heat is kept low to keep coconut milk from curdling.) As soon as coconut milk is mixed in with the sauce, add tortellini, and stir gently to coat with the sauce. Garnish with cilantro. Best served immediately. If allowed to stand, tortellini will drink up some of the sauce, reducing its volume, although the dish will still taste good. *Yield: 2 to 3 entrée servings*

SERVING SUGGESTIONS: Serve with a side dish of Crostini with Chutney (page 29), steamed carrots or a baked sweet potato, and a lightly dressed salad of romaine, apples, and toasted walnuts. Chocolate-Glazed Banana Cake (page 242) will add the crowning touch.

PIZZAS, TARTS, AND SAVORY PASTRIES

Making pizza is a leisurely affair that allows me time to watch the world outside my kitchen window. For the yeast, it's always a lazy summer afternoon; it can't be rushed. The warm-water base in which it sits eventually becomes frothy. Then I knead flour into the liquid and my kitchen fills with a pleasant yeasty smell.

In the summer, I may water the herb bed outside the kitchen door while the dough rises. Several bees cluster on a dill plant flowering in the late August heat. Basil leaves are curled up, protecting their moist essence from the intense sun. My beloved tarragon is slowly spreading to cover an entire corner of the bed. A few leaves from each will go into my pizza.

Assembling a sauce to top the pizza affords an opportunity for creativity. Among my favorites are a rich peppery tomato purée, a light tomato curry, and a bold combination of Chinese hoisin and plum sauces laced with chile pepper. Occasionally I add a splash of tamarind to the tomato sauce to impart a rich tartness.

Shortly after the pizza goes into the oven, a wonderful fragrance of baking dough permeates the kitchen, raising expectations of a fine meal. On this particular day, while I smell the pizza, a squirrel on the lawn furiously burrows a hole to hide nuts. Both of us are working toward a future meal. I gather an assortment of salad greens. Only the freshest and most tender are fit to accompany an oven-fresh pizza. By now, dinner isn't far away.

Some days, I prepare dough-based dishes, such as tarts, that take less time. An onion tart is one of the most basic, and requires few ingredients. The region of Alsace-Lorraine in northeastern France is famous for such tarts. While in Paris, I had occasion to visit that area, and my first encounter with this Alsatian specialty was at a restaurant that listed *tarte d'oignon* on its menu. To my surprise, it was served as the first course. It came as a slender wedge, rich, warm, and tasty, but with less cheese than I had expected. From this first experience, I recognized numerous possibilities for preparing and serving onion tarts.

Today I make a Leek-Onion Tart (page 198), substituting leeks for part of the onions in the recipe, because they impart a more delicate flavor. I use skim milk rather than cream, and eliminate the traditional hard cheeses entirely.

Another French delicacy that I am fond of is potato nests, crispy brown cups made of deep-fried grated potatoes filled with bright green peas and orange-red carrots. When I prepare a lowfat version of the recipe, I use commercial puff pastries that are shaped like cups, and fill them with vegetables simmered in a light, spicy Indian-style sauce. The dish, Peas and Carrots in a Pastry Nest (page 204), looks attractive, and the contrast of flaky pastry and subtly spiced vegetables is a dance for the taste buds.

This chapter also contains recipes for a variety of bean- or vegetable-filled puff pastries, such as Savory Bean Pie (page 202). These easily prepared pastries make elegant, substantial dishes that are equally appropriate for everyday meals or entertaining.

Quick breads such as biscuits and breadsticks take only minutes to whip up. One of my favorites is a variation of that American classic—cornbread. I roast the cornmeal for a nutty taste, add carrots for sweetening, and shape the dough like bread or muffins to prepare Chile-Cumin Cornbread (page 206).

Whether it's a pizza, tart, or quick bread, these appealing dough-based dishes can be served either as entrées or as an accompaniment to other dishes.

QUICK PIZZA DOUGH
International

This whole wheat pizza dough is quick and easy, yet produces a hearty, chewy crust.

> 1 package (¼ ounce) quick-rise active dry yeast
> 1 cup lukewarm water (110 to 115 degrees F)
> 2 cups whole wheat flour plus additional flour
>   for dredging
> 1 teaspoon salt
> 2 teaspoons sugar
> 1 tablespoon olive oil
> Olive oil for the bowl, the pizza pan, and for brushing
> ½ teaspoon kalonji seeds (optional)
> Coarse cornmeal for dusting
> Sauce of choice
> Toppings of choice

1. Dissolve yeast in warm water. (For accuracy, use an instant thermometer or even a meat thermometer.) If using a food processor, place flour, salt, sugar, and 1 tablespoon oil in the work bowl. Process for a few seconds. With food processor running, pour yeast mixture in a slow stream through feed tube. Process until dough forms a ball. If you don't have a food processor, combine flour, salt, sugar, and 1 tablespoon oil in a large oiled bowl. Add yeast mixture and beat vigorously with a spoon until a dough forms. In either case, turn dough out onto a floured board and knead by hand 10 to 12 times. The dough will be slightly sticky. Allow to rest for 5 minutes.

2. Preheat oven to 450 degrees F. Generously oil a 12-inch pizza pan and sprinkle with cornmeal.

3. Roll the dough out on a lightly floured board to a 12-inch round. Or roll dough out partially, then stretch it out with floured hands. Fit into the pizza pan, pressing it up at the sides to form an elevated border, which will keep the sauce from running off the dough. Sprinkle with kalonji seeds and press lightly. Prick all over with a fork. Brush the entire surface with olive oil. Let rest for another 5 to 10 minutes.

4. Ladle sauce of choice over the crust, carefully avoiding the edges. (You may not need to use all of the sauce.) Arrange topping of choice. Bake for 20 to 30 minutes, or until the crust is crisp and nicely browned and the topping is piping hot. (Baking time will vary; start to check after 20 minutes, and check frequently after that.) Overbaking will harden the crust.

Yield: One 12-inch pizza

ARTICHOKE, GOAT CHEESE, AND OLIVE PIZZA
International

This dish features all three elements a good pizza should have: a crispy crust, a tasty combination of compatible topping ingredients, and a well-balanced sauce whose flavor complements those of the topping ingredients without overwhelming them. The sauce, called Green Rouille, is not only a refreshing change from common tomato variety, but provides a subtle yet delicious contrast in flavor with artichoke, goat cheese, and olive. With each bite you experience sharp, pungent, and salty taste sensations.

Green Rouille (page 74)
Quick Pizza Dough (preceding recipe)
One 4-ounce can artickoke hearts, or ½ cup thawed
    frozen artichokes, drained and quartered
6 Kalamata (black) olives, pitted and thinly sliced
1 heaping teaspoon capers, drained, rinsed, and
    chopped
1 to 2 ounces goat cheese, such as feta or Montrachet,
    slivered or crumbled depending on texture

1. Prepare Green Rouille and set aside.

2. Prepare Quick Pizza Dough through Step 3.

3. In Step 4, spoon Green Rouille evenly over the crust. Arrange artichoke hearts, olives, and capers decoratively over the sauce. Dot with cheese. Bake as suggested in Quick Pizza Dough recipe.

Yield: One 12-inch pizza; 2 entrée or 4 side-dish servings

SERVING SUGGESTIONS: Start with a salad of Bibb lettuce, radish, and red onions, dressed with olive oil and a squeeze of lemon; finish with Poppy Seed Fruit Ring (page 246). On another occasion, start with Sweet Potato Bisque (page 54) and serve the pizza with a side dish of grilled vegetables and Chile-Basil Dip (page 229).

SWISS CHARD, ROASTED GARLIC, AND MUSHROOM PIZZA
International

Shredded Swiss chard on a pizza may come as a surprise to some, but this topping is a treat. Ingredients that complement Swiss chard are whole garlic cloves, made tender and brown by roasting; succulent, sautéed mushrooms; and rich, earthy feta cheese. For sauce I use Red Rouille, a fine sauce of red bell pepper.

18 whole garlic cloves, peeled (about 2 whole heads)
1 tablespoon Garlic Oil (page 231) or olive oil
1 firmly packed cup medium-fine chopped Swiss chard
    (see Note)
¼ pound fresh mushrooms, sliced
Dash of dried red pepper flakes to taste
Quick Pizza Dough (page 193)
Red Rouille (page 73)
1 to 2 ounces feta cheese

1. Preheat oven to 425 degrees F.

2. Place the garlic cloves on a baking sheet and at bake for 10 to 12 minutes, or just until soft and lightly browned. Check often and remove each clove as it's done.

3. Heat oil in a large skillet until sizzling. Add Swiss chard, mushrooms, and red pepper flakes. Cook, uncovered, for a few minutes, stirring often. Lower heat, cover, and cook for a few minutes just until Swiss chard is tender but still retains its color. Remove from heat, keep uncovered, and allow to cool.

4. Prepare Quick Pizza Dough through Step 3.

5. In Step 4, spoon Red Rouille evenly over the crust. Arrange Swiss chard mixture over the sauce. Distribute garlic cloves over the Swiss chard mixture. Crumble cheese on top. Bake as suggested in Quick Pizza Dough recipe.

Yield: One 12-inch pizza; 2 entrée or 4 side-dish servings

NOTE: When chopping Swiss chard, remove the stem and central rib from each leaf. Retain these for stews, stocks, and other dishes.

SERVING SUGGESTIONS: This makes a complete meal when accompanied by a mixed green salad dressed with Chile-Sesame Vinaigrette (page 223). Put out a platter of bite-sized raw vegetables and Peanut Mayonnaise (page 224) to start. A good ending is Almond Pear Tart (page 250) or some ripe Bosc pear slices.

VARIATION: For a most delightful treat, prepare half the pizza using this recipe and the other half using the recipe for Artichoke, Goat Cheese, and Olive Pizza (preceding recipe).

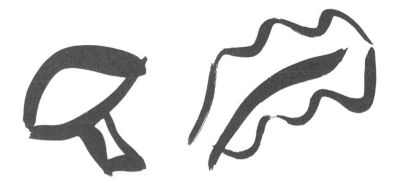

LEEK-ONION TART
France

This easy, lowfat tart is filled with caramelized onions and sweet, tender leeks in a light, airy custard of egg and skim milk.

2 tablespoons Garlic Oil (page 231) or olive oil
2 cups thinly sliced onions
8 cups sliced leeks (⅛ to ¼ inch thick) (whites and
    2-inches of green parts only)
1 tablespoon chopped fresh tarragon or thyme, or
    1 teaspoon dried
Salt and freshly ground black pepper to taste
2 large eggs plus 1 egg white, lightly beaten
¼ cup evaporated skim milk or regular nonfat or
    lowfat milk
Basic Pie Crust (Deep-Dish Consideration;
    the following recipe or other pie crust, rolled and
    placed in a deep tart or quiche pan)
A sprinkling of grated Parmesan or other hard cheese
    (optional)

1. Heat oil in a large skillet. Sauté onions until richly browned, 12 to 15 minutes, stirring often. Adjust heat as necessary to prevent burning. Add leeks and herbs and cook for an additional 7 to 10 minutes, or until leeks are soft. Sprinkle with a little water from time to time if the onion sticks. Season to taste with salt and pepper. Remove from heat and transfer to a large platter or bowl. Allow to cool completely (so that the custard in the next step will not become lumpy when in contact with this mixture).

2. Preheat oven to 425 degrees F.

3. Gently whisk eggs and milk together in a bowl. Arrange onion-leek mixture in a layer on the pie crust. Pour the egg-milk mixture over the top.

Bake for 10 minutes, then lower heat to 350 degrees F. Bake for another 30 to 35 minutes, or until the custard is set and the crust is golden brown. If using cheese, sprinkle it over the top during the last 10 minutes of baking and let it melt. Allow to cool slightly, then cut into wedges and serve.

Yield: 4 entrée or 6 to 8 side-dish servings

SERVING SUGGESTIONS: This dish is a complete light meal on its own. Add a salad of spinach, radish, and orange segments. An appropriate dessert would be Almond Pear Tart (page 250) and Indian-Style Tea (page 262). It also makes a tasty appetizer served in thin wedges.

BASIC PIE CRUST
United States

1 to 1½ cups unbleached white flour
4 tablespoons butter, or 2 tablespoons butter and
    2 tablespoons canola oil
1 to 4 tablespoons ice water

1. Combine flour, butter, and oil in the work bowl of a processor. With motor running, slowly pour water in a steady stream through the feed tube just until the dough forms a ball.

By hand, use a pastry blender or 2 knives to work butter and oil into the flour so that it resembles coarse meal. Add water gradually just until the mixture holds together.

2. Roll out dough on a floured board to a 10-inch circle. Invert a 9-inch pie pan onto dough to check size. Place dough in pie pan and trim excess. Flute the edges by pinching the dough between thumb and index finger. Chill at least 15 minutes.

Yield: One 9-inch pie crust

DEEP-DISH CONSIDERATION: If preparing a vegetable tart or quiche with a substantial amount of filling, use the larger amount of flour. Also use a deep pie pan or quiche or flan pan that is at least 1½ inches deep, instead of a shallow pie pan.

GINGERY SQUASH QUICHE
South Asia/United States

Here is a fine marriage of winter squash, gingerroot, green chile, and coconut. Although it looks like a pumpkin pie, it's actually a savory entrée. This bright orange quiche, with its tender, smooth texture, is easy to put together, especially if the crust is made ahead of time. It's perfect for buffets and picnics as well as family meals. Or serve the filling alone, as a tasty side dish.

1 pound winter squash (butternut, Hubbard, or
    Delicata squash) or sweet potatoes, peeled and
    cubed (leave butternut unpeeled)
1½ tablespoons olive oil
1 cup finely chopped onion
¼ teaspoon ground turmeric
1 tablespoon grated gingerroot
1 teaspoon seeded, minced jalapeño or other fresh
    green chile, or to taste
¼ cup plus 2 tablespoons nonfat or low-fat milk
¼ teaspoon ground nutmeg
Salt to taste
Ground red pepper to taste (start with a scant pinch)
2 large eggs plus 2 egg whites, lightly beaten
Basic Pie Crust (preceding recipe) or your favorite (9-inch)
    pie crust rolled and placed in a pie plate

1. Steam squash about 15 minutes, or until tender. Mash thoroughly.

2. Heat oil in a large steep-sided skillet until sizzling. Sauté onion until richly browned, but not burned, 8 to 10 minutes. Sprinkle turmeric over the onion. Stir in gingerroot, jalapeño, mashed squash, and ¼ cup milk. Cook, stirring often, until the mixture is heated through. Add nutmeg, salt, and red pepper. Remove from heat, transfer to a large bowl, and allow to cool.

3. Preheat oven to 350 degrees F.

4. Combine eggs and 2 tablespoons milk in a large bowl. Add the squash mixture and stir with a fork to mix well. Pour into the prepared pie crust. Bake for 45 to 50 minutes, or until a knife inserted near the center comes out clean. Remove from oven. Let stand on a wire rack to cool for a few minutes. Best served warm. If made ahead, cover with a piece of aluminum foil, and reheat in a 350-degree oven for 10 minutes, or until just heated through. *Yield: 2 to 3 entrée or 6 side-dish servings*

SERVING SUGGESTIONS: A large salad, Garlic Toast (page 41), and Sweet Hot Swiss Chard (page 110) make lovely accompaniments. Because of the sweetness of the squash a dessert is not absolutely essential, but Anise-Pistachio Biscotti (page 260) have the requisite crispness and flavor to go with the meal. Serve the squash filling alone as a side dish topped with toasted garlic chips, chopped cilantro, and a sprinkling of balsamic vinegar and ghee or butter.

SAVORY BEAN PIE
Latin America/United States

Black beans are tasty even when cooked simply. They are spectacular when crushed, mixed with cumin, jalapeño, ground red pepper, and plenty of onion and garlic, and made into a smooth, savory pie filling as in this recipe. This most desirable entrée takes the guesswork out of what to serve when you have a vegetarian guest.

1½ cups cooked black beans, or one 15-ounce can black
    beans, drained, cooking or can liquid retained
¼ cup bean liquid or water, or more, as needed
1 to 1½ tablespoons canola oil
1 cup finely chopped onion
3 large garlic cloves, forced through a garlic press
¼ teaspoon ground turmeric
2 teaspoons ground cumin
1 to 2 teaspoons seeded, chopped jalapeño or other
    green chile of choice to taste
Ground red pepper to taste (use ground chipotle
    pepper, if available)
2 large eggs, lightly beaten
Salt to taste
Basic Pie Crust (page 199) or your favorite 9-inch
    pie crust rolled and placed in a pie plate
Chopped scallions for garnish
Dollop of plain yogurt or a sprinkling of Parmesan
    cheese for garnish

1. Preheat oven to 425 degrees F.

2. Purée ½ cup beans and ¼ cup bean liquid in a blender or food processor until smooth, adding a little more bean liquid if necessary.

3. Heat oil in a large skillet, and sauté onion until lightly browned, about 5 minutes, stirring often. Add garlic, turmeric, and cumin and stir until evenly distributed. Add jalapeño and ground red pepper. Add puréed beans and bring to a simmer. Add the remaining 1 cup beans. Simmer, covered, 5 to 8 minutes to heat the mixture through and blend the flavors. Transfer to a large bowl and allow to cool to room temperature. (Up to this point the dish can be prepared ahead and refrigerated.)

4. Add eggs and mix well. Season to taste with salt.

5. Pour filling into the prepared crust. Bake for 10 minutes, then reduce heat to 325 degrees F. Bake for another 15 to 18 minutes, or just until the mixture has set (it will feel firm to the touch). Allow to cool slightly, then cut into wedges. Serve garnished with scallions and a dollop of yogurt or a sprinkling of Parmesan.   *Yield: 2 to 3 entrée or 4 to 6 first-course servings*

SERVING SUGGESTIONS: Accompany at a luncheon with Nut-Topped Savory Rice (page 174) or a baked potato, and a salad of Bibb lettuce, watercress, and Rosemary-Garlic Croutons (page 42). Finish with Chocolate-Macadamia Temptation (page 258).

A man must eat a peck of salt with a friend before he truly knows him.

> —*Latin saying*

PEAS AND CARROTS IN A PASTRY NEST
India/United States

This recipe is a happy combination of techniques and ingredients from East and West. A spicy peas-and-carrots preparation fills flaky puff pastry shells and is served either as an entrée or as an appetizer.

½ pound carrots, cut into ¼ inch cubes (about 2 cups)
1 tablespoon canola oil
¼ teaspoon cumin seeds
1 tablespoon grated gingerroot
3 large garlic cloves, forced through a garlic press
¼ cup evaporated skim milk
¾ cup thawed frozen peas
Salt and freshly ground black pepper to taste
6 unbaked puff pastry shells (one 10-ounce package)

1. Steam carrots until fork-tender, 6 to 8 minutes. Set aside.

2. Heat oil in a large skillet until a light haze forms. Add cumin seeds and cook until they are lightly browned. Add gingerroot and garlic and cook until they are golden. Add milk. As soon as the mixture sizzles, add peas and carrots. Cook, uncovered, for a few minutes to heat the mixture through. Season to taste with salt and pepper. Remove from heat and keep covered. (Up to this point the recipe can be prepared ahead of time and refrigerated.)

3. About 30 minutes before serving, preheat oven to 400 degrees F.

4. Bake the pastry shells, top side up, until golden brown, 20 to 25 minutes. Remove from oven and lift off the top lid from each pastry shell, exposing the hollow center. Reheat the pea and carrot mixture just until heated through. Divide the filling among the hollows of the shells. Serve immediately. *Yield: 6 shells; 2 entrée or 4 side-dish servings*

SERVING SUGGESTIONS: This is especially good served at a luncheon with Wild and Brown Rice Salad (page 77) and Mint-Cilantro Chutney (page 213). Peach Flan (page 238) will complete a memorable meal.

SPANISH EGG-POTATO OMELETTE
Spain

The Spanish serve a potato omelette called *tortilla de patata* for breakfast, lunch, and dinner. It differs from the better-known French omelettes in that it is more like a tart with a golden brown crust on the outside and a succulent, soft inside. Richly browned potato rounds, a tender yellow veil of eggs, and fresh green herbs make this dish both attractive and filling. An East-West combination of cumin seeds and tarragon adds a delightful accent to this Spanish classic.

2 tablespoons olive oil
½ pound new potatoes (about 2 medium), peeled or
    unpeeled, cut into ⅛-inch-thick rounds
2 to 4 large eggs, lightly beaten
2 tablespoons thinly sliced scallions
1 tablespoon chopped fresh tarragon, or
    1 teaspoon dried
¼ teaspoon cumin seeds
1 cup thinly sliced onions

1. Heat 1 tablespoon oil in a 12-inch steep-sided skillet. Tilt the skillet so that the oil coats its entire bottom. Lower the heat. Add the potatoes and sauté until they are richly browned and tender, 15 to 20 minutes, turning

often. Adjust heat to prevent potatoes from burning. With a slotted spatula, remove each potato slice as soon as it is ready and place on a platter between layers of paper towels to absorb any excess oil.

2. In a medium bowl, combine eggs, scallions, and tarragon and stir gently with a whisk until smooth.

3. Heat the remaining 1 tablespoon oil in a 10-inch skillet. Add cumin seeds and cook until the seeds are lightly browned. Add onion and cook until it is translucent, about 2 minutes. Lower the heat. Arrange the potatoes on top of the onions so that the entire bottom is covered. Pour in the egg-herb mixture and spread it with a spatula to distribute evenly over the potatoes. Cook over low heat until the eggs are firm but not dry, 3 to 8 minutes. (The timing will vary with the number of eggs.) Tilt the skillet occasionally so that any uncooked egg will run to the sides. Remove from the heat, cover the skillet with a large platter, invert the omelet, then slide it into the skillet again to cook the underside. Cook over low heat for a few minutes, or just until the bottom is set. *Yield: 2 to 4 servings*

SERVING SUGGESTIONS: Start with Crostini with Chutney (page 29) and follow with fresh fruit and Nutty Cream (page 264). Or serve with a salad of crisp greens and olive.

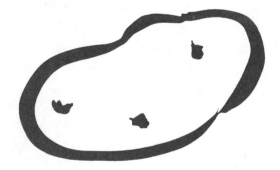

Today's egg is better than tomorrow's hen.

—*A Turkish proverb*

CHILE-CUMIN CORN BREAD
United States

I have always liked corn bread, but it is only recently that I have come to appreciate the opportunities it offers for creative spicing, as in this recipe. First I lightly roast the cornmeal to intensify its flavor. The batter is mixed with grated carrots and judiciously spiced with cumin powder, jalapeños, and ground chipotle, all of which have an affinity with cornmeal. The final result is a gently hot, sweet, and spicy dish that will be a welcome substitute for bread at most meals.

¾ cup coarse cornmeal
2 large eggs
¼ cup sugar
2 tablespoons melted butter or canola oil
1 cup low-fat buttermilk
¾ cup unbleached white flour
2 teaspoons baking powder
½ teaspoon baking soda
½ teaspoon salt
1 tablespoon ground cumin
2 teaspoons seeded, minced jalapeño or other fresh
    green chile of choice, or to taste
Dash of ground chipotle to taste (start with a scant
    pinch; available in specialty food shops and some
    supermarkets)
¾ cup grated carrots
¾ cup thawed frozen corn

1. Roast the cornmeal in an ungreased skillet over low heat. Stir often to prevent browning the bottom. In a few minutes, when a nutty aroma is exuded, remove from heat. Transfer to a large bowl and allow to cool.

2. Preheat oven to 425 degrees F. Oil an 8-inch-square baking pan or an 8-cup muffin tin.

3. Beat together eggs and sugar. Add oil and buttermilk and stir well. Set aside.

4. Add flour, baking powder, baking soda, salt, and cumin to the cornmeal and stir to distribute evenly. Add jalapeño, chipotle powder, carrots, corn, and the egg mixture. Mix well. Pour into the prepared pan or muffin cups.

5. Bake for 15 to 25 minutes, or until a toothpick inserted in the center comes out clean. *Yield: 8 to 10 servings*

SERVING SUGGESTIONS: A hearty soup or bean stew is the most appropriate accompaniment, a good choice being Two-Bean Shorba (page 58) or Chipotle Chick-peas (page 150). The salad should be kept simple, perhaps some mixed greens with sliced tomatoes. A compatible dessert is Bosc pear slices or fresh strawberries in season.

CHUTNEYS, SALSAS, AND OTHER CONDIMENTS

Our family dinners in India included at least one chutney prepared only minutes before the meal. A cooling blend of gingerroot and yogurt would complement rich, roasted potatoes; delicate tomato chutney accompanied a robust eggplant stew; an assertively spiced carrot chutney was served with a more simple meal of rice and lentils.

Our traditions did not encourage using standardized recipes. Rather, the cook's mood and the seasonal availability of ingredients made each chutney a profusion of unique flavors, running the gamut from subtle to wildly intense. A mango chutney could result in a gently sweet or strongly sour note. A cilantro chutney, laced with fresh green chile, would be pungent, and a plum chutney decidedly tart.

Salsa is to Mexicans what chutney is to Indians. A tomato salsa requires only chopped tomatoes, onions, chile, cilantro, and time for the mixture to create its own delicious juice. This all-purpose sauce serves as a dip for corn chips, is equally suitable as a base for a stew, and adds zest to tortillas filled with vegetables. Mexican friends have taught me to prepare more complex salsas by roasting dried ancho or pasilla chiles. Once softened and puréed, these chiles are blended with other seasonings to produce a rich salsa with a deep flavor. They fill the kitchen with a smoky fragrance.

In my French cooking school, part of each day's lesson was devoted to sauces. Our teacher paid much attention to sauce making and the selection of fresh ingredients. The chef was a portly man who would stoop over a tiny bowl in which he blended oil, vinegar, Dijon mustard, sage, thyme, and oregano with great care. Even the tougher leaves of these herbs would cooperate with him and melt into a fragrant purée, glossy and smooth.

One day when the time came to dress fresh fruit, I wondered what sauce the master would prepare. He had arranged a beautiful platter of sliced apples, apricots, orange and grapefruit sections that looked complete. Without appearing to give the matter a second thought, he brought out lemon and orange juices and sugar. His mixture added a fragrant, slightly tart citrusy flavor to the composed salad. I realized that one measure of an accomplished cook is his sauces.

Condiments help create zesty and interesting meals in a hurry, even when there is little on hand beyond rice and vegetables. Sometimes, instead of preparing a sauce, I finely chop apples, cucumbers, and sweet onions, drizzling the mixture with a fine vinegar and ginger juice. I call such a blend a "natural" chutney—one that requires only a few fresh ingredients and little time or energy, but serves as a stimulating condiment at the table.

I once attended a dinner party in which every course, including the bread, was homemade, except the salad dressing. The sight of the familiar Thousand Island dressing nearly spoiled the effect of that delicious meal. Yet one can whisk together a vinaigrette, that classic, infinitely variable oil-and-vinegar combination, in minutes. You can go fancy with raspberry vinegar or garlic-flavored olive oil, or omit the oil entirely and fold in a puréed banana or yogurt as the base. Top it off with a sprinkling of poppy seeds or a splash of honey mustard.

When preparing lasagna, I once omitted the customary cheese and enriched the dish with tofu and spinach. I set it out with a large platter of grilled vegetables and a pungent Mint-Cilantro Chutney (page 213). Despite the distinctive main dish and elaborate vegetables, the guests raved about the chutney. I was reminded once again how condiments can make or break a meal.

NATURAL CHUTNEY
International

This fresh condiment, composed of spices, fruits, and vegetables with their aromatic natural juices provides an excellent way to incorporate crisp, uncooked food in a meal. Apples and cucumber are the main ingredients, but you can use other combinations—Asian pear and radish, for instance.

Juice of ½ lemon
1 sweet apple (about ½ pound), cored but not peeled,
    finely chopped
1 small cucumber, peeled, seeded, and finely chopped
½ sweet red or other mild onion, finely chopped
1 tablespoon chopped fresh tarragon
Raspberry or balsamic vinegar
Ginger juice or grated gingerroot (optional; see Note)
1 teaspoon toasted cumin seeds.

Sprinkle lemon juice over the chopped apple to keep it from discoloring Combine apple, cucumber, and onion in a large serving bowl or platter. Scatter tarragon over the mixture. Sprinkle with raspberry vinegar and ginger juice or grated gingerroot. Top with cumin seeds.   *Yield: 4 small servings*

NOTE: To prepare ginger juice, grate ginger, then squeeze through several layers of cheesecloth.

CHILE CHUTNEY
India

A relish for chile enthusiasts! In India, this chutney is made entirely from chiles, both mild and hot. Since supermarket chiles in the West vary in their degree of hotness, I use a combination of sweet bell pepper and such hot chiles as serrano or jalapeño. By tasting the chiles beforehand to test for spiciness, you can control the hotness of this relish.

2 teaspoons canola oil or mustard oil
1 tablespoon grated gingerroot
3 to 4 large garlic cloves, forced through a garlic press
¼ teaspoon turmeric
1 teaspoon ground cumin
½ teaspoon black mustard seeds, ground to a powder
    and mixed with 1 teaspoon water
1 medium green bell pepper, seeds and inner ribs
    removed, finely chopped
1 teaspoon to 1 tablespoon seeded, minced serrano or
    jalapeño (to taste)
½ teaspoon sugar
¼ teaspoon salt
3 tablespoons rice vinegar

1. Heat oil in a small skillet over medium-low heat until sizzling. Add gingerroot and garlic and sauté until golden, 2 to 3 minutes, stirring constantly. Add turmeric, cumin, and black mustard paste and stir several times. Add bell pepper, green chiles, sugar, and salt and mix well. Add vinegar.

2. Turn heat to low. Simmer, covered, just until the vegetables are tender, 3 to 5 minutes. Remove from heat and allow to cool. Serve at room temperature or chill for 45 minutes. Stored in the refrigerator, it lasts for a few days.

Yield: About ⅔ cup

MINT-CILANTRO CHUTNEY
India

This versatile green sauce, which can be made in a blender, is a regular on my table. Deriving its flavor from chile, lime, scallions and cilantro, it can be served with most meals, but is especially good with grain dishes and on top of bean stews. Use it as a spread for sandwiches or a dip for chips.

1 cup firmly packed mint leaves (see Notes)
1 cup firmly packed cilantro leaves
1 cup chopped scallions
1 teaspoon seeded, chopped jalapeño, or to taste
    (see Notes)
¼ cup freshly squeezed lime juice
4 teaspoons sugar
½ teaspoon salt

Combine all the ingredients in the container of a blender or food processor and process until smooth. Serve at room temperature or chill for 45 minutes. Stored in the refrigerator, it lasts for a few days.   *Yield: 1 cup*

NOTES: Instead of a mixture of mint and cilantro, you can use all mint or all cilantro, 2 cups of either one.

You can use other flavorful chiles such as serrano or habanero. Use a smaller amount with either of these hotter chiles, especially habanero.

In Jamaica they say, "A little bit of chile pepper

can burn a big man's mouth."

MARINATED
CARROT CHUTNEY
India

Because of their sweet taste and ability to blend with spices, carrots are used in India for preparing condiments. In western India, people pickle them expertly, using plenty of cumin and mild vinegar, whereas in the south, carrots are treated with black mustard and curry leaves. This recipe combines both of these techniques to produce a tasty relish that can double as a side dish.

1 pound carrots, cut into ¼ to ½-inch cubes
   (about 4 cups)
½ cup rice vinegar
Salt to taste
1 tablespoon canola oil or mustard oil
2 whole dried red chiles
½ teaspoon black mustard seeds
6 to 8 fresh or dried curry leaves
¼ teaspoon ground turmeric
½ teaspoon ground cumin
1 teaspoon sugar
1 tablespoon chopped peanuts

1. Steam carrots until tender, 6 to 10 minutes. Combine them with rice vinegar and salt and let rest at room temperature at least 15 minutes, several hours or overnight in the refrigerator, if possible.

2. Heat oil in a large skillet until sizzling. Add dried chiles and cook until they blacken. Add mustard seeds and cook until they start to pop. Hold the cover briefly over the skillet to keep the seeds from flying out. Stir in curry leaves, turmeric, cumin, and sugar; stir until evenly distributed. Add carrots. Cook,

uncovered, for a few minutes to heat the mixture through. Taste and adjust salt. Sprinkle peanuts over the top. Serve warm or at room temperature.

Yield: Over 2 cups; enough for 4 side-dish servings

VARIATIONS: For a special richness, sprinkle with 1 tablespoon toasted shredded coconut before serving. Another alternative is to add browned onions. For this, sauté ¾ cup thinly slivered onions in 1½ tablespoons canola oil until richly browned, 6 to 9 minutes, stirring often. Add the onions just before removing from the heat in Step 2.

ASIAN PESTO
Italy/East Asia

This Asian-style pesto is light and fragrant. It is enriched by vinegar-soaked bread, rather than the customary cheese. Either peanuts or pine nuts will thicken it.

1 slice whole wheat or white bread, cut into cubes
Rice vinegar
2 tablespoons freshly squeezed lime juice
2 to 4 large garlic cloves, coarsely chopped
½ cup firmly packed, coarsely chopped fresh basil leaves
1 tablespoon peanut butter
2 tablespoons pine nuts
Salt to taste
¼ to ½ cup extra-virgin olive oil, hazelnut oil, or
    walnut oil

1. Cover the bread pieces with rice vinegar and let soak a few minutes. Squeeze out the liquid and place the bread in the container of a blender or food processor. Retain the soaking liquid.

2. Add lime juice, garlic, basil, peanut butter, pine nuts, and salt. Process until smooth, using a bit of the soaking liquid if necessary. Transfer to a medium bowl. Add oil, a drop at a time, stirring constantly, until thoroughly mixed. Refrigerate until ready to serve. Stir before using. *Yield: 1 cup*

ANCHO AND RED PEPPER SALSA
Mexico

Some say they love the chocolatelike flavor of ancho chiles, whereas others rave about their fruity quality. Regardless, these dried brown chiles blend well with roasted bell peppers and caramelized onions to produce a vivid orange-colored salsa. This deep-flavored sauce goes well with any bean dish and can be used as a spread for baked potatoes.

2 large red bell peppers
2 dried ancho chiles
1 tablespoon canola oil
1 cup minced onion
1 large garlic clove
1 teaspoon vegetable bouillon powder
2 tablespoons freshly squeezed lime juice
2 tablespoons chile soaking water, or more, as needed (see below)
Salt to taste

1. To roast bell peppers, follow directions on page 3. Set the flesh and accumulated juices aside.

2. Toast the ancho chiles by placing in an ungreased skillet over low heat for a few minutes. Soak chiles in boiling water to cover until soft, about 15 minutes. Drain, retaining soaking water. Cut each chile in half. With the help of a spoon, scrape off any red flesh and put in a small bowl. Do not include the brown skin, which has a bitter taste, or the seeds, which are extremely hot.

3. Heat oil in a medium skillet until sizzling. Sauté onion until it is richly browned, but not burned, 7 to 10 minutes, stirring often. Add garlic and cook for a minute until it softens slightly. Place sautéed onion, garlic, bell pepper flesh and juices, a dash of ancho chile flesh, bouillon, lime juice, and 2 tablespoons chile soaking water in a blender or food processor and purée until smooth, adding a bit more chile water if necessary. Taste and add more ancho chile flesh if you prefer a hotter flavor. Add salt to taste.

Yield: 1 cup

"To be united in the pickle jar" is a Tamil expression that applies to two people born far from each other, but who have much in common.

SUN-DRIED TOMATO AND CUCUMBER RAITA
India/Italy

A raita is a yogurt-based sauce or salad from India. The vegetable most commonly used in a raita is cucumber. In this incarnation, cucumber raita travels to Italy and gets an extra zip from an Italian friend: sun-dried tomatoes.

1 cup plain nonfat yogurt, lightly beaten until smooth
1½ teaspoons sugar
¼ teaspoon salt
Ground red pepper to taste (start with a scant pinch)
½ cup peeled, seeded, and finely chopped cucumber
1 ounce sun-dried tomatoes (about 10), soaked in
    boiling water to cover for 5 to 15 minutes, or until
    softened, then drained and finely chopped
1 teaspoon mustard oil or canola oil
¼ teaspoon black mustard seeds

1. Combine yogurt, sugar, salt, and red pepper in a medium bowl and stir until smooth. Add cucumber and sun-dried tomatoes.

2. Heat oil in a small skillet until sizzling. Add mustard seeds and sauté until the seeds pop. Remove from heat and pour over the yogurt mixture; mix well. Taste and adjust salt. Can be served immediately, but for best results chill for 30 minutes. *Yield: 1½ cups, 2 servings*

PEACH SALSA
Mexico

When ripe peaches come to the marketplace in summer, I prepare this invigorating salsa. The natural juices from lime, tomato, jalapeño, and cilantro combine to form a sweet-sour sauce. This salsa so refreshes the palate that you almost don't need a dessert.

½ pound ripe peaches (about 2), pitted and finely chopped
½ pound tomatoes (about 1 medium), seeded and finely chopped
1 tablespoon chopped fresh basil
1 tablespoon grated gingerroot
1 jalapeño, cut in half lengthwise, seeded and thinly sliced
1 scallion (green part only), very thinly sliced
1 tablespoon finely chopped cilantro
3 tablespoons freshly squeezed lime juice

Combine all the ingredients in a medium bowl. Let stand at least 15 minutes for flavors to develop.   *Yield: Over 1 cup*

Condiments are like old friends—highly thought of, but often taken for granted.

—Marilyn Kaytor

CHERRY TOMATO "CHALSA"
India/Mexico

This sauce combines techniques of both chutney and salsa. Here the usual salsa combinations of tomatoes, jalapeño, sweet onion, and lime juice are spiced with black mustard seeds for a chutneylike taste. This "chalsa" goes with just about any meal and is especially good with a platter of steamed vegetables.

1 tablespoon canola oil
¼ teaspoon black mustard seeds
¾ cup thinly sliced onion
1 pound cherry tomatoes, halved
1 jalapeño, cored, seeded, and minced
   (see Note for the Gardener)
1 tablespoon sugar
½ teaspoon salt, or more to taste
3 tablespoons freshly squeezed lime juice
½ cup coarsely chopped red or other sweet onion
2 tablespoons finely chopped cilantro

1. Heat oil in large skillet, and sauté mustard seeds until they pop. Add sliced onion and cook until soft, 3 to 5 minutes. Lower the heat. Add tomatoes to the skillet, reserving about ½ cup for garnish. Stir in jalapeño, sugar, and salt. Cook, uncovered, for 2 minutes. Remove from heat and transfer to a large bowl.

2. Add the reserved tomatoes, lime juice, chopped onion, and cilantro. Let rest at room temperature for at least 30 minutes.   *Yield: 4½ cups, 6 servings*

NOTE FOR THE GARDENER: If you grow habanero or other flavorful chiles, you can prepare a chile paste, which will distribute the hot flavor more evenly in this dish. For this, pound the seeded, chopped chile in a mortar and pestle with a little water until smooth. Use a few drops of this paste in this dish instead of minced jalapeño, and retain the rest for cooking bean or vegetable stews.

LIME-ORANGE VINAIGRETTE
International

Fresh lime and orange juices cut down the amount of oil needed for this dressing and impart a fresh, clean taste. It is perfect with crisp greens, as a dressing for lentil salads, and as a topping for steamed green beans.

1 cup freshly squeezed orange juice
2 tablespoons freshly squeezed lime juice
2 tablespoons rice vinegar or white wine vinegar
½ teaspoon salt
2 teaspoons sugar
2 tablespoons extra-virgin olive oil or avocado oil
2 teaspoons chopped fresh tarragon, or
    1 teaspoon dried

Combine all the ingredients in a screw-top jar. Shake to combine and thicken the dressing. Chill until needed. Shake again before using.

Yield: 1 cup

LIME-PEANUT VINAIGRETTE

East Asia

This vinaigrette will delight peanut lovers, as well as those who are looking for something a bit different with which to dress their greens. It also works well with bean, potato, and cabbage salads.

6 tablespoons freshly squeezed lime juice
2 tablespoons Chinese sesame oil
1 teaspoon fish sauce (see Note)
½ teaspoon salt
2 teaspoons sugar
1 teaspoon seeded, minced jalapeño or other fresh
   green chile (a ripe red one, if available)
1 teaspoon finely chopped cilantro
1 tablespoon chopped dry roasted peanuts

Combine all ingredients except cilantro and peanuts in a medium bowl and whisk until thickened. Add cilantro and peanuts. Refrigerate until ready to use. Stir before using. *Yield: ½ cup*

NOTE: Fish sauce, *nam pla*, is available in Asian markets. Strict vegetarians can substitute vegetarian oyster sauce for fish sauce.

CHILE-SESAME VINAIGRETTE
International

A tart-sweet dressing with a sharp edge. Pecan bits add an unexpected crunch. Use it to moisten crisp greens or potato salad, as a marinade for carrots, and as a dip for grilled zucchini or butternut squash.

½ cup Chinese sesame oil
½ cup rice vinegar
2 teaspoons low-sodium soy sauce
3 teaspoons sugar
½ teaspoon salt (optional)
A few drops of Chinese chile oil
3 teaspoons spicy prepared mustard
8 pecans, finely chopped

Combine sesame oil and vinegar in a screw-top jar. Shake thoroughly. Add the remaining ingredients except pecans. Add salt, if desired. Taste for sugar and add more if needed. Add pecans. Refrigerate until ready to serve. Shake thoroughly before using. *Yield: Over 1 cup*

SHISO VARIATION: For an extra zip, add finely chopped shiso leaves. Shiso is better distributed in the salad this way and its flavor is more pronounced than if simply added to the greens.

The Chinese liken a superficial person to a "half-filled bottle of vinegar," which makes a lot of bubbles when shaken.

PEANUT MAYONNAISE
International

A fine-textured mayonnaise with the unusual touch of peanut. Best if made several hours ahead of serving for the flavors to develop.

2 garlic cloves, coarsely chopped
1 large egg (see Note)
1 tablespoon peanut butter
2 tablespoons freshly squeezed lime juice
¼ to ½ cup extra-virgin olive oil
Salt to taste

Place garlic, egg, peanut butter, and lime juice in a blender and spin on medium speed until thoroughly mixed. Set blender on low speed. With the motor running, add oil, a drop at a time at first, then in a slow steady stream as the mixture thickens. Remove to a small bowl, add salt, and refrigerate until ready to use.

You can also do this by hand. Place the first 4 ingredients in a large bowl and whisk them together. Add oil as described above, whisking until the mixture is thick. *Yield: ½ to 1 cup*

NOTE: If you'd rather not use a raw egg, substitute 1 tablespoon commercial mayonnaise for the egg, as Jacques Pépin, the noted French chef, suggests.

HONEY YOGURT SPLASH

United States/India

In America, honey and yogurt form a wonderful base for fruit dressing. Following an Indian technique, the honey-yogurt mixture is heated briefly in cumin-infused oil to remove its "raw" flavor. This is excellent for drizzling over cooked grains and for dipping warm tortillas.

1 cup plain nonfat yogurt
2 tablespoons honey, or to taste
2 tablespoons freshly squeezed lime juice
Salt to taste
1 teaspoon canola oil
¼ teaspoon cumin seeds

1. Combine yogurt, honey, lime juice, and salt in a small bowl and stir with a spoon until smooth. Taste and adjust the amount of honey and salt, if necessary.

2. Heat oil in a medium skillet until sizzling. Add cumin seeds and cook until they are lightly browned. Remove skillet from heat. Pour the yogurt mixture over. It will sizzle immediately. Stir a few times, then transfer to a medium-sized serving bowl. Serve at room temperature or chill for 45 minutes.

Yield: About ¾ cup

TOFU CREAM
International

Made from rich soy milk, this tofu is the base for an excellent thick dressing. Lime and sesame further enrich this "cream," which is lower in fat than most mayonnaise or sour cream spreads. The dressing goes well as a topping for baked potatoes or sweet potatoes, as a dip for chips or raw vegetables, and with potato salads.

One 10-ounce carton silken soft tofu, drained
(don't substitute other types of tofu)
2 tablespoons toasted sesame tahini (preferred
over raw tahini)
3 large garlic cloves, coarsely chopped
¼ cup freshly squeezed lime juice
1 tablespoon rice vinegar or mild white vinegar
1 teaspoon sugar
1 teaspoon Chinese sesame oil
3 tablespoons low-fat buttermilk
½ teaspoon salt
1 tablespoon finely chopped scallion

Process all ingredients except scallions in a blender or food processor until smooth. Taste and adjust salt. Scatter scallions on top. Refrigerate until ready to use.

Yield: 1½ cups

VARIATIONS: For an extra zip, add a dash of black salt and ½ teaspoon or more balsamic vinegar. You can also add an extra garnish of toasted sesame seeds.

SESAME-BANANA WHIP
International

Whip up this rich, creamy sauce by blending roasted banana, buttermilk, and sesame powder. Add sautéed mustard seeds for a spicy effect.

1 medium-size ripe banana, unpeeled
1 tablespoon freshly squeezed lime juice
2 teaspoons sesame seeds, toasted and ground
¾ cup low-fat buttermilk, or more as needed
Salt to taste
1 teaspoon canola oil
¼ teaspoon black mustard seeds

1. Place the unpeeled banana on a baking sheet. Broil 8 to 10 minutes, or until the skin is thoroughly blackened, turning once. Allow to cool completely. Peel and discard skin. Mash the pulp and measure to ½ cup.

2. Process banana pulp, lime juice, ground sesame seeds, and buttermilk in a blender or food processor until smooth. The mixture should have the consistency of mayonnaise. If too thick, add a little more buttermilk. Add salt.

3. Heat oil in a small skillet until sizzling. Add mustard seeds and cook until they pop. (Hold the cover briefly over the skillet to keep the seeds from flying out.) Pour this mixture over the banana purée; stir. Serve at room temperature or chill for 45 minutes. *Yield: 1 cup*

CHIPOTLE BARBECUE SAUCE
United States/Mexico

What makes this barbecue sauce stand out among others is the use of three choice ingredients: fresh tomatoes, balsamic vinegar, and chipotle chile. Chipotle is a dried smoky jalapeño pod with a definite character. The spicy sauce isn't just for barbecueing, but serves as a table condiment with just about any meal. I never seem to make enough of it.

2 tablespoons olive oil or canola oil
1 cup finely chopped onion
3 large garlic cloves, minced
2 teaspoons ground cumin
¼ cup balsamic vinegar
2½ tablespoons sugar
1 tablespoon spicy prepared mustard
1 pound Roma (plum) or regular tomatoes,
    peeled, seeded, and coarsely chopped
¾ teaspoon salt
Ground chipotle pepper or chipotle sauce from a
    can to taste (start with a small amount; see Note)

Heat oil in a large saucepan, and sauté onion and garlic until onion is softened, 2 to 3 minutes. Add cumin and stir until well-mixed with oil. Add vinegar, sugar, and mustard and stir until evenly distributed. Stir in tomatoes, salt, and chipotle pepper. Bring to a boil, reduce heat slightly, and cook, uncovered, until a thick sauce forms, 6 to 12 minutes, stirring often to prevent sticking. Remove from heat and allow to cool. Working in batches, purée the mixture in a blender or food processor until smooth. Taste and adjust seasoning. If possible, let rest in the refrigerator overnight to blend the flavors. If using as a table sauce, reheat gently before serving just until warmed through. *Yield: Over 2 cups*

NOTE: Ground chipotle pepper is available in specialty and natural food stores. Chipotle sauce is available canned in Latin American groceries. Use small amounts to start with, adjusting according to taste.

CHILE-BASIL DIP
International

A lovely dip for crusty bread. It is also excellent with steamed Chinese (or regular) broccoli, spinach, or carrots, or over baked potatoes. If you eat seafood, spread over grilled fish or use as a dip for boiled shrimp.

> 1 cup olive oil
> ¼ cup balsamic vinegar
> Several dashes of salt
> 1 tablespoon chopped fresh herbs (basil, thyme, oregano)
> 1 teaspoon jalapeño, seeded and chopped

Combine all the ingredients together. Best made ahead, preferably the night before, and refrigerated. Stir before using.

PEPPERY TOMATO SAUCE
United States

This rich tomato sauce derives its flavor from roasted tomatoes and bell peppers. The sweetness of the sauce is complemented by the tart touch of tamarind. Easy to prepare, this sauce can be used in any recipe that calls for tomato sauce, such as spaghetti.

2 large red bell peppers
2 pounds Roma (plum) tomatoes
    (see Note for the Gardener)
1 tablespoon olive oil
½ cup minced shallot or onion
3 to 5 large garlic cloves, minced
1 tablespoon chopped fresh basil, or
    1 teaspoon dried
1½ teaspoons sugar
¾ teaspoon tamarind concentrate
Salt and freshly ground black pepper to taste

1. Preheat broiler.

2. Place the peppers and tomatoes on a baking sheet and broil them 5 to 8 minutes, or until their skins wrinkle and are charred in places. Remove each vegetable as it's done. When all the peppers are done, put them in a paper bag and close the top. Let stand for 10 minutes, then remove from the bag. Peel off the skin, and discard it along with the seeds and inner ribs. Remove the charred parts of the tomato skins and discard.

3. Heat oil in a medium skillet, and sauté shallot and garlic until shallot is translucent and soft, 3 to 4 minutes. Process the pepper flesh, tomatoes and any accumulated juices, and the shallot-garlic mixture, in batches, in a blender or food processor until smooth. Transfer to a large saucepan. Add basil and cook, uncovered, over gentle heat. When the sauce is thoroughly

heated and is starting to bubble, add sugar and tamarind. Season to taste with salt and pepper. Remove from heat.   *Yield: 3 to 4 cups, 4 servings*

NOTE FOR THE GARDENER: During summer, when Roma tomatoes grow abundantly in my garden, I make several batches of this sauce. Stored in the refrigerator, it lasts a few days. It can also be frozen.

Russian riddle: **Who ran all over the world and dined at the czar's?** *Answer:* **Black pepper; it was brought from the East especially to be used at the czar's table.**

GARLIC OIL
International

Garlic-infused olive oil can be bought in specialty food shops, but it's a snap to do at home. The warm, mellow aroma and flavor of roasted garlic permeate the oil. Use Garlic Oil in cooking, as a dip for bread, or in salad dressings.

4 to 5 large garlic cloves
1½ cups olive oil

1. Roast garlic cloves by following directions in Roasted Garlic Soup (page 61).

2. Cut the larger cloves in half, if desired. Add to the oil and cover tightly. Let stand in the refrigerator for at least 15 days. Shake occasionally.

Yield: 1½ cups

TWO-TOMATO JAM
Italy/India

When serving grilled or roasted vegetables, I seek a robust sauce for dipping, and this is one I use often. The reddish brown jam of fresh and sun-dried tomatoes derives a hint of sourness from tamarind. It is especially good with grilled eggplant, can be slathered on crusty bread, or used on top of bean stews. For those who eat meat it's an excellent accompaniment for pork.

1 pound Roma (plum) tomatoes
8 sun-dried tomatoes, soaked in boiling water
    to cover for 5 to 15 minutes, or until softened,
    drained
½ teaspoon ground cumin
3 tablespoons sugar
¼ teaspoon tamarind concentrate
Salt to taste (optional)

1. To peel tomatoes, plunge them in boiling water for 30 seconds, or just until the skin starts to crack. Drain and cool. Remove skin from each and discard it. Cut each in half and, into a sieve placed over a bowl, gently squeeze out most of the seeds. Discard the seeds in the sieve and reserve the juices. Chop the flesh coarsely.

2. Process tomato flesh and drained sun-dried tomatoes in a blender or food processor until smooth. Place in a medium saucepan over medium heat and add cumin and sugar. Bring to a boil. Lower heat and cook, uncovered, for 20 to 25 minutes or until the mixture is thick, stirring often. Add tamarind and salt and mix well. Taste for salt, sugar, and tamarind. The sauce should be gently sweet with a hint of tartness. Best served warm, but can also be served at room temperature or chilled.   *Yield: Over 1 cup*

GARLIC BREAD CRUMBS
United States

With this recipe, it's easy to prepare fresh bread crumbs any time. Whether you're making your own or buying bread crumbs, follow the tip below to give them a fresher, more garlicky taste.

2 slices whole wheat or white bread, cubed
1 teaspoon garlic chips or dehydrated garlic flakes
    (preferred) or garlic powder (see Note)

1. Preheat oven to 350 degrees F.

2. Arrange bread cubes in a single layer on a large baking sheet. Bake for 15 minutes, or until crisp and medium brown in color. Process along with the garlic chips or flakes to a coarse powder in a blender or food processor.

Yield: ½ cup

NOTE: An alternative to using dried garlic is to rub the bread cubes, after they have been baked for 10 minutes, with the cut end of half a garlic clove.

ENHANCING STOREBOUGHT PLAIN BREAD CRUMBS: Toast the crumbs by placing on an ungreased skillet over low heat until heated through, stirring often. Grind the garlic chips or flakes to a powder as above and mix with the crumbs.

DESSERTS

Your guests may forget the coconut-mustard beans, the eight-green salad, even the dahlia arrangement, but they'll remember forever an astonishing dessert. "Ah! your peach tart," someone will recall months later. Whether it's because we love a sweet taste or because dessert is the surprise finale of a meal, most of us associate a dessert with dining pleasure.

So when planning a menu, select your dessert with care. If the meal is a simple bean stew, dessert can be an intriguing Poppy Seed Fruit Ring (page 246), served with Lemon Satin (page 263). If the meal offers many courses, a few bites of a simple, but spectacular treat such as Hazelnut Lime Bars (page 257) will do. Dessert can also be fresh fruit ripened to perfection or biscottis served with a cup of rich Indian-Style Tea (page 262).

Many of the desserts we grew up loving are loaded with fat and refined sugar. In my preparations, I reduce the use of both and substitute a blend of fruits or vegetables for a natural sweetness, to add moistness and enhance the nutritional content. When I serve rich desserts, it is in small portions, often garnished with extra fruit or sprightly sauces.

A dessert sauce makes a thin slice of Chocolate-Glazed Banana Cake (page 242) or Mango-Apricot Bread Pudding (page 247) seem thicker. A sauce like Lemon Satin is easy to make, yet adds an aura of luxury. If the sauce is appropriate, it will enrich your dessert. You will have to linger over every bite, savoring its richness, recalling memories of good things past.

BAKING POINTERS

- Set the oven to the correct temperature before baking. Many oven thermostats are unreliable; an oven thermometer will give an accurate reading.

- When working with chocolate, be aware that it is susceptible to heat; it stiffens and turns bitter if overcooked. Melt chocolate in a double boiler or heavy pan over very low heat, stirring often to prevent scorching. Don't overbake chocolate cakes or cookie bars.

- When beating eggs, sugar, and other ingredients, don't cut it short. Do it for the requisite length of time to help develop the texture of the finished dish.

- A baked dessert cools best on a wire rack, which allows air to circulate at the bottom and prevents it from sticking.

- During baking, dough shrinks. When fitting pastry in a pie tin, make sure it is slightly loose, not stretched too tightly.

- Slide a piece of aluminum foil on the oven rack below a baking pan to catch spillovers during baking.

- Dusting decoratively with confectioners' sugar is best done just before serving. Otherwise the sugar may be absorbed by the moisture in the dessert. Place the sugar in a sifter or a small sieve and shake it gently over the food. Instead of putting confectioners' sugar on food, a chef's trick is to dust the serving plate lightly and then place the dessert amid the design.

LEMON MOUSSE SURPRISE
France/Spain

This elegant chiffon dessert satisfies a lemon craving. With its surprise caramel bottom and full-bodied lemon flavor, this makes a lovely light ending to a meal.

CARAMEL (SEE NOTE):
¼ cup dark brown sugar
1 tablespoon water

MOUSSE:
2 tablespoons cornstarch
1 cup evaporated skim milk
½ cup plus 1 tablespoon sugar
3 large eggs, separated
½ teaspoon vanilla
¼ cup freshly squeezed lemon juice

1. To prepare the caramel, heat brown sugar and water in a small pan. Cook over low heat, stirring often. In a few minutes when the mixture thickens and starts to become sticky, divide quickly among 6 custard cups. Swirl each cup to coat the entire bottom and partly up the sides. The mixture will harden as it sits.

2. Preheat oven to 350 degrees F.

3. To prepare the mousse, put milk in a medium-size heavy saucepan and add cornstarch gradually, stirring to break up any lumps. Add sugar and stir to dissolve. Cook, uncovered, over medium-low heat to bring it to a full boil, stirring often. Lower the heat and simmer, uncovered, until the mixture thickens, a few minutes, stirring constantly. Remove from heat and transfer to a large mixer bowl and allow to cool completely. Using an electric mixer, gradually blend in the egg yolks. Add vanilla and lemon juice.

4. In a separate bowl, beat the egg whites until stiff peaks form. Fold them gently into the milk-yolk mixture. Divide among the custard cups. Don't overfill; leave ¼-inch space on top for expansion. Set the cups into a large baking pan (such as a 9 × 12 × 2-inch size) partly filled with hot water. Bake 40 to 45 minutes, or until the top springs back when lightly touched and a toothpick inserted into the center comes out clean. Serve in custard cups warm or chilled.

Yield: 6 servings

NOTE: Omit the caramel if lowering sugar intake. The mousse will still taste good.

SERVING SUGGESTIONS: This mousse is a delightful ending to a meal that features Peas and Carrots in a Pastry Nest (page 204), and steamed vegetables tinged with Sesame-Banana Whip (page 227).

Squeeze a lemon too hard and it gets bitter.
—*Indian proverb*

PEACH FLAN
Spain

Over the years flan, Spain's most popular dessert, has become one of my favorites. Flan, or caramel custard, is basic, simple to prepare, and complements most meals. "There's no dessert but flan," say the Spanish. This peach version is a pleasant variation on the original Spanish dessert.

CARAMEL:
¼ cup dark brown sugar
1 tablespoon water

FLAN:
2 to 3 fresh very ripe peaches
3 large eggs
3 tablespoons sugar
1 quart low-fat milk (see Note)
½ teaspoon vanilla

TOPPING:
¼ cup peach preserves

GARNISH:
Sliced ripe peaches

1. Heat brown sugar and water in a small skillet over medium-low heat. In a few minutes, the sugar will melt and start to thicken. When it begins to get sticky, divide quickly among 6 custard cups. Swirl each cup to coat the bottom and partly up the sides.

2. Remove pits from peaches and purée enough pulp in a blender to measure ½ cup.

3. Using an electric mixer, beat eggs and sugar together in a large mixer bowl until thoroughly combined.

4. Lightly coat the bottom and sides of a large pan with oil to prevent milk from sticking. Place milk in this pan and bring to a boil over medium-high heat. Lower heat and stir vigorously until the foam subsides. Turn heat to medium and cook for about 15 minutes, or until reduced to about half its volume. During this period, stir often, scraping the sides and bottom to incorporate any milk solids that have formed.

5. Preheat oven to 350 degrees F.

6. Add vanilla and the peach pulp to egg-sugar mixture. Gradually add hot milk, stirring constantly. Divide this mixture among 6 custard cups. Fill a baking pan, large enough to hold the cups, partway with hot water. Carefully place the cups in this pan. Bake for 35 to 45 minutes, or until custard is set. If overbaked, custard will start to separate. Allow to cool, cover, and refrigerate for at least 30 minutes.

7. Just before serving, run a blunt knife around the sides of the custard. Place a saucer on top of each custard. Invert the cup and the saucer, tap the bottom of the cup lightly, and lift the cup. The custard will now sit, upside down, on the saucer with the caramel sauce oozing over the top.

8. Heat peach preserves in a small saucepan until melted and a sauce is formed, stirring often to break any lumps. Allow to cool. Pour this sauce over the custard. Serve garnished with sliced peaches.   *Yield: 6 servings*

NOTE: For a quick and low-fat custard, replace low-fat milk with a 12-ounce can of evaporated skim milk. In Step 4, just scald the milk, instead of cooking it for 15 minutes.

SERVING SUGGESTIONS: Some entrées that go beautifully with this flan are Artichoke, Goat Cheese, and Olive Pizza (page 195), Garlicky Chard and Chick-peas (page 153), or Sweet-Spiced Millet with Cabbage and Pine Nuts (page 178).

CARROT-APPLE HALWA
India

Halwa, as found in India, is a thick, rich pudding often made with vegetables and warming spices. For special occasions, halwa is covered with edible silver leaves, which are sold in tissue-thin sheets. They have no flavor but dazzle the eye with their brilliance. This wholesome, orange-colored treat is made simply with carrot or butternut squash and cooking apples. A dessert-loving friend once told me that when it first touches your palate, it's like a "brief, warm kiss."

1 quart low-fat milk (see Note)
2 cups grated carrots
¼ cup slivered almonds, toasted
2 tablespoons golden raisins
¾ cup grated tart apple
3 tablespoons plus sugar
Splash of rose water

1. Lightly oil the bottom and sides of a large steep-sided saucepan to prevent milk from sticking. Place milk in this pan and bring to a boil over medium-high heat. Lower heat and stir vigorously until the foaming subsides. Turn heat to medium and cook for about 10 minutes, until slightly thickened, stirring often. Scrape the sides and bottom to incorporate any milk solids that form.

2. Add carrots, almonds, and raisins. Cook for another 20 to 25 minutes, or until quite thick, stirring and scraping the pan as before. Add apple and mix well. Stir in 3 tablespoons sugar. Taste and add more sugar, if necessary. Remove from heat and allow to cool slightly. Sprinkle rose water on top. Serve warm or, if serving later, refrigerate. Bring to room temperature before serving for maximum flavor. *Yield: 4 servings*

NOTE: For a creamier texture, use whole milk or a mixture of whole milk and half-and-half.

SERVING SUGGESTIONS: This halwa makes a good dinner companion to Kale-Apple Soup (page 68) and Nut-Topped Savory Rice (page 174).

Even bruised figs make a sweet pudding.
—Jamaican proverb

MAPLE PEARS
United States

Asian pears are juicy sweet when raw and make delicious side dishes when cooked. Here Asian pear slices are tossed in butter and maple syrup, then coated with crushed hazelnuts. A simple yet pleasant side dish or dessert.

1 to 2 tablespoons butter or ghee
1 tablespoon pure maple syrup
1 large Asian Pear or tart apple (about ¾ pound), cored
    but not peeled, cut into ¼-inch-thick slices
2 tablespoons hazelnuts, toasted and finely chopped

Melt butter in a medium skillet. Lower heat slightly, add maple syrup and cook until bubbly. Add pear. Cook for 1 or 2 minutes, or until the sauce caramelizes and forms a glaze around the fruit, turning gently but often. Add hazelnuts and mix well. Serve immediately.   *Yield: 4 small servings*

SERVING SUGGESTIONS: For a main meal, team with a grain dish such as Red Rice with Five Vegetables (page 171) and Scrambled Tempeh (page 131).

CHOCOLATE-GLAZED BANANA CAKE

United States

Bananas and chocolate have a special affinity for each other, deliciously demonstrated in this coffee cake. Ripe bananas produce a delicately sweet, moist cake, which is perfectly balanced by a thin film of chocolate topping. The total effect is enhanced by a middle layer of streusel made by rich, buttery cashews. Although somewhat lower in fat than most coffee cakes, this dessert has the rich moistness that discerning food lovers treasure.

STREUSEL (SEE NOTE):
¼ cup chopped raw, unsalted cashew halves
1½ tablespoons dark brown sugar

CAKE:
2 tablespoons canola oil
½ cup sugar
2 large eggs
½ teaspoon vanilla
2 large very ripe bananas, cut in chunks, puréed in a
    blender or food processor, and measured to 1¼ cups
½ cup low-fat buttermilk
1¾ cups whole wheat flour
1 teaspoon baking powder
1 teaspoon baking soda
¾ teaspoon cardamom powder
¼ cup raisins

TOPPING:
Light Chocolate Glaze (recipe follows) or
    confectioners' sugar (optional)

1. To prepare the streusel, combine cashews and brown sugar in a small bowl. Set aside.

2. Preheat oven to 350 degrees F. Oil a 9-inch tube or Bundt pan.

3. With an electric mixer, beat oil and sugar together in a large bowl. Add eggs, 1 at a time, and beat until lemon-colored, about 10 minutes. Fold in vanilla, banana purée, and buttermilk.

4. Sift together flour, baking powder, and baking soda. Add cardamom powder. Add one-third of the dry mixture to the banana mixture and beat until smooth. Add the remaining dry ingredients in two more batches. Add raisins. Pour half the cake batter into the prepared pan. Sprinkle with streusel topping. Pour the remaining batter over it. Bake for 30 to 35 minutes, or until a toothpick inserted near the center comes out clean. Place the pan on a rack and allow to cool for 15 minutes.

5. Run a knife along the edges to loosen the cake. Invert the cake onto the rack to cool the bottom for a few minutes. Place, right side up, onto a serving platter. Spoon some Light Chocolate Glaze over the top and spread evenly. Pass the rest at the table. Alternatively, dust confectioners' sugar lightly on top (page 235). *Yield: 10 servings*

NOTE: For a lower fat dish, omit the streusel entirely, or reduce the amount by half.

SERVING SUGGESTIONS: The lightness of this cake suggests heartier entrées such as Seven Vegetable Stew (page 138), Cool-Hot Cabbage (page 126), or New Touch to Stuffed Peppers (page 162). It also goes well with a lunch of Tofu-Walnut Burgers (page 104).

LIGHT CHOCOLATE GLAZE

A thin luscious glaze that can also serve as a sauce.

½ cup evaporated skim milk or
    regular skim milk
2 ounces unsweetened chocolate
2 tablespoons butter
1 cup confectioners' sugar, or more if required
1 teaspoon vanilla

1. In a small heavy saucepan or a double boiler, heat milk, chocolate, and butter together over very low heat just until chocolate melts, about 5 minutes. If the heat is too high or if cooked too long, chocolate may turn bitter. Remove from heat immediately and transfer to a medium bowl. Allow to cool.

2. Add sugar a little at a time, beating with a spoon after each addition until smooth. (Break any lumps in confectioners' sugar before adding by sieving it.) Add vanilla. Add more sugar for a stiffer frosting or if you like it sweeter.

Yield: 1 cup

COCONUT VARIATION: For a richer flavor, add ½ cup shredded sweetened coconut along with sugar. Reduce sugar to ¾ cup in this case.

**When something unpleasant is kept under control,
the Tamils say, "The milk boiled, but didn't boil over."**

MANGO, APPLE, AND BLUEBERRY DELIGHT

International

There's an art to putting together a fruit salad. The colors and textures of fruits should complement each other. Fruits that discolor should be added at the end and the dressing should enhance, but not overpower the flavor. This attractive fruit salad is composed of orange-fleshed mango and intense blueberries. Apples add the requisite crispness.

2 sweet apples (each about 10 ounces)
2 large very ripe mangoes (about 1 pound each),
    peeled, pit removed, flesh coarsely chopped
1 cup fresh blueberries
Honey Yogurt Splash (page 225)

1. Just before serving, core the apples but don't peel them. Chop them coarsely.

2. Combine mango flesh and the accumulated juice, apples, and blueberries in a large bowl. Spoon fruit into individual plates and swirl the dressing over. To preserve the distinct colors and shapes of the fruits don't mix the fruits with the dressing. If appearance is less of a concern, prepare the fruits ahead of time, stir them gently with the dressing, and store in the refrigerator. The fruit juices and the dressing will combine to form a thick sauce. Before serving, bring to room temperature and mix thoroughly with the sauce.

Yield: 4 servings

SERVING SUGGESTIONS: Serve following a meal of Spuds and Black Bean Casserole (page 160) and a mixed green salad. Also enjoy at snacktime and at picnics.

VARIATION: Another fruit combination that works here is strawberries, kiwi, seedless grapes, and peaches.

POPPY SEED FRUIT RING
Eastern Europe

I have always enjoyed both carrot cake and poppy seed cake. Once, on impulse, I used carrot and poppy seeds together in a cake and discovered a joyful synergy. Grated carrots, enhanced by figs, dates, and raisins, produce a moist cake with a delicate sweetness. Poppy seed paste adds a complex, buttery taste and imparts a delightful crunchiness to the texture. When baked in a Bundt pan, the result is a rich brown dome with lovely fluted edges, which makes a showy, attractive dessert.

2 tablespoons canola oil

½ cup sugar

One 12-ounce can poppy seed filling

2 large eggs, separated

1 cup low-fat buttermilk (see Note)

1½ cups grated carrots

1½ cups unbleached white flour

1 teaspoon baking soda

1 teaspoon ground cardamom

½ cup mixed dried fruit (raisins, chopped dates, and chopped figs)

Confectioners' sugar for dusting (optional)

1. Preheat oven to 350 degrees F. Generously oil a 9- or 10-inch tube or Bundt pan.

2. With an electric mixer, beat oil and sugar together in a large bowl for several minutes. Beat in poppy seed filling. Add egg yolks, 1 at a time, beating for 3 to 4 minutes after each addition. Fold in buttermilk. Add carrots. Set aside.

3. Beat egg whites in a separate mixer bowl until stiff.

4. Sift together flour and baking soda in a large bowl. Add cardamom. Gradually add dry ingredients to the yolk mixture, beating well after each addition. Add mixed fruits. Fold egg whites into the batter. Turn batter into prepared pan. Bake for 45 to 50 minutes, or until a toothpick inserted near the center comes out clean. Allow to cool on a rack for 15 to 20 minutes.

5. Run a blunt knife around the inside edges of the pan to loosen the cake. Invert onto the rack to allow the bottom side to cool for a few minutes. Place the cake, right side up, on a large platter. Just before serving, dust with confectioners' sugar (page 235). Covered and stored in the refrigerator, this cake stays fresh for several days. *Yield: 10 or more servings*

NOTE: To lower the fat content even more, replace buttermilk with ½ cup plain nonfat yogurt and ½ cup nonfat milk, thoroughly combined.

SERVING SUGGESTIONS: Serve alone, or topped with Lemon Satin (page 263). For a full meal, it is luscious with Zucchini Vichyssoise (page 97) served warm, Cherry Tomato Chips (page 37), and a mixed green salad.

MANGO-APRICOT BREAD PUDDING
United States

On a trip to New Orleans I discovered that the city has a well-developed sweet tooth. The dessert that most impressed me was their bread pudding. Dense, syrupy, and rich, it was even served in candy shops. After tasting many versions I was inspired to come up with my own. This easy bread pudding leaves out the butter and cream and uses ripe mangoes and dried apricots to create a subtle fruity undertone. A light apricot glaze forms a glossy top. The whole wheat variation is dense and filling, while the french bread version has a lighter texture.

5 cups chopped baguette pieces (crust included)

2¾ cups evaporated skim milk

½ cup plus 3 tablespoons sugar

3 large eggs

½ teaspoon cardamom powder

¼ teaspoon ground cinnamon

1 large very ripe mango, peeled, pit removed,
   flesh puréed in a blender and measured to ½ cup

¼ cup chopped, dried apricots (see Note)

2 tablespoons golden raisins

6 to 8 pecans, chopped

Apricot Glaze (recipe follows) or confectioners' sugar
   (optional)

1. Preheat oven to 400 degrees F. Generously oil a 9-inch-square cake pan or a deep baking dish.

2. Put bread in large mixer bowl. Add milk. Press with a spoon so that all the bread pieces are soaked in milk. Let rest for 5 minutes. Using an electric mixer, blend at low speed for a few minutes until the mixture becomes a thick purée. Let stand another 10 minutes to allow the bread to absorb the milk.

3. Add sugar and stir until dissolved. Blend in eggs, cardamom, and cinnamon; beat for 5 minutes. Fold in mango purée, apricots, raisins, and pecans. Pour into prepared cake pan. Bake for 45 to 50 minutes, or until the top is golden brown and a toothpick inserted in the center comes out clean.

4. Spread Apricot Glaze over the top while still hot. Pass any leftover Apricot Glaze at the table. Cool pudding for a few minutes, then serve from the pan. If using confectioners' sugar, dust on top just before serving. Best served warm, but can also be served at room temperature or chilled.

Yield: 12 servings

NOTE: Some varieties of dried apricots are very dehydrated and hard to chew; they will require soaking in warm water for 30 minutes or longer. If possible, buy the plumper, moister Turkish apricots, which are ready to be used.

SERVING SUGGESTIONS: For a special treat, place a dollop of Nutty Cream (page 264) on top of or next to each individual serving. This pudding is a lovely addition to a summer luncheon of Chilled Cucumber-Buttermilk Soup (page 66), Pear Slaw with Honey Pecans (page 84), and Leek-Onion Tart (page 198). In autumn, pair this pudding with a hearty entrée such as Fusilli in Chick-pea–Walnut Cream (page 188). Enjoy as a snack accompanied by a cup of aromatic Indian-Style Tea (page 262).

WHOLE WHEAT VARIATION: Substitute 5 slices of whole wheat bread for the baguette. Reduce the quantity of evaporated skim milk to 2 cups, and the sugar to ½ cup. Bake in an oiled 8-inch-square pan for 35 to 45 minutes.

You can't eat a mango in one bite.
—Caribbean proverb

APRICOT GLAZE

¼ cup apricot jam or preserves
1 to 2 teaspoons freshly squeezed lime juice (to taste)

Heat jam in a small saucepan over low heat, stirring often. When it melts and forms a sauce, remove from heat. Mix in lime juice.

Yield: Over ¼ cup

ALMOND PEAR TART
International

This beautiful tart is both quick and simple to prepare. A flaky pastry is used for the bottom crust. The filling consists of thinly sliced ripe Bosc pears, topped with a streusel-like layer of almond paste and studded with pistachios. In about an hour, this tart will be on the table, warm and brown, filling the room with a heady aroma of almond and pear.

One 6-inch wide puff pastry sheet (see Note)
Sugar for sprinkling
1 medium egg, lightly beaten
2 large ripe Bosc pears, peeled, cored, and thinly sliced
One 8-ounce can almond paste
1 tablespoon raw, unsalted pistachio halves, chopped

1. On a lightly floured board, roll out the puff pastry to a size slightly larger than a 9 × 13-inch baking pan. Handle gently and don't stretch the pastry any more than necessary. Cover the pan bottom and ½ inch up the sides with the sheet. Lightly prick in several places with a fork, and sprinkle with sugar. Brush with the beaten egg. (You will not need all of it.) Refrigerate for at least 15 minutes.

2. Preheat oven to 450 degrees F.

3. Arrange the pears, edges slightly overlapping, on the crust. Remove almond paste from the can and divide into 8 equal parts. Shape each portion into a ball. Place each ball on a lightly floured cutting board. Using a floured rolling pin, roll into strips. Using a flat spatula, pick up the strip and gently place on top of the pears. Repeat procedure with all the balls. Use your fingers to gently pinch the almond paste strips together to form a solid crust; sprinkle with pistachios on top. Bake for 22 to 25 minutes, or until the crust is richly browned in places. Be careful not to let it burn. Best served warm, but you can refrigerate and serve chilled.   *Yield: 10 servings*

NOTE: Puff pastry sheets are available refrigerated in supermarkets. If using pastry sheets of narrower width, join them lengthwise to form a larger sheet. Using moist fingers, seal the edges together well. Trim off any excess dough. Reroll these trimmings, sprinkle them with sugar and minced crystallized ginger (or ground cinnamon), shape them into twists and bake them to serve as a snack.

SERVING SUGGESTIONS: This tart is a perfect finish to a meal of Red Lentils in Coconut Cream (page 158), Green Beans and Red Pepper Gratin (page 142), and briefly steamed cauliflower sprinkled with Lime-Peanut Vinaigrette (page 222).

PEACH TART
France

While living in Paris, I often lingered at the windows of the ubiquitous neighborhood pâtisseries just to stare. Even the thinnest tart would have a flaky crust and a lush, shining glaze on top. Back in the United States, I started to prepare my own tarts using a variety of fruits. In this recipe, I poach peaches in wine and arrange them over a lowfat cream cheese filling that tastes like cheesecake. I finish the tart in traditional French fashion by brushing it with melted fruit preserve for the glossy, professional look found in French pâtisseries.

PASTRY:
One 6-inch wide puff pastry sheet (see Note)
Sugar for sprinkling
1 large egg, lightly beaten

FILLING:
4 ounces Neufchâtel or low-fat cream cheese
¼ cup evaporated skim milk
¼ cup plus 2 tablespoons sugar
2 tablespoons freshly squeezed lime juice
3 ripe peaches, sliced no thicker than ½ inch
½ cup mirin (Japanese cooking wine) or other white or
    red cooking wine

GLAZE:
2 tablespoons peach preserves

1. Roll out the pastry sheet on a lightly floured board to a size slightly larger than a 9 × 13-inch baking pan. Handle gently and don't stretch the pastry any more than necessary. Place it on the pan so that the bottom is covered

entirely and the sides are raised to at least ½ inch. Lightly prick with a fork and sprinkle with sugar. Brush with the beaten egg. (You will not need it all.) Refrigerate for at least 15 minutes.

2. Preheat oven to 350 degrees F.

3. About 40 minutes before serving, place some pastry weights or uncooked dry beans on top of the crust to prevent it from overpuffing. Bake for about 15 minutes, or until golden. Remove pastry weights or beans. Set crust aside.

4. Process cheese, milk, and ¼ cup plus 1 tablespoon sugar in a blender or food processor until smooth, while crust is baking. Place in a small saucepan and cook over low heat just until it is heated through and is starting to bubble. Don't let it boil. Remove from heat and allow to cool.

5. In another saucepan, cook peaches, wine, and 1 tablespoon sugar over low heat for 3 to 5 minutes, or just until peaches have softened slightly. Remove from heat and allow peaches to marinate in the cooking liquid until ready to be used, 30 minutes if possible.

6. Spread a layer of cheese filling evenly over the crust. Drain the peaches and discard cooking liquid. Place the peaches in a single, slightly overlapping row.

7. Just before serving, heat preserves in a small saucepan for 3 to 5 minutes, or just until melted and a sauce is formed, stirring to break any lumps. Pass through a small sieve if any lumps still remain. Brush glaze over the peach slices. Place under the broiler very briefly just to melt the glaze. Watch carefully and don't let it burn. Allow to cool before serving.

Yield: 8 servings

NOTE: For serving a larger number of guests, select a baking pan of desired size. Use several 6-inch pastry sheets and join the sheets lengthwise by pinching together with moistened fingers. Fit pastry in baking pan of desired size and trim off any excess. Increase the amount of cheese filling and fruits proportionately.

SERVING SUGGESTIONS: The cheese filling is delicious when used as a dressing for fresh fruits or cole slaw. Dishes that go well with this tart are Lentil Salad in Pepper Cups (page 81), Beans with Fancy Toppings (page 146), or Saffron-Baked Quinoa (page 172). It can also be served as an afternoon snack with rich coffee, a strong tea such as Assam, or an herbal tisane.

VARIATION: FOURTH OF JULY BERRY PLEASURE For the Fourth of July, I prepare this red, white, and blue tart by substituting a mixture of blueberries, strawberries, and raspberries for peaches. This variation is even easier because the berries require no cooking. You'll need about ½ cup of each berry. Hull the strawberries and slice them in half lengthwise. Follow above directions through Step 4. Skip Step 5. In Step 6, place the berries gently over the cheese filling, with strawberries cut side down. In Step 7, substitute apple jelly for peach preserves.

PLUM KUCHEN
Germany

This German-style cake-tart boasts a substantial crust, a rich, ripe plum filling, and a thin custard topping.

CRUST:
¾ cup unbleached white flour
1 teaspoon baking powder
2 tablespoons sugar
2 tablespoons butter, softened
1 large egg, lightly beaten
1 tablespoon low-fat milk

FILLING:

2 tablespoons raisins

¼ cup brandy or water

¾ pound ripe plums, pitted and thinly sliced
   (see Notes)

Sugar for sprinkling

2 tablespoons bread crumbs (see Notes)

TOPPING:

1 egg yolk

2 tablespoons low-fat milk

GLAZE:

2 tablespoons apple jelly

Confectioners' sugar

1. Sift the flour and baking powder together. Add sugar and mix thoroughly. Work in butter until the mixture resembles coarse crumbs. Make a well in the center and in it place the egg and milk. Using a fork, mix wet ingredients into the flour. Gather with your hands into a ball and knead lightly. The dough will be sticky. With floured hands, press into the bottom and sides of a 9-inch pie tin. Press the edge of the dough against the sides of the tin with a fork. Chill for at least 15 minutes.

2. Heat raisins in the brandy until the liquid comes to a boil. Remove from heat and let rest at least 15 minutes, or until plump. Drain, discarding the liquid. Sprinkle 1 tablespoon sugar (more if the plums are tart) over the plums and toss gently.

3. Preheat oven to 350 degrees F. Beat egg yolk and milk until light and fluffy, 3 to 4 minutes. Scatter bread crumbs over the crust. Arrange plum slices in concentric circles with edges slightly overlapping on top of the crust. Pour the yolk mixture over the plums. Bake for 18 to 20 minutes, or just until the crust is golden brown around the edge of the pan and the

plums are soft. Don't overbake or the crust will harden. Heat jelly in a small pan until it melts. Brush the plums carefully with the melted jelly. Sprinkle the top lightly and evenly with a small amount of confectioners' sugar. Place very briefly under the broiler to glaze the top. Watch carefully and don't let the kuchen burn. Serve immediately. Can also be served at room temperature or chilled. *Yield: 8 servings*

NOTES: Use Italian prune plums or any other firm European cooking plums. Don't substitute Santa Rosa or Japanese plums, which are too juicy.

Bread crumbs catch the dripping juices from the plums, keeping the crust crisp. Prepare plain bread crumbs following instructions given in Garlic Bread Crumbs (page 233), omitting garlic chips. A pleasant alternative to white or whole wheat bread is cinnamon raisin or other sweet bread.

SERVING SUGGESTIONS: For a wholesome and filling meal, Leeks, Leafy Greens, and Navy Bean Soup (page 70) and Grilled Eggplant and Toasted Pecan Salad (page 78) are most appropriate. Intensify the fruity flavor at teatime with a steaming cup of Darjeeling, orange pekoe, or other black tea of choice.

VARIATION: AUTUMN FRUIT TART During autumn, substitute a mixture of thinly sliced apples, pears, and plums for plums in the above recipe.

HAZELNUT LIME BARS
United States

Lime-flavored desserts are among the most popular in the United States, so I have some sure-fire recipes in my repertoire. These bars with a mouth-puckering, sweet-and-sour lime filling, also have the attraction of a dense hazelnut crust. I am particularly fond of this dessert during spring and summer. It goes well with most meals, but is especially good with rice, pasta, and, I don't know why, with asparagus!

CRUST:
½ cup unbleached white flour
½ cup hazelnuts, ground in a blender or
    food processor to a coarse powder
2 tablespoons sugar
8 tablespoons butter, or 4 tablespoons butter and
    4 tablespoons canola oil
½ teaspoon ground cardamom (optional)

FILLING:
2 large eggs
¾ cup sugar
2 tablespoons unbleached white flour
¼ teaspoon baking powder
½ cup freshly squeezed lime juice

1. Preheat oven to 350 degrees F.

2. Sift flour into a large bowl. Add ground hazelnuts, sugar, butter, and cardamom. Place in the bowl of a food processor and pulse a few times so that a meal-like consistency results. Or, work with a pastry cutter or your fingertips

to blend the ingredients until the mixture resembles coarse crumbs. Pat into the bottom of an 8-inch cake pan. Bake 15 to 18 minutes, or until the top is lightly browned.

3. Just before the crust is ready, prepare the filling. With an electric mixer, beat eggs and sugar until beige and smooth, 5 minutes. Beat in flour, baking powder, and lime juice. Pour into the crust. Bake for 20 to 25 minutes, or until set. If overbaked, the top will start to crack. Allow to cool, then cut into squares.   *Yield: 8 to 10 servings*

SERVING SUGGESTIONS: These bars are sensational at a summer brunch with Orzo and Asparagus Salad (page 83) and Chilled Jicama-Buttermilk Soup (page 67). In winter, the lime flavor hits the spot after a meal of Soba Noodles and Smoked Pepper Fantasy (page 184) and steamed asparagus sprinkled with Spiced Ghee (page 13).

CHOCOLATE-MACADAMIA TEMPTATION
United States

A good chocolate cake recipe is a staple in everyone's repertoire, and here is mine. It's fudgy, moist, and all-American. The ring of macadamia nuts around the edge of the cake adds a hint of luxurious richness. I serve this indulgence on special occasions. The one-layer cake is simple to make. A thin chocolate glaze, a light dusting of confectioners' sugar, and a mint sprig are all the decoration this sensuous treat needs.

    3 squares (1-ounce each) unsweetened chocolate
    4 tablespoons butter
    1¾ cups unbleached white flour
    ¾ cup plus 1 tablespoon sugar
    1 teaspoon baking soda
    1 cup regular or nonfat sour cream (see Note)

2 large eggs
1 teaspoon vanilla
½ cup nonfat or low-fat milk
2 tablespoons whole macadamia nuts or whole
    hazelnuts, toasted
Light Chocolate Glaze (page 244; Coconut Variation
    preferred)
Confectioners' sugar for dusting
A mint sprig for garnish (if available)

1. Preheat oven to 350 degrees F. Oil a 9 × 13-inch cake pan.

2. Melt chocolate and butter together over very low heat in a heavy-bottomed saucepan. As soon as both have melted, remove from heat and transfer to a medium bowl.

3. In a large mixer bowl, place flour, sugar, baking soda, sour cream, eggs, and vanilla and beat at low speed for 1 to 2 minutes. Add milk and the chocolate-butter mixture and beat for 2 minutes more. Pour into the prepared pan. Lightly press macadamia nuts all around the edges at even intervals. Bake for 30 to 35 minutes, or until a toothpick inserted into the center comes out clean. Place on a wire rack to cool for 20 minutes.

4. Frost with Light Chocolate Glaze. (You can spread the entire amount of frosting over the cake. This results in an accumulated puddle at the bottom of the cake, creating a marvelous effect. Or spread half for frosting and pass the rest at the table.) Just before serving, dust with confectioners' sugar (page 235) and place mint sprig at the center.   *Yield: 10 or more servings*

NOTE: Nonfat sour cream produces a surprisingly moist cake. For a richer taste or for a special occasion use regular sour cream.

SERVING SUGGESTIONS: Serve thinly sliced following a rich holiday dinner, or take to a potluck supper. It is the perfect finish to a glamorous meal of Sesame-Sauced Spinach (page 125), Thai Tortellini (page 189), and Plum-Glazed Squash Rings (page 89).

ANISE-PISTACHIO BISCOTTI
Italy

Long ago, I spotted biscottis in a Manhattan deli, where the sign simply said ANISE COOKIES. I liked the flavor and experimented making these Italian specialties, adding pistachios for color and a nutty flavor. Biscottis are baked twice. This double-baking process intensifies the flavor and keeps these versatile cookies fresh longer. Italians often dunk them in their coffee. You can also serve them with regular tea or Indian-Style Tea (page 262), and with fruit or frozen yogurt.

2 large eggs plus 1 egg white
¾ cup plus 2 tablespoons sugar
2 cups unbleached white flour
1 teaspoon baking powder
1 teaspoon ground cardamom
¼ teaspoon ground ginger
1 teaspoon anise seeds
¼ cup unsalted raw pistachios, finely chopped
1 egg yolk or egg white, lightly beaten (for brushing)

1. Preheat oven to 350 degrees F.

2. Beat together eggs, egg white, and sugar in a large bowl until pale lemon-colored, 3 to 4 minutes. Set aside.

3. Sift together flour and baking powder in a medium bowl. Add cardamom, ginger, anise seeds, and pistachios and stir to distribute evenly. Add dry ingredients to the egg mixture and work into a dough, which will be sticky.

4. With floured hands, divide into 2 equal portions. Shape each into a log, about 12 inches in length, 1¾ inches wide, and with the narrow ends rounded. Smooth the top. The log will resemble a baguette. Place both on

a large lightly oiled baking sheet, at least 2 inches apart. Brush with beaten egg yolk or white, which will impart a rich brown color during baking.

5. Bake for 30 to 35 minutes, or until the tops are golden. They will remain slightly soft at this point. Remove from oven, but don't turn oven off. Allow to cool on the baking sheet for 7 to 8 minutes. Transfer to a cutting board. Cut each loaf diagonally into slices that are ¾ inch wide. Place the slices with one of the cut sides up, at least ½ inch apart on the baking sheet. Bake for another 15 to 20 minutes, or until they are dry to the touch and have a lightly toasted look. Halfway through this period, turn the biscottis to make the other side crisp and lightly browned. Transfer to a large platter and place the platter on a wire rack. Allow to cool completely before storing.

Yield: 25 to 30 biscottis

SERVING SUGGESTIONS: Indian-Style Roasted Potatoes (page 32), scrambled eggs, and Maple Pears (page 241) will ensure a lovely brunch. At a main meal, Chinese Broccoli with Shiitake Mushrooms (page 130) or Orzo-Stuffed Maple Squash (page 167) are two of the possible serving options. Carry these crisp cookies to the workplace for coffee break, or take them along on a picnic.

INDIAN-STYLE TEA
India

One of the pleasures of traveling in India by train is watching the country-side pass by your window while sipping fragrant hot tea. As soon as the train stops at a station, vendors rush over to the windows and offer rich, spicy tea in unglazed terracotta cups for a few rupees. Tourists soon become accustomed to the phrase *"chai, garam chai"* (tea, hot tea), at all hours of the day. Throughout India, tea is served late in the afternoon with snacks. Many American friends who have grown to appreciate this flavorful brew claim that it serves just as well as dessert. Here is an excellent low-calorie answer to the craving for "something sweet."

> 1 cup water
> 4 teaspoons Indian black tea (such as Assam,
>   Darjeeling, orange pekoe; can be decaffeinated;
>   can substitute 4 teabags)
> 3 cups milk (see Note)
> ½ teaspoon ground cardamom
> ½ teaspoon ground cinnamon
> One ¼-inch-thick piece peeled gingerroot
> Sugar or other sweetener of choice

Bring water and tea to a boil. Lower the heat and cook, uncovered, until the water takes on a deep amber color, a few minutes. Add milk, cardamom, cinnamon, and gingerroot. Cook, uncovered, until the mixture comes to a boil. Strain into cups. Sweeten to taste. *Yield: 4 servings*

NOTE: This tea can be made with whole, low-fat, or nonfat milk. Low-fat or nonfat milk is adequate for everyday dining, but for special occasions consider using whole milk or a mixture of whole milk and half-and-half. Alternatively, thicken 1 quart low-fat or nonfat milk by the method used in Carrot-Apple Halwa (page 240). It will reduce to about 3 cups after cooking.

SERVING SUGGESTIONS: This "tea latte," so to speak, is perfect after most meals and at teatime alone or with Anise-Pistachio Biscotti (preceding recipe). Dishes that go particularly well with it are Saffron-Baked Quinoa (page 172), Roasted Eggplant Relish (page 27), and Yam Masala (page 144).

LEMON SATIN
United States

This tart, creamy low-fat dessert sauce bursts with lemon flavor. It is a wonderfully refreshing pudding on its own and also serves well as a tasty topping for cakes.

1 tablespoon cornstarch
2 tablespoons cold water
¼ cup sugar
1 large egg
½ cup boiling water
⅛ teaspoon salt
2 tablespoons freshly squeezed lemon juice
    (don't substitute bottled lemon juice)

Combine cornstarch and water in a small bowl and stir until smooth. Place cornstarch mixture, sugar, egg, boiling water, and salt in a blender or food processor and spin until smooth. Transfer to a medium-size heavy saucepan. Over low heat, cook for a few minutes stirring constantly to avoid any lumps and scraping the bottom. When it thickens slightly, remove to a medium bowl. Stir in lemon juice. Smooth the top with the back of a spoon and allow to cool to room temperature. Refrigerate until ready to use. Best served chilled.   *Yield: Over 1 cup*

NUTTY CREAM
India

Instead of preparing dessert sauces with cream, I follow a technique that originated in India centuries ago. First boil milk, then cook slowly until it thickens and develops a nutty flavor. Lowfat and even nonfat milk tastes rich and delicious when cooked this way. This saffron-flavored thickened milk can be used on its own as a pudding, or use it as a dip for fresh fruit and for topping cakes.

4 cups low-fat or nonfat milk
½ teaspoon saffron threads
2 tablespoons sugar, or more to taste

Lightly oil the bottom and sides of a large steep-sided nonstick pan to prevent milk from sticking. Place milk in this pan and bring to a boil over medium to high heat. Lower the heat to prevent milk from boiling over and stir vigorously until bubbling subsides. Turn heat to medium. Add saffron. Cook until milk thickens to the consistency of heavy cream, 15 to 25 minutes. Watch carefully, as milk will try to rise over and over again. If it does, stir until it subsides. Stir the mixture frequently and scrape the bottom and the sides to loosen any milk solids and incorporate them into the milk mixture. If any skin forms on the surface, gently stir it into the liquid mixture as well. Add sugar, adjusting the amount to your taste. Remove from heat. Serve hot or chilled. Will keep in the refrigerator for 2 days.

Yield: 1 cup; 2 small servings

SUGGESTED MENUS

Most of the recipes suggested below serve 4 to 6 people. Double or triple the recipes as necessary when serving a larger number of guests.

ONE-HOUR MENU #1

Garlicky Chard and Chick-peas (page 153)

Basmati or jasmine rice

mixed green salad

baked butternut or acorn squash

ONE-HOUR MENU #2

Saffron-Baked Quinoa (page 172)

Sweet Hot Swiss Chard (page 110)

spinach and orange salad

NONFAT DINNER

Soy-Glazed Napa Cabbage (page 114)

brown Basmati rice

baked sweet potato

Mint-Cilantro Chutney (page 213)

SOUP AND SANDWICH SUPPER #1

Roasted Garlic Soup (page 61)

Grilled Eggplant and Toasted Pecan Salad (page 78)

Peas and Potatoes in a Pocket (page 98)

SOUP AND SANDWICH SUPPER #2

Thai Pea Soup (page 64)

Roasted Eggplant Burritos (page 100)

Beets and Feta Cheese in a Spinach Nest (page 86)

SUNDAY DINNER #1

Soba Noodles and Smoked Pepper Fantasy (page 184)

Pesto-Laced Broccoli (page 120)

Marinated Carrot Chutney (page 214)

Chocolate-Glazed Banana Cake (page 242)

SUNDAY DINNER #2

Chipotle Chick-peas (page 150)

Crostini with Chutney (page 29)

mixed green salad

warm tortillas

Peach Flan (page 238)

SUNDAY DINNER #3

Sweet Potato Bisque (page 54)

Thai Tortellini (page 189)

Bok Choy in Miso-Tamarind Sauce (page 121)

Almond Pear Tart (page 250)

BROWN-BAG SURPRISES #1

Sweet Tempeh Burgers (page 102)

Easy Baked Potato Chips (page 34)

carrot and celery sticks

BROWN-BAG SURPRISES #2

Hazelnut Rice Burgers (page 107)

mixed green salad

Indian-Style Tea (page 262)

TEATIME

Pear and Cheese Tea Sandwiches (page 95)

Sweet-Sour Carrot Roll-ups (page 100)

Hazelnut Lime Bars (page 257)

Chocolate-Glazed Banana Cake (page 242)

an assortment of teas

HOT AND COLD BUFFET

Orzo and Asparagus Salad (page 83)

Thai Tortellini (page 189)

Green Beans and Dried Tofu Foogath (page 123)

Glazed Carrots with Elephant Garlic (page 90)

Anise-Pistachio Biscotti (page 260)

SPRING CELEBRATION

Wild and Brown Rice Salad (page 77)

Peas and Carrots in a Pastry Nest (page 204)

Sesame-Sauced Spinach (page 125)

Sweet-and-Sour Pomegranate Tofu (page 118)

Almond Pear Tart (page 250)

SUMMER BRUNCH

Spanish Egg-Potato Omelette (page 205)

toast or focaccia bread

Maple Pears (page 241)

LIGHT SUMMER LUNCHEON

Chilled Cucumber-Buttermilk Soup (page 66)

Chile-Cumin Cornbread (page 206)

Peach Salsa (page 219)

AUTUMN HARVEST DINNER

Carrot-Lentil Soup with Rosemary-Garlic
Croutons (page 52)

Chile-Ginger Parsnips (page 128)

Nut-Topped Savory Rice (page 174)

Poppy Seed Fruit Ring (page 246)

HEARTY WINTER FARE

Roasted Garlic Soup (page 61)

Spicy Tofu and Pea Stew (page 140)

Sweet-Spiced Millet with Cabbage
and Pine Nuts (page 178)

Lemon Mousse Surprise (page 236)

WINTER BRUNCH

Indian-Style Roasted Potatoes (page 32)

eggs any style with Chipotle Barbecue Sauce (page 228)

warm chapati

APPETIZER BUFFET

Caramelized Garlic (page 26)

Spicy Roasted Chick-peas (page 24)

Sweet Potato Chips (page 35)

Curry Gyozas (page 38)

CHUTNEY PARTY

Mint-Cilantro Chutney (page 213)

Chile Chutney (page 212)

Marinated Carrot Chutney (page 214)

Sun-Dried Tomato and Cucumber Raita (page 218)

papads (page 24)

SOUP AND TART PARTY

Kale-Apple Soup (page 68)

Two-Bean Shorba (page 58)

Leek-Onion Tart (page 198)

mixed green salad

PIZZA PARTY

Orzo and Asparagus Salad (page 83)

Artichoke, Goat Cheese, and Olive Pizza (page 195)

fresh fruit with Nutty Cream (page 264)

EAST ASIAN DINNER

Snow Pea–Mushroom Stir-Fry (page 112)

Soba Noodles with Smoked Pepper Fantasy (page 184)

Wilted Spinach Banchan (page 87)

green tea

INDIAN DINNER

Split Pea and Sweet Potato Sambhar (page 148)

Roasted Eggplant Relish (page 27)

brown Basmati rice

Carrot-Apple Halwa (page 240)

STUFFED VEGETABLE DINNER

Orzo-Stuffed Maple Squash (page 167)

New Touch to Stuffed Peppers (page 162)

Warm Mustard Green Salad (page 80)

Anise-Pistachio Biscotti (page 260)

INDEX

Tahini, 19
tamarind, 19
    -miso sauce, bok choy in, 121–22
tapas, 21
tart(s), dessert:
    almond pear, 250–251
    berry pleasure, Fourth of July, 254
    fruit, autumn, 256
    kuchen, plum, 254–256
    peach, 252–254
tart(s), savory, 192
    basic pie crust for, 199–200
    bean pie, savory, 202–204
    gingery squash quiche, 200–201
    leek-onion, 198–199
    Spanish egg-potato omelette,
        205–206
tea, Indian-style, 262–263
tempeh, 19–20
    balls, spaghetti and, 103
    burgers, sweet, 102–103
    scrambled, 131–132
temperature, appropriate serving, 7
Thai pea soup, 64–65
Thai tortellini, 189–190
toast(ing):
    garlic, 41–42
    of nori, 16
    of nuts, spices, and grain, 5
tofu, 20
    cream, 226
    dried, and green beans *foogath,*
        123–125
    and pea stew, spicy, 140–141
    sweet-and-sour pomegranate,
        118–119
    walnut burgers, 104–105
tomato(es; ey):
    in baguette, roasted, 101
    cherry, "chalsa," 220–221
    curry, linguine with, 182–183
    green beans, super, 154–155
    grilled, 4
    jam, two-, 232

-peanut soup, 63–64
    sauce, peppery, 230–231
    slow-roasted, 36–37
    sun-dried, and cucumber raita,
        218
tortellini, Thai, 189–190
tortilla rolls, curried vegetables in, 100
two-bean *shorba,* 58–59
two-tomato jam, 232

Vegetable(s):
    appropriate temperature for serving
        of, 7
    bouillabaisse, 72–74
    five, red rice with, 171–172
    grilled, 3–4
    and salsa, bite-size raw, 23
    in a "pillow," seven little, 100
    spices in cooking of, 6
    stew, seven, 138–139
    stock, 45–46
    in tortilla rolls, curried, 100
    variety of, 6
    see also specific vegetables
vegetables, stuffed, 133
    maple squash with orzo, 167–168
    peppers, new touch to, 162–164
    sesame eggplant, 182
vegetable side dishes, 75–76, 87–91
    carrots with elephant garlic, glazed,
        90–91
    spinach *banchan,* wilted, 87–88
    squash rings, plum-glazed, 89–90
vegetarian cooking basics, 3–7
    cooking methods, 3–5
    tips, 6–7
vichyssoise, zucchini, 47–49
vinaigrette(s):
    chile-sesame, 223
    chile-sesame-shiso, 223
    lime-orange, 221
    lime-peanut, 222
vinegar, 20